LAW, IDEOLOGY, AND COLLEGIALITY

Law, Ideology, and Collegiality

Judicial Behaviour in the Supreme Court of Canada

DONALD R. SONGER, SUSAN W. JOHNSON,
C.L. OSTBERG, AND MATTHEW E. WETSTEIN

McGill-Queen's University Press
Montreal & Kingston • London • Ithaca

ISBN 978-0-7735-3928-0 (cloth)
ISBN 978-0-7735-3929-7 (paper)

Legal deposit second quarter 2012
Bibliothèque nationale du Québec

Printed in Canada on acid-free paper that is 100% ancient forest free (100% post-consumer recycled), processed chlorine free

This book has been published with the help of a grant from the Canadian Federation for the Humanities and Social Sciences, through the Aid to Scholarly Publications Program, using funds provided by the Social Sciences and Humanities Research Council of Canada.

McGill-Queen's University Press acknowledges the support of the Canada Council for the Arts for our publishing program. We also acknowledge the financial support of the Government of Canada through the Canada Book Fund for our publishing activities.

Library and Archives Canada Cataloguing in Publication

Law, ideology, and collegiality : judicial behaviour in the Supreme Court of Canada / Donald R. Songer ... [et al.].

Includes bibliographical references and index.

ISBN 978-0-7735-3928-0 (bound). – ISBN 978-0-7735-3929-7 (pbk.)

1. Canada. Supreme Court. 2. Political questions and judicial power – Canada. 3. Judicial process – Canada. 4. Judges – Canada – Attitudes. I. Songer, Donald R.

KE8244.L39 2012 347.71'035 C2011-907117-7
KF8764.ZA2L39 2012

Typeset by Jay Tee Graphics Ltd. in 10.5/13 Sabon

Contents

List of Tables

List of Figures

List of Cases

Attorney General of Ontario v. Attorney General of Canada, [1940] AC 348.

Béliveau St-Jacques v. Fédération des employées et employés de services publics Ins., [1996] 2 SCR 345.

British Coal Corporation v. The King, [1935] AC 500.

Canadian Broadcasting Corp. v. Canada (Labour Relations Board), [1995] 1 SCR 157.

Canadian Pacific Ltd. v. Matsqui Indian Band, [1995] 1 SCR 3.

Co-operative Committee on Japanese Canadians v. Attorney General for Canada, [1947] AC 458.

Dagenais v. Canadian Broadcasting Corp., [1994] 3 SCR 835.

Dagg v. Canada (Minister of Finance), [1997] 2 SCR 403.

Edwards v. Attorney General of Canada, [1930] AC 125.

Egan v. Canada, [1995] 2 SCR 513.

Finlay v. Canada (Minister of Finance), [1993] 1 SCR 1080.

Ford v. Quebec, [1988] 2 SCR 712, 54 DLR 4.577.

Friesen v. Canada, [1995] 3 SCR 103.

Galaske v. O'Donnell, [1994] 1 SCR 670.

Gold v. Rosenberg, [1997] 3 SCR 767.

Gould v. Yukon Order of Pioneers, [1996] 1 SCR 571.

Haig v. Canada, [1993] 2 SCR 995.

Hickman Motors Ltd. v. Canada, [1997] 2 SCR 336.

Hodgkinson v. Simms, [1994] 3 SCR 377.

Hunter v. Southam, [1984] 2 SCR 145.

Hy and Zel's Inc. v. Ontario (Attorney General), [1993] 3 SCR 675.

In the Matter of a reference as to the Meaning of the Word "Persons" in Section 24 of the British North America Act, 1867, [1928] SCR 276.

Kienapple v. The Queen, [1975] 1 SCR 729.
Law Society of Upper Canada v. Skapinker, [1984] 1 SCR 357.
Miron v. Trudel, [1995] 2 SCR 418.
Morgentaler v. The Queen, [1976] 1 SCR 616.
Morgentaler v. The Queen, [1988] 1 SCR 30.
R. v. Belnavis, [1997] 3 SCR 341.
R. v. Boucher, [1951] SCR 265.
R. v. E. (A. W.), [1993] 3 SCR 155.
R. v. Feeney, [1997] 2 SCR 13.
R. v. Heywood, [1994] 3 SCR 761.
R. v. Hydro-Québec, [1997] 3 SCR 213.
R. v. Jones, [1994] 2 SCR 229.
R. v. McDonnell, [1997] 1 SCR 948.
R. v. N.T.C. Smokehouse Ltd., [1996] 2 SCR 672.
R. v. Nikal, [1996] 1 SCR 1013.
R. v. Noble, [1997] 1 SCR 874.
R. v. O'Connor, [1995] 4 SCR 411.
R. v. P. (M. B.), [1994] 1 SCR 555.
R. v. R. (D.), [1996] 2 SCR 291.
R. v. Seaboyer, [1991] 2 SCR 577.
R. v. Swietlinski, [1994] 3 SCR 481.
R. v. Van der Peet, [1996] 2 SCR 507.
RJR-MacDonald Inc. v. Canada (Attorney General), [1995] 3 SCR 199.
Reference Re Anti-Inflation Act, [1976] 2 SCR 373.
Reference Re Persons of Japanese Race, [1946] SCR 248.
Robertson and Rosetanni v. The Queen, [1963] SCR 651.
Royal Bank of Canada v. Sparrow Electric Corp., [1997] 1 SCR 411.
Slattery (Trustee of) v. Slattery, [1993] 3 SCR 430.
Symes v. Canada, [1993] 4 SCR 695.
The Queen v. Drybones, [1970] SCR 282.
University of British Columbia v. Berg, [1993] 2 SCR 353.
Wallace v. United Grain Growers Ltd., [1997] 3 SCR 701.
Weber v. Ontario Hydro, [1995] 2 SCR 929.
Winnipeg Child and Family Services (Northwest Area) v. G. (D. F.), [1997] 3 SCR 925.

LAW, IDEOLOGY, AND COLLEGIALITY

1 Introduction

Toronto's *Globe and Mail* suggested in August 2005 that Canadian prime ministers should be careful when selecting justices to serve on the Supreme Court of Canada because of its profound impact on society. Indeed, the article notes: "The court's rulings have far-reaching effects, particularly in the age of the Charter of Rights and Freedoms" (*Globe and Mail* 2005). Although Canadians may view the court as a substantial policy maker in a wide range of issues, that has not always been the case. At its inception in 1875, no newspaper would have made such a claim. Even as late as the mid-1970s, the same was probably true. But since the adoption of the Charter in 1982, many observers acknowledge that the Supreme Court has come to play a central policy-making role in the resolution of politically important issues.

The heightened political role and increasing activism appear to be part of a world-wide phenomenon, in which courts involve themselves more in politics in various democracies around the globe. Scholars in many countries have recently devoted more attention to this "judicialization of politics." In more and more countries, "judges are making public policies that previously had been made or that, in the opinion of most, ought to be made by legislative and executive officials" (Tate and Vallinder 1995, 2). In many places this role has followed increasing consciousness of rights. In Europe, for example, the European Convention and the European Court of Human Rights in Strasbourg have helped "spread the gospel" of judicialization (Tate and Vallinder 1995, 3). In Canada, this rights consciousness is reflected in the establishment of the Charter and various groups' use of the law to secure rights and advance their status in society.

Given the Supreme Court of Canada's new centrality in resolving disputes over public policy, scholars have questioned whether its new mandate to protect Charter rights and freedoms has triggered greater attitudinal disagreement among the justices serving on the contemporary Canadian court. Yet, given the politically charged nature of many of the policy disputes that the court hears, justices might well disagree over how to solve cases and face increasing criticism for their more activist rulings. Even the justices have noticed increasing conflict within their own court, with one suggesting that academics need to devote more energy to understanding the nature of conflict that has emerged on the top court since the Charter's adoption (Iacobucci 2002).

This book seeks to take up this charge in two ways. First, it explores the relevance of the attitudinal model, which US political scientists set up, to explain judicial decision making in Canada's Supreme Court. Second, it examines what the justices say about their work and the patterns of conflict and consensus that emerge in their rulings. Specifically, it employs three strategies for quantitative research to see how much ideology influences their decision making in non-unanimous cases and explore cleavages that divide the justices. We use three methods – factor analysis, bivariate correlation analysis, and logistic regression – to explore the effects of ideology on judicial voting under the Charter. Moreover, we also use qualitative research, relying on our extensive interviews with the justices to explain their thinking about their decisions. The blending of these four methods allows a robust and comprehensive assessment of the impact of attitudes on decision making, and the data and interviews help answer the book's central foci: the nature and extent of attitudinal decision making on the court and the influence of ideology on its decisions.

Although the impact of ideology plays out differently in each chapter and varies substantially throughout, the book makes the following claim: justices' personal ideologies affect their approach to policy issues and help explain divisions among them. Thus attitudinal decision making does indeed profoundly affect a prominent high court outside the United States.

We hope to present a systematic examination of the attitudinal model in a non-American context while also revealing much about the Supreme Court of Canada. The book offers a unique contribution to attitudinal literature by using several methods to examine the impact of ideology qualitatively and quantitatively. It builds on earlier assessments of attitudinal decision making in Canada by applying a macro-level perspective of judicial decision making in three broad areas of law rather than taking a micro-level look at specific sub-fields of law (see Ostberg and Wetstein 2007a). It also expands on the method that earlier studies of the court used but applies several methods to generate a more sweeping assessment of ideology's role in the making of judicial decisions. In short, the book makes a singular contribution to the growing body of literature on the judicialization of politics around the world, using the Supreme Court of Canada as a test case to explore the nature and extent of high courts' ideological decision making.

A NOTE ON AUDIENCE AND IDEOLOGY

We designed this study to address at least three audiences with an interest in judicial behaviour in high courts such as the Supreme Court of Canada. On one level, we seek to educate US readers about the operation, collegiality, and ideological leanings of justices on Canada's top judicial body. We hope thereby to prompt American scholars and students to consider the hyper-ideological tendencies of their own Supreme Court in the light of the more modest and subtle ideological behaviour in its Canadian counterpart, which possesses similar rules of operation and power of docket control. US readers tend to concentrate on their own institutions, so we hope this volume can introduce some of them to the collegial making of law in Canada's high court and to ways to study attitudinal behaviour in a non-American judicial body.

On a second level, we introduce the attitudinal model to scholars of Canadian public law, many of whom underestimate the extent to which ideological proclivities influence Canadian justices. Although the justices' collegiality masks the impact of ideology, in highly contentious cases attitudinal dynamics inform that conflict.

On a third level, we address a wider audience of judges, lawyers, politicians, and lay readers who wonder how the Supreme Court of Canada works and how to apply to its study the theory and methods that have emerged in the US literature on public law. For this wider audience, we seek to explain our quantitative techniques in an accessible way, while maintaining methodological rigour. In the end, this volume attempts to describe how justices of the Supreme

Court of Canada address sometimes-competing tensions as they try to write sound judgments that meet three criteria: they must have a firm legal grounding, comport with the norms of their colleagues, and reflect their ideological vision of the law. These tensions are sometimes in conflict and aptly reflect the title of the book: *Law, Ideology, and Collegiality*.

We wish to make as clear as we can what we mean by "ideology" and how we distinguish it from terms such as "judicial philosophy" and "jurisprudence." "Ideology" in this context refers to the personal political values and attitudes of the judges, which US observers often couch in the language of liberalism and conservatism. "Judicial philosophy" typically refers to a justice's approach to constitutional or legal interpretation: whether strict construction of the legal text, balancing various interests, or advocating preferred freedoms. Ultimately, "ideology" refers to an individual's tendency to hold consistent perceptions about the appropriate scope and purpose of government's role in society. For example, an ideological question might ask: Do justices favour government intervention into the economy or not? Do they tend to lean towards government more often when they are assessing the prosecution of criminals, or do they support defendants' rights to due process? Do they usually champion economic underdogs or corporate and government interests in the economic sphere? As we discuss below, sometimes the way a justice supports a particular party can unmask his or her ideological orientation, and in attitudinal scholarship a justice's legal opinion becomes a kind of smokescreen to mask ideological preferences.

One of the critical findings of our research is that the typical US scholar's understanding of judicial ideology tends to derive from notions of liberalism and conservatism, which misses out on other potentially relevant ideological dimensions, as becomes evident in the Canadian court. Two obvious ones are communitarianism and federalism, which frequently influence Canadian justices. This finding may have implications for the study of justices elsewhere as well.

In contrast to judicial ideology, judicial philosophy – activist, restraintist, originalist, or organicist – is not about ideology per se, but about a justice's vision (within the Canadian context) of how to undertake judicial review in a Westminster parliamentary system and how to interpret the textual description of constitutional powers and rights. Some justices will take an activist judicial philosophy, demonstrating willingness to read the constitution and Charter of Rights to imply expansive rights, and they will invoke the power of courts to strike down laws much more readily than others. Restraintists take the opposite tack, presuming that laws that democratically elected officials enact should receive considerable deference from the court and that judges should strike down only egregious infringements. Originalists will want to hold hard and fast to the words in a historical document, so as to remain faithful to the "intent of the framers," or what those who wrote the provision intended it to mean. Organicists see the constitution as a "living tree" that needs to grow and expand as society changes over time.

Thus we can frequently distinguish a justice's ideology from his or her philosophy about judicial review and how to interpret the text of laws and the constitution. To put it simply, a liberal justice can be either activist or restraintist, and so can a conservative, a communitarian, or a libertarian. Our aim is to examine how much one can uncover justices' ideology by using several methods to examine their writings and votes. We focus on their ideological proclivities rather than on their judicial philosophies

A ROADMAP FOR THIS BOOK

The structure of the book takes the following form. In chapter 2 we explore the history and development of the Supreme Court of Canada as a policy-making institution, tracing its evolution from its founding in 1875 to its current status as a critical institution in Canadian politics. In contrast to the development of the US Supreme Court, for its first 75 years the Canadian court did not always have the ultimate say on legal and constitutional matters: appeals were possible in some matters to the Judicial Committee of Britain's Privy Council in London, and the principle of parliamentary supremacy in Canada severely limited its power.

In its early years, turnover of justices was very high, and the institution lacked legitimacy in the eyes of many citizens and government officials (McCormick and Greene 1990). However, in 1949 Canada's Parliament abolished appeals to the Privy Council, rendering the court the final arbiter. Its adoption of a statutory *Canadian Bill of Rights* in 1960 gave the court more influence, although its rulings vis-à-vis civil rights and liberties disappointed many observers. Between 1960 and 1982, the court decided 34 claims under the Bill of Rights and ruled in favour of the individual in only five (Russell

1987, 343; Morton et al. 1991, 61–2). Its acquisition of control over its own docket in 1975 allowed it greater judicial power.

Proclamation of the Charter of Rights and Freedoms in 1982 made the Supreme Court a central policy-making body. The Charter has resulted in growing judicialization of politics in Canada and has triggered many normative debates among scholars, journalists, and laypeople over the legitimacy of its power of judicial review in a parliamentary system. The Supreme Court's centrality in deciding a wide range of contentious political issues raises a fundamental concern about how justices' individual attitudes and ideology influence their voting behaviour. As the findings in this volume demonstrate, such an inquiry is very necessary.

Readers familiar with the court's history and legacy (chapter 2) may want to skip to chapter 3, which lays out the theory underlying the empirical analysis of chapters 5–7. Chapter 3 reviews scholarship that catalogues the increasing judicialization of politics in courts around the world, assesses the Charter's impact on the role of the Supreme Court of Canada in the political process, and describes the normative debate over its greater power of judicial review. As judges around the world have become increasingly activist and influential in the policy process, scholars have begun to examine the influence of their personal ideology on their decisions, both in Canada's high court and in tribunals elsewhere. The research in Canada has taken both a normative frame of reference, by examining the tension between the exercise of judicial power and majoritarian values, and an empirical frame of reference, which tests factors that shape who wins and loses in the legal system.

From a normative perspective, some observers have suggested that elites in Canada have won Charter litigation at the expense of other people and that this undermines democratic values (Mandel 1994). Others argue that justices have used Charter litigation to advance the interests of a constellation of leftist social groups that they label the "court party," trumping majoritarian values in the process (Morton and Knopff 2000). Others have suggested that members of Parliament and justices in effect tussle over the appropriate scope of judicial review; some have spoken of a "Charter dialogue" (see Hogg and Bushell 1997; Manfredi and Kelly 1999; Kelly 2005). Still others contend that judicialization of politics requires broad support within the public and the legal profession and mobilization of rights advocacy groups (Epp 1998).

Many empirical scholars have instead explored specific factors that decide winners and losers and ideological factors that divide justices. These studies focus on the degree to which justices' personal attitudes and background influence their decisions and on links between the process of judicial selection and ideological patterns of voting (for examples, see Tate and Sittiwong 1989; Heard 1991; Morton et al. 1992; McCormick 1993; Ostberg and Wetstein 1998).

Chapter 3 highlights three models that social scientists have developed to explain judicial decision making – legal, attitudinal, and strategic. The oldest and most traditional account – the legal model – envisions justices as applying settled rules of law or precedents to the facts of a case. This approach, the favourite of many law professors and lawyers, sees justices as rule appliers and fact finders, not policy makers. It often presents judicial decision making as mechanical and largely devoid of any discretionary authority.

Other social scientists follow an attitudinal model and focus on other factors, most notably ideological preferences, especially in senior appeals bodies. The most strident American advocates of this approach argue that the personal attitudes and values of justices explain all decisions by the US Supreme Court.[1] Unlike judges in lower appellate courts, Supreme Court justices face no legal, institutional, or political constraints because they work in a unique institutional environment that allows them to vote freely according to their own policy preferences (Segal and Spaeth 1996; 2002).

More recently, an alternative, strategic model has emerged. Although the attitudinal approach has dominated the literature on US jurisprudence over the past fifty years, some scholars have found that appellate court justices, since they work in small groups, often must act strategically in relation to each other and politicians when ruling on cases (see Epstein and Knight 1998; 2000; Spriggs et al. 1999).

While all three models are compelling, each has flaws and seems to provide a separate piece to explaining the larger puzzles of judicial behaviour. Consequently, an increasing number of scholars consider them complementary to each other and think that pulling them together may provide a more robust and complete explanation of judicial behaviour both in the United States and abroad. Even though a multi-level approach is gaining favour, in this volume we assess the extent to which justices on the Supreme Court of Canada have adopted the attitudinal model in the Charter era.

Chapter 3 also explores how the justices view the three models and examines the problems with measuring ideology. Our in-depth interviews with ten current and former Canadian justices (see Appendix A) suggest strongly that they think each model revealing. While all of them rely extensively on law and precedent when preparing for oral argument, most acknowledge that personal philosophies do divide justices in resolving more complex disputes. Although none claim to be "strategic" per se, most believe that they react strategically to other justices by trying to negotiate and bargain over the content of rulings in the conference and opinion-writing stages in an effort to obtain a unified court ruling. Overall, the justices admit that their personal attitudes do affect rulings but think that legal, strategic, and institutional considerations often outweigh these factors and that they often sacrifice their own views for the sake of unanimity. This analysis seems to confirm the value of a multi-level approach. The chapter ends with an exploration of the methods that we use to assess the relationship between ideology and voting behaviour on the Canadian court.

While chapter 3 lays out the theory underlying the analysis and explores the literature on the Supreme Court's role in Canadian politics, chapter 4 looks at the decision-making process through the eyes of the justices. Our interviews provide a unique first-person account of their appointment process, their procedures and criteria for selecting cases for oral argument, their preparation for cases, their degree of reliance on clerks for assistance, their desiderata in oral arguments, and their assignment of opinions and reaching of final decisions.

Although there are no formal guidelines for evaluating petitions for review, the justices agree that the most important criterion is whether the case raises an important national issue or whether provincial courts of appeal differ with each other and therefore challenge national uniformity in the law. Yet, in contrast to US Supreme Court justices, the Canadians do not feel pressure to turn away cases because their docket is full. Overall, the interviews suggest that the leave to appeal process is much less political in Canada than across the border and that most decisions to grant leave are unanimous.

Unique in the Canadian court is the chief justice's full discretion to decide who will hear a particular case. While this raises the specter of political gamesmanship, the interviews reveal that most justices feel that chief justices do not construct panels to reach a particular outcome or to advance a policy agenda. Although each justice prepares cases for oral argument differently, they all follow certain norms: they do not consult each other's chambers before oral argument and prepare extensively. They all find that the oral argument reveals information and exposes the strengths and weaknesses of counsels' positions and that the informal exchanges that take place during oral argument can help the court develop a consensus.

At the conference stage, the justices, in reverse order of seniority, briefly outline how they would resolve the case and generally do so in a polite and collegial manner, with little give and take. Assignment of opinions in the McLachlin court does not seem to follow any hard-and-fast rules. Factors at play include justices' legal expertise, willingness to volunteer, workload pressures, and seniority (although seniority was more significant in the Dickson and Lamer courts).

All the justices consider writing of opinions the key stage in decision making and observe much more give and take there. The interviews reveal strong emphasis on reaching unanimous decisions and collaborative effort, despite justices' willingness to express preferences on important matters. Consequently, more than 75 per cent of decisions in the Charter period have been unanimous. Moreover, several interviews reveal that justices act strategically and are comfortable with compromise over use of language or interpretation of law if it will lead to common ground and allow unanimity. This behaviour contrasts sharply with patterns in the US Supreme Court, where ideological preferences tend to dominate.

While chapter 4 looks at decision making through the eyes of the justices, chapter 5 turns to empirical analysis of their voting behaviour. In chapters 5, 6, and 7, we examine the extent of attitudinal voting in the Supreme Court of Canada. Although the justices claim that all three approaches to judicial decision making inform their voting behaviour, we seek to evaluate that self-assessment. We assume that the same types of institutional safeguards allow Canadian and US justices to express their preferences in judicial policy and thus that attitudinal voting should be equally prevalent in both courts. We believe that our findings are persuasive and compelling because we use three quantitative techniques, triangulating our methods, to determine robustly and definitively the extent to which Canadian justices engage in attitudinal decision making.

Chapter 5 examines the attitudinal model in the Canadian court. We employ factor-analytic techniques on cases decided by the Lamer court (1992–7), since it constituted one of the most stable periods of membership on the court. We look at latent factors of conflict in order to assess whether ideology divides the justices. Factor analysis weds quantitative analysis with qualitative reading of cases and starts from the presumption that liberal/conservative tensions are not the sole predictor of conflict. The chapter describes the two most prominent fulcrums of conflict in each key issue area: criminal, economic, and civil rights and liberties. Our overall results demonstrate that liberal/conservative tensions were the strongest predictor of split outcomes. We also present evidence that justices do not always vote consistently across issue areas in such cases. Indeed, one of our most striking findings is frequently conflicting voting patterns, juxtaposing justices' clear liberalism in economic cases against their clear conservative slant in criminal cases. These findings contrast starkly with voting patterns on the US Supreme Court. Ultimately, we offer an interesting blend of findings: strong attitudinal behaviour in divided rulings of Lamer's court, but with an incredible degree of ideological nuance and complexity.

Chapter 6 builds on these results with a holistic assessment of attitudinal decision making in career-long voting patterns of 23 justices under the Charter (1984–2002). We assess the bivariate relationships between ideology and judicial voting by using two a priori measures of ideology common in the discipline – namely, party affiliation of the appointing prime minister and a measure based on newspapers' ideology scores. Although the first measure is self-explanatory, we borrow newspapers' ideology scores for justices from earlier research by two of us authors (Ostberg and Wetstein 2007a). Ostberg and Wetstein derived this measure from commentary on justices at the time of their appointment in nine regional newspapers across Canada. For each justice they gave each ideological reference in articles or editorials a score that ranged from +2 (for very liberal comments) to –[minus]2 (for very conservative) and added them up to reach a cumulative score. Because newspaper coverage of judicial appointments varied so much in the papers, they decided to calculate a summary listing of each justice's ideological score from four perspectives. In other words, each justice received a score from the *Globe and Mail*, from the *Ottawa Citizen*, for the seven remaining papers, and cumulative – equal treatment of comments in all the papers. They tested the relationship between the various newspaper measures and found that they all correlated highly with each other, which suggested the method's validity.

In the last section of chapter 6, we turn to the bivariate relationship between ideology and long-term voting records. Overall, the bivariate equations suggest strongly that justices' political preferences relate to their overall support for liberal or conservative outcomes. These results reinforce our factor-analytic findings (chapter 5) and demonstrate that justices' ideological predispositions do provide a robust explanation of their voting.

Chapter 7 builds on chapter 6 by assessing the ideological measures in conjunction with other independent influences on decision making. Specifically, it highlights the importance of personal attributes that might explain disagreement among justices better than does party affiliation of the appointing prime minister. The background attributes in our multivariate models derive from prior research in this area and include justices' religion, region, gender, and previous jobs, such as law professor, lower-court judge, or federal official. We consider each variable in relation to non-unanimous decisions in criminal cases, economic cases, and civil rights and liberties.

One major finding is that party affiliation shapes liberal/conservative voting patterns in criminal cases, but not in economic cases or civil rights and liberties. In other words, Liberal appointees were more likely to vote in favour of criminal defendants than their Conservative counterparts, yet no more likely to take liberal stances in the other two fields.

Some other characteristics appear to matter in ways that differ from the period before 1982. Most intriguing, the appointment of female justices has resulted in an unmistakable gender gap across all three areas of law. Female justices are substantially more likely than men to side with rights claimants vis-à-vis civil rights and liberties and with economic underdogs, but less likely to favour criminal defendants. As well, regional and religious distinctions differ from the pre-Charter era. For example, the court appears to centre around a new regional split, with justices from Ontario, like those from Quebec in prior decades, most strongly supporting rights claimants and criminal defendants. In addition, religious differences have less impact now, particularly vis-à-vis economic cases and civil rights and liberties. Overall, religion seems to have given way to gender differences; Ontario justices are now most likely to support the underdog; ideology seems to matter in criminal law.

The empirical approaches in chapters 5–7 demonstrate that ideology, regardless of how one measures it, helps explain voting behaviour in the three areas of law. Moreover, these chapters reinforce the argument that personal characteristics that shape ideology illuminate divided outcomes.

Chapter 8 looks at empirical factors that might explain the puzzle of pervasive unanimous rulings. Using material from interviews, we present a logistic-regression equation that explores the impact of ideological differences on unanimity, along with other variables, such as legal constraints, panel size, and the presence of interveners. Not surprising, ideological differences have little effect on unanimous decisions. Instead, panel size shapes the probability of consensus. Additionally, legal constraints such as precedent, a constitutional issue, statutory interpretation, and scope of legal issues can either foster or discourage unanimity. Thus non-attitudinal factors seem to best explain how justices reach unanimous outcomes. Our picture of decision making on the Supreme Court of Canada comes full circle, providing strong empirical support for ideological behaviour in divided rulings but recognition that legal factors and collegiality foster consensus and suppress ideological disagreement. This fits with the way the justices themselves talk about their work.

Chapter 9 summarizes our major findings and discusses their relevance for democratic politics in Canada and for judicialization of politics in courts around the world. It also discusses attitudinal distinctions between Canadian justices and their US counterparts, stressing the Canadians' ideological complexities as we see them in our interviews and empirical findings. Specifically, Canadian justices approach cases in a more nuanced and complex fashion than US justices. Moreover, there is an emerging gender gap on the Canadian court that is unlike anything on the US Supreme Court. Lastly, there seems to be only a tenuous relationship between party of prime minister and liberal/conservative voting patterns in the Canadian court, which differs drastically from the US context. The book closes with some discussion of the political implications of attitudinal behaviour for the Canadian judicial-appointment process and of the larger theoretical implications of our findings for the literature on politicization of courts around the world.

2 The Supreme Court's Evolving Role

In exploring the relevance of the attitudinal model of judicial decision making in the Supreme Court of Canada, it is important to understand and assess the background and history of the Supreme Court as an institution of government in Canada. Many scholars and court observers mark 1982 as the date when the Supreme Court became a substantial policy maker because of proclamation that year of the Charter of Rights and Freedoms. The court's place as a political and legal institution, however, can best be understood against the backdrop of its historical development during the century prior to the Charter's enactment. This history illuminates its institutional arrangements and relations with the evolving federal and provincial governments and – until 1949 – the Judicial Committee of the Privy Council in London, as well as the social and political differences that would emerge over the decades in Canadian society and on the court itself.

BEFORE THE SUPREME COURT (TO 1875)

Confederation

The Constitutional Act of 1791 divided the Quebec colony into two colonies: Upper Canada in the west (the future southern Ontario), with an English-speaking majority, and Lower Canada in the east (the future southern Quebec) with a French-speaking majority (Russell 1993). In 1840, in response to a report by Lord Durham, Britain's Act of Union created a legislature for the United Province of Canada (Russell 1993). Then, in 1867, Westminster passed the

British North America Act, 1867 (BNA Act), which provided for Confederation. The legislation created the Dominion of Canada, with four provinces – New Brunswick, Nova Scotia, Ontario, and Quebec – and divided powers between the federal and provincial legislatures. Commerce, communications, criminal law, currency, defence, postal service, and trade were to be under dominion control, and the provinces took power over private-law interests, including contracts and torts, municipalities, and property.

A two-chamber Parliament in Ottawa was to consist of an elected House of Commons, which apportioned seats by population, and the federal government was to appoint representatives from each province to the Senate, with equal representation for the regions. The cabinet, under the prime minister, would formally derive its legal powers from the Privy Council to act in the name of the Crown and its representative, the governor general (British North America Act, 1867). The BNA Act did not create a Supreme Court of Canada, but it did provide the federal government with the power to establish and provide procedures for a national judiciary. The act permitted anglophones to use their language in the legislature and courts of Quebec and reciprocal rights for francophones outside Quebec (Russell 1993).

Each colony prior to 1867 had had its own court system. Lower Canada had established its own judicial system, much of it based in the French civil law tradition, while Upper Canada's derived largely from English common law. Under the Constitutional Act of 1791, each province enjoyed new courts alongside the ones established by the colonies prior to their uniting. When the two provinces united, the old court systems remained. After Confederation, provincial courts remained the general courts of Canada, but the federal government and Parliament would appoint and remove judges (Russell 1993, 24). Section 101 of the BNA Act authorized Parliament to create a "General Court of Appeal for Canada," but, Russell notes, the "Fathers of Confederation did not discuss judicial review" and saw no immediate need for such a body (Russell 1993, 44), and Parliament did not immediately set one up. Many people believed that appeals from the provincial courts should go not to Ottawa, but to the Judicial Committee of Britain's Privy Council in London (Snell and Vaughan 1985; McCormick and Greene 1990).

Early Drafts (1868–1875)

Conservative Prime Minister Sir John A. Macdonald in 1868 wanted to create a Supreme Court but was concerned over its jurisdiction (McCormick and Greene 1990; Snell and Vaughan 1985). He rejected the American model of dual federal and state courts, with federal courts having no jurisdiction over provincial law; in fact, he considered abolishing provincial courts (Snell and Vaughan 1985) but knew that the provinces would never agree. Macdonald also wanted to give the Supreme Court oversight vis-à-vis the provinces but not the federal government (McCormick and Greene 1990). In his view, the court would provide uniformity of law across Canada without encroaching on parliamentary supremacy (Snell and Vaughan 1985).

Macdonald presented the first bill to establish a Supreme Court of Canada to Parliament in 1869 (Snell and Vaughan 1985), giving it "exclusive jurisdiction" in interpreting provincial statutes. It created a Supreme Court but with no requirements about members' province of origin or training in civil versus common law. The bill created a very strong judicial institution, but its provisions were not widely accepted. The prevailing view was that the bill did not protect Quebec's civil law tradition or leave provinces enough control over their own laws (Snell and Vaughan 1985). Macdonald withdrew the measure in 1870, after support for it from his Conservatives in Parliament began to decline (McCormick and Greene 1990).

Creation (1875)

The issue did not die, however. Alexander Mackenzie's Liberal government in 1874 proposed to create a central appellate court. It submitted a bill in 1875 that created "two courts, one of appellate jurisdiction, the Supreme Court of Appeal; and another, a tribunal of first instance, composed of the same members but being a totally different court" (Snell and Vaughan 1985, 8). This draft dealt with some of the criticisms of Macdonald's proposal. The Supreme Court's jurisdiction was to be strictly appellate. A separate Exchequer Court would handle tax matters (Snell and Vaughan 1985; McCormick and Greene 1990; Ian Bushnell 1992). The legislation proposed limits on the dollar amount appealable to the Supreme Court from Quebec. At least two justices were to come from that province's bar. The bill would have ended provincial and federal appeals to the Judicial Committee of the Privy Council (JCPC), but London overruled that provision the next year (see below). The act did retain a provision from Macdonald's bill whereby the governor-in-council and the provinces could submit questions to the Supreme Court for advisory opinion (Snell and Vaughan 1985).

Parliament adopted Mackenzie's bill, with its appeals to the JCPC, in 1875 as the Supreme Court Act (Snell and Vaughan 1985; Ian Bushnell 1992). The act created a Supreme Court with six seats, two for Quebec justices. It also established an Exchequer Court consisting of the same six justices, which would exercise a very narrow original jurisdiction over cases involving admiralty law, citizenship and immigration, copyright, estate law, and trademark. The Supreme Court would have appellate jurisdiction over matters of both provincial and federal law.

The Supreme Court would, in the words of future chief justice Bora Laskin, remain a "captive court" until well into the twentieth century (McCormick 1994; Ian Bushnell 1992), with its decisions still appealable to the JCPC.

BETWIXT AND BETWEEN (1875–1949)

The First Decades (1875–1900)

The first appointments to the Supreme Court by Prime Minister Mackenzie established several traditions. The law insisted on two justices from Quebec, and Mackenzie began the tradition of an equal number of justices from Ontario (Snell and Vaughan 1985). The other two came from New Brunswick and Nova Scotia (British Columbia, Manitoba, and the Northwest Territories had very few people). Five justices had political experience, and two had been provincial chief justices (Ian Bushnell 1992). One of the latter, Sir William Richards of Ontario, became first chief justice of Canada.

Some observers thought the early court unimaginative in decisions and administration. Snell and Vaughan (1985) note " a strong tendency to adopt, copy, or emulate the practices found in Ontario courts" (19). Undoubtedly the chief justice played a role there. Most cases dealt with civil and commercial matters involving minor issues of law or of law and fact and related to both private and public law (McCormick and Greene 1990). Because of the court's low prestige, many appeals skipped it and proceeded *per saltum* directly to the JCPC (Russell 1993). As Russell notes, the court was "supreme in name only" (1993, 40). Many people who favoured strong provincial rights were suspicious of the institution and its personnel. Justices Ritchie and Strong viewed the British North America Act in centralist terms, which concerned observers who regarded the document as limited in scope over the provinces (Snell and Vaughan 1985; McCormick and Greene 1990).

Most critics considered the Supreme Court a failure in its first two decades (Snell and Vaughan 1985; McCormick and Greene 1990; Ian Bushnell 1992; Russell 1993). It was not the crucial institution that its proponents in Parliament had maintained (Snell and Vaughan 1985). In 1888 a Conservative MP called for its abolition (Ian Bushnell 1992). The bill had some Conservative support, but the Liberals defeated it. The legislation represented rural animosity in some provinces, especially Quebec, towards large, central, expensive government (Snell and Vaughan 1985). Some observers viewed the justices as outsiders and legal novices who knew little about provincial law. Quebec, in particular, was very critical of justices who lacked training in civil law, with some Quebec MPs voting to abolish the court (Ian Bushnell 1992).

The debate also related to the issue of whether Canada was a federation or a legislative union. People who thought it a federation viewed the Supreme Court as an encroachment on provincial power. Believers in a legislative union wanted the court even stronger, to ensure uniformity of law throughout the dominion.

The Supreme Court's early practices were somewhat timid and conservative (Snell and Vaughan 1985; Ian Bushnell 1992; Russell 1993). The court relied on seriatim opinions partly as common law tradition (as only the US Supreme Court under Chief Justice John Marshall and the JCPC gave full court opinions) and partly as convenience. The justices were not often in Ottawa, as many served on special commissions within their home provinces (Snell and Vaughan 1985; Ian Bushnell 1992). The fact that the court did not harmonize in its judgments may partially explain its lack of legitimacy at the time (McCormick and Greene 1990).

The Supreme Court published its first decision only in 1877 – it lacked organization, and some justices simply forgot to turn in their opinions or misplaced them (Snell and Vaughan 1985). During these early years, the justices operated independent of each other rather than by holding conference (Ian Bushnell 1992). Problems were blamed mostly on poor leadership, but inexperience was also a crucial factor. As well, the JCPC overturned several of the Supreme Court's earliest cases vis-à-vis the BNA Act.

Despite these setbacks, appeals sent to the Supreme Court, rather than bypassing it, continued to grow in number – to an average of 71.9 per year from 1879 to 1892. During the 1880s, only 53 of the approximately 1,000 cases that it decided were appealed to London (Snell and Vaughan 1985).

In 1882 the Supreme Court moved into its first permanent building (Supreme Court of Canada website 2005) from vacant rooms in the Parliament buildings (Snell and Vaughan 1985), and the issue of abolition never surfaced again (Ian Bushnell 1992). In 1895, Westminster's Judicial Committee Amendment Act made it possible for the monarch to summon a handful of colonial justices to sit, without pay, on the JCPC (Ian Bushnell 1992). In 1897, Chief Justice Strong became the first Canadian to do so, but this appointment began the tradition of divided loyalties (Snell and Vaughan 1985).

The Twentieth Century to 1949

In the first decades of the twentieth century, turnover among justices was extremely high (Snell and Vaughan 1985; Ian Bushnell 1992), with more senior government positions frequently being a lure. In 1900, Liberal Prime Minister Sir Wilfrid Laurier named the first westerner to the court, Justice Albert Clements Killam from Manitoba. Thereafter a westerner usually took one of the seats that had formerly gone to a Maritimer (Snell and Vaughan 1985). Killam resigned only 18 months later to become head of the Board of Railway Commissioners for Canada. In 1906, Laurier appointed the most famous justice in the court's history, Lyman Duff. Duff was only 41, had lived in Ontario, but had moved to and practised law in British Columbia. Unlike most of the appointments, his did not involve patronage (Ian Bushnell 1992). He was well qualified and would become one of the most influential chief justices ever to serve.

The 1900s and 1910s were very conservative decades for the court (Snell and Vaughan 1985; McCormick and Greene 1990; Ian

Bushnell 1992; Russell 1993). The justices followed precedent to the letter, even when opportunities arose for them to distinguish precedent. Snell and Vaughan (1985) suggest that most justices lacked experience and were unsure of themselves, sticking very close to *stare decisis* and overturning only 24 per cent of lower courts' decisions. At the same time, appeals to London were at an all-time high in the 1910s, rising from 5 per cent in the decade prior to 14 per cent (Snell and Vaughan 1985).

Justice Duff joined the JCPC in 1918 after gaining prominence on the Supreme Court. He was instrumental in the 1910s and 1920s in leading the court to use advisory opinions and in tackling constitutional issues (Ian Bushnell 1992). He became chief justice of Canada in 1933. During his years on the court (1906–44), it decided nearly 200 constitutional cases (Snell and Vaughan 1985). Yet most members were patronage appointees who served also in other government posts, and the institution remained conservative and narrow in its decisions, much more so than the JCPC.

William Lyon Mackenzie King's Liberal governments in the 1920s made many patronage appointments. According to Snell and Vaughan (1985), the "tendency to partisan use of judicial appointments ... caused a good deal of concern in this period. With the return of the practice under Mackenzie King, protests increased, though with little apparent impact" (156). In 1927, Parliament expanded the court to seven justices – the recommendation in the original bill to create the body. But Parliament also viewed ageing justices as a problem – some were approaching or over 75 years of age (McCormick and Greene 1990). The new law mandated retirement at 75, so John Idington, 86, stepped down immediately. When Chief Justice Duff turned 75, the government, because of his towering reputation, waived the requirement, and he served three more years (Ian Bushnell 1992).

Thibaudeau Rinfret, who would replace Duff as chief justice in 1944, had sat on the Royal Commission on Dominion–Provincial Relations beginning in 1937. In 1945, Justice Kellock headed a royal commission on the VE-day riots in Halifax, and Justices Taschereau and Kellock investigated Soviet espionage in Canada. Other royal commissions also used justices for non-judicial purposes (see Snell and Vaughan 1985 for further examples). Some critics saw such non-judicial tasks as blatant patronage; others thought that it trivialized the court (Ian Bushnell 1992).

The Long Struggle: The Appeal to London (1833–1949)

After the British Parliament created the Judicial Committee of the Privy Council (JCPC) in 1833, that body served as arbiter of disputes arising throughout the British Empire (Swinfen 1987). The committee was to "consist of all Privy Councillors who held, or had held, certain specified high judicial offices" (Swinfen 1987, 7). This rule gave it legitimacy in deciding cases arising from various colonial regions whose laws differed from each other. However, by the 1870s, many commentators began to challenge the need for a right to appeal from the colonies and dominions (Swinfen 1987). Some critics thought that the committee served only the wealthy, and others criticized the impracticality of overseas appeals and of the committee's slow decisions (Swinfen 1987).

Canada abolished appeals to the JCPC in 1875 with clause 47 of the Supreme Court Act (Snell and Vaughan 1985). In passing the legislation on to the British government in 1875, Ottawa made the case that, since Parliament had the authority to regulate appeals to the JCPC, it could also abolish them. London, however, viewed clause 47 as an attempt to break ties between Canada and Britain completely (Ian Bushnell 1992). In 1876 it rendered clause 47 inoperative (Ian Bushnell 1992) but allowed Canada to regulate appeals to the committee.

By the 1920s and 1930s, both Canada and Australia were anxious for the appeals to the JCPC to end, but federal arrangements in both countries slowed change (Swinfen 1987). Quebec valued the right to appeal to London to protect the French majority in the province. The committee itself cited the same concern vis-à-vis the Irish Free State (which came into being in 1922) (Swinfen 1987). In fact, symbolism seems to be the main reason why the right to appeal lasted so long. The committee's decisions have almost always been unanimous: "Occasionally the fact of dissent has been recorded but, prior to 1966, the grounds of such dissent could not be made public" (Swinfen 1987, 19). This fact, and the symbolism surrounding the institution, perpetuated the perception that it was a neutral third party, especially in federal–provincial disputes.

Canadians could appeal to the JCPC from decisions by the Supreme Court and by provincial courts. During the 74 years before abolition of appeals in 1949, the Supreme Court "suffered the further indignity that if the litigants so elected appeals from provincial appellate decisions could be taken directly to the Privy Council, and in practice often were" (Ziegel 2001, 135). In fact, McCormick (1994) reports that the majority of appeals were *per saltum* rather than from the Supreme Court of Canada. Vaughan (2001) concludes that the JCPC overshadowed the Supreme Court. It decided between 50 and 60 appeals from Canada during the late nineteenth century. The figure increased to over 100 for the 1910s and 1920s, decreased slightly to 84 in the 1930s, and fell dramatically to only 36 in the 1940s (Snell and Vaughan 1985; McCormick 1994), probably because of the end of criminal appeals in 1933.

The Canadian Parliament had abolished criminal appeals to the JCPC in 1888. However, in 1926, the Privy Council ruled such action *ultra vires* of Parliament, as it conflicted with a British statute of 1844 that expressly extended the committee's jurisdiction to Canada (Ian Bushnell 1992). In 1931, the *Statute of Westminster* granted Ottawa control over Canada's external affairs and any other matters previously under British control (Snell and Vaughan 1985), and in 1933 Parliament re-enacted the prohibition of criminal appeals in section 1025 of the Criminal Code. In *British Coal Corporation v. The King* (1935), the JCPC upheld the validity of section 1025, officially sanctioning abolition of criminal appeals.

The issue of the end of the appeal was not dead, however. In 1930, a decision by the JCPC set off a firestorm of controversy. In 1928, the Supreme Court of Canada decided the famous *Persons* case (*In the Matter of a reference as to the Meaning of the Word "Persons" in Section 24 of the British North America Act, 1867*). The case was a reference to the Supreme Court about whether Ottawa could appoint a woman to the Senate under section 24 of the BNA Act: did the word "persons" there include females? All senators had been male, and the court reasoned that the framers of the act could not have intended to permit female senators (Ian Bushnell 1992). The act used the word "he" exclusively in reference to senators. Five of the seven justices decided the case. Only Justice Duff refused to confront the central issue directly: he suggested that it was Parliament's role, not the court's, to decide who "qualified persons" were.

The JCPC received the case in 1929 and renamed it *Edwards v. Attorney General of Canada* to reflect the name of the petitioner who sought the Senate seat. The committee found the Supreme Court's ruling completely erroneous, calling the exclusion of women from public office "a relic of days more barbarous than ours" (*Edwards v. Attorney General of Canada*, 1930). The decision caused a deeper rift between people who viewed the Supreme Court as incompetent and those who felt that the committee was out of touch with Canada. The Supreme Court's decision in the *Persons* case damaged its public image, but legal professionals worried much more about the JCPC's judicial activism (Snell and Vaughan 1985; Vaughan 2001). The case sparked an editorial debate in law professional journals in Canada, in which proponents of abolition of appeals argued that the committee was no more impartial than the Supreme Court. Others maintained that it would uphold only provincial rights, which the Supreme Court would trample. Quebec was especially sceptical about ending appeals (Ian Bushnell 1992).

To fathom the nature of the decades-long debate, we can consider a 1946 case before the Supreme Court. In 1945, responding to concerns of British Columbia about Japanese-Canadian residents during and after the Second World War, the federal government passed three orders-in-council that authorized deportation to Japan of people over sixteen who had requested repatriation under earlier government policy. These persons would cease to be British subjects or Canadian nationals. One order required that wives and children return to Japan with their husbands, even if only the man made the request. Under public pressure, the government submitted the orders-in-council to the Supreme Court in *Reference Re Persons of Japanese Race* (Ian Bushnell 1992). In February 1946 the court upheld the orders, but a 4–3 majority invalidated the provision forcing wives and children to join their husband/father. Justices Estey and Hudson reasoned that Ottawa had not deemed such action necessary for national security under the War Measures Act, while Justices Rand and Kellock directly confronted the racism of the orders-in-council and also reasoned that expulsion of wives and children was not essential for national security.

The government appealed the decision to the JCPC. The latter upheld Ottawa's power to issue the orders-in-council under national security powers and maintained that deportation of dependants fell within its power of security and defence, even without explicit provision of the necessity under the War Measures Act (*Co-operative Committee on Japanese Canadians v. Attorney General for Canada*, 1947). In this case the committee overturned the Supreme Court's limits on government intrusion into civil liberties.

The push for complete abolition of appeals had been continuing (Snell and Vaughan 1985; Ian Bushnell 1992). An understandable backlog of appeals during the Second World War created concern about the system's practicality (Snell and Vaughan 1985). As well, the JCPC was losing some of its popularity in Canada: in a series of cases in the late 1930s, it overturned the New Deal–style legislation of R.B. Bennett's Conservative government (1930–5), and the resulting outcry spurred Ottawa's desire to abolish all appeals. The Liberal government submitted a reference question to the Supreme Court in 1940 about the constitutionality of abolition (*Attorney General of Ontario v. Attorney General of Canada*, 1940), and the court found that it could do so. The JCPC heard the case in 1946 and announced in early 1947 that it concurred (Ian Bushnell 1992). The government soon introduced a bill to that effect. There was little debate, and the measure passed easily (Snell and Vaughan 1985). In December 1949, the Supreme Court became Canada's final court of appeal; its membership increased from seven to nine justices.

Establishing the court's status as a legitimate and fully competent final arbiter had been a long, hard-fought battle, but by 1949, its reputation had grown steadily in the public and legal profession's eyes (Snell and Vaughan 1985; Ian Bushnell 1992). Its new authority meant that it would have more opportunity to exercise judicial review and become more activist (Vaughan 2001).

While the appeal certainly was symbolic in maintaining provincial versus federal interests, it is not at all clear that the JCPC favoured the provinces. According to Swinfen, many decisions in the later nineteenth century expanded the provinces' legislative power, but he wonders about the significance of this trend (1987, 28). However, some scholars argue that the provinces gained a great deal of power in that period (Russell 1993). In the 1870s, as Russell (1993) notes, in several key constitutional challenges the Supreme Court interpreted federal power broadly, declaring provincial laws *ultra vires* (outside [the provinces'] power). By the 1880s, however, the JCPC had reversed many of these cases, deciding 75 per cent of them for the provinces (Russell 1993).

Some scholars see the end of the appeal not as Ottawa's winning a federal–provincial struggle but as the result of attacks on the quality of the JCPC's decisions (Ian Bushnell 1992). Vaughan (2001) thinks that criticisms of the committee really targeted the principle of judicial review from London. "Those calls [for abolition] were never to abandon the use of the courts as instruments of constitutional adjudication. Rather, they were to allow our own Canadian courts, especially the Supreme Court of Canada ... to become the final court of appeal" (Vaughan 2001: 6). Whatever the case, the evidence about reasons for abolition tells us nothing about how appeals to the committee constrained justices' decisions. The evidence does suggest, however, that the committee's reversal of so many of the Supreme Court's decisions on federalism further delegitimized the court.

FINAL ARBITER (1949–1982)

The 1950s

In *R. v. Boucher* (1951), the Supreme Court overruled the conviction under sedition charges of Aimé Boucher, a member of the Jehovah's Witnesses. Jehovah's Witnesses challenged the views of the Roman Catholic church in Quebec, and during the war the Canadian government allowed the province to ban the group as an illegal organization under the War Measures Act (Ian Bushnell 1992). The ban had ended in 1945, but in 1946 provincial authorities charged Boucher with "seditious intention" for distributing religious tracts. The Court of King's Bench upheld his conviction on appeal. The full bench of the Supreme Court rendered its verdict on the appeal in June 1950 and ruled 5–4 in favour of acquittal.

Prior to Boucher's arrest, the meaning of "seditious intention" had derived from Britain's Royal Commission on Codification of the Criminal Law (1880), which defined "seditious intention" as "to promote feelings of ill will and hostility between different classes of subjects" (Ian Bushnell 1992, 298). The Supreme Court, 8–1, reasoned that "ill-will and hostility" were not enough to constitute "seditious intention." Chief Justice Ivan Rand met with great support for his seriatim opinion. One journalist wrote, "The judgments inspire pride and confidence in the court that is now in all matters Canada's final court of appeal" (Ian Bushnell 1992, 300). Another observer noted, "*Boucher* is a textbook example of judicial craftsmanship and demonstrates that Canadian judges are perfectly capable of it" (Weiler 1974). The ultimate result in the *Boucher* case is striking when compared to the civil liberties claim made in *Reference Re Persons of*

Japanese Race. In that case, the Judicial Committee overturned the Supreme Court's expansion of civil liberties; in *Boucher*, the court's expansion of civil liberties was the final word. Heading into the latter half of the twentieth century, protection of civil liberties by the Supreme Court seemed hopeful.

Under the Bill of Rights (1960–1982)

After the end of appeals to the Judicial Committee of the Privy Council in 1949, the Supreme Court became more active vis-à-vis civil liberties. Passage of the Canadian Bill of Rights in 1960 aided this process. The legislation has been described as a response to the postwar human rights movement in Europe and indication of Canada's desire to be a leader in that field (Vaughan 2001). The new Bill of Rights instructed the Supreme Court to "construe and apply" all laws of the government of Canada to ensure that they did not infringe on the rights that the document protected. The statute did not affect provincial laws (Vaughan 2001). Many civil libertarians were hopeful that the Supreme Court would continue its efforts of the 1950s (McCormick and Greene 1990).

The court decided its first case under the Bill of Rights in 1963. In *Robertson & Rosetanni v. The Queen*, it addressed the Lord's Day Act, a long-standing federal law. Robertson and Rosetanni were bowling-alley operators who had opened on Sundays. The court refused to strike down the Lord's Day Act, and a majority ruled that the Bill of Rights applied only protections as they existed before its enactment – it did not create new rights (*Robertson & Rosetanni v. The Queen*, 1963). Notably, Justice John Robert Cartwright, who joined the court in 1949, wrote a sharp dissent. He argued that the act ought to confer new rights as well as confirm existing ones and that the only way for it to do so was by striking down any legislation to the contrary. His view was very controversial and seemed to some critics to challenge parliamentary supremacy. In 1967, when he became chief justice, many civil libertarians were hopeful that under his leadership the court would become more activist in its application of the Bill of Rights (Ian Bushnell 1992).

The opportunity for activism presented itself in 1970 in *The Queen v. Drybones*. In the case, the court for the first time ruled a section of federal legislation inoperative. A majority held that section 94 of the Indian Act of 1947 violated the guarantees of equality before the law in the Canadian Bill of Rights. In this decision, Weiler (1974) argues, the Supreme Court "abruptly shifted from its path in *Rosetanni* ... The judges seized the opportunity to carve out a visible and full fledged judicial role as the protector of our civil liberties against Parliamentary intrusion" (195).

Yet Cartwright disappointed many civil libertarians by dissenting from this decision. In his dissent, he stated that he had earlier interpreted the Canadian Bill of Rights incorrectly (Vaughan 2001): Parliament could not have intended that the Supreme Court be able to overturn existing statutes by ordinary statute, he explained. He was particularly concerned about the burden placed on lower government officials at all levels in implementing such judicial decisions (*The Queen v. Drybones*, 1970).

After Cartwright retired in 1970, the court remained quite reluctant to use the Bill of Rights to overturn legislation. Leeson (2001) describes the judicial interpretation of the statute as "cautious and restrictive" (Leeson 2001, 303). That trend continued under Chief Justice Gérald Fauteux (Ian Bushnell 1992). Fauteux, whom Liberal Prime Minister Louis St-Laurent appointed in 1949 from Quebec, became chief justice in 1970, serving until December 1973. Liberal Prime Minister Pierre Trudeau's elevation of Fauteux might have been surprising to some observers, as he was so close to retirement age at 75. He acted perhaps to help give French Canadians a more prominent role in Ottawa (Snell and Vaughan 1985). Fauteux retired from the bench early, as did Justice Douglas Charles Abbott, perhaps, some historians suggest, because of internal tensions in the court (Ian Bushnell 1992).

Those tensions arose in response to the court's decision in *Kienapple v. the Queen*. A court had convicted Kienapple of statutory rape of a female under the age of fourteen. The Supreme Court reversed the conviction, formulating a new criminal defence that prohibited conviction of an accused for multiple crimes for the same act. The court divided 5–4, with justices Abbott, Fauteux, Martland, and Ritchie dissenting. Shortly afterwards, but before announcement of the decision in February 1974, Abbott and Fauteux resigned. The new chief justice, Bora Laskin, who had joined the court in 1970, announced the decision. Laskin had attended Harvard Law School for graduate study and become a law professor at the University of Toronto and Osgoode Law School. He had written extensively on civil rights and liberties and believed that the Canadian Bill of Rights gave the Supreme Court a basis for judicial activism.

Still, despite the decision in *Kienapple*, Laskin was unable to "nudge a Court majority into a more activist role even after he became chief justice" (Snell and Vaughan 1985, 223). Instead, a majority "held firmly to the tradition of legislative deference; they wanted a more explicit invitation to judicial activism than the Bill of Rights contained" (Snell and Vaughan 1985, 223). In writing about this period, Paul Weiler (1974) criticizes the court's approach to cases: "My diagnosis of the malady of the Supreme Court is quite simple and can be summed up in one short sentence: Our judges share an outmoded and unduly narrow conception of the rule of law in courts" (1974, 4).

Laskin's appointment as chief justice in 1973 (he served until his death in 1984) stirred hopes for more active application of the Canadian Bill of Rights (Weiler 1974; McCormick and Greene 1990; McCormick 1994). Laskin hoped to increase the court's status vis-à-vis Parliament and thought that the Bill of Rights gave it special status in interpreting federal laws. However, the majority of his colleagues disagreed, and Laskin was frequently in the minority on issues of civil liberties, with the majority continuing to interpret the Bill of Rights narrowly (Snell and Vaughan 1985). The Supreme Court had seemed to many observers in the early 1960s as the body to enforce Canadians' rights and freedoms, but it turned out to be much weaker and less effective than many supporters had hoped (Snell and Vaughan 1985).

By the 1970s, many lawyers were blaming its inaction not on justices' lack of activism but on the court's workload (Weiler 1974; Ian Bushnell 1992). In response, Parliament in 1975 gave it virtually complete discretionary control of its docket. Previously it had to hear all appeals except for civil cases dealing with less than $10,000. Now it could decide which civil cases of "public importance" it would review (Statutes of Canada 1974–75–76). It still had to hear criminal cases where dissent existed in the court below, but there was now no automatic right to appeal to it in writs of mandamus or habeas corpus when the decision below was unanimous (*Statutes of Canada* 1974–75–76).

A reference case soon afterwards would have broad implications for federal policy. In *Reference Re Anti-Inflation Act* (1976) the court ruled on the constitutionality of the Anti-Inflation Act of 1975. Canada could not amend much of its constitution (the British North America Act, 1867) without Westminster's approval. The Trudeau government had argued that it lacked the constitutional authority to control wages and prices, but under enormous public pressure it proposed the Anti-Inflation Act, which Parliament passed in late 1975. Unions and business groups attacked the measure. A teacher's group challenged it, and the government referred it to the Supreme Court.

Over five days in late May and early June 1976, the full bench heard the case, which involved unprecedented amounts of information and participation by interveners. The court rushed to judgment and issued its decision on 12 July. It split 7–2 in favour of the government and its authority to enact the Anti-Inflation Act under Parliament's "emergency power." Laskin, for the majority, commented: "A Constitution designed to serve this country in years ahead ought to be regarded as a resilient instrument capable of adaptation to changing circumstances" (*Reference Re Anti-Inflation Act*, 1976). While the decision was not activist in tone, a constitutional scholar argues that Laskin had accomplished a "significant piece of law reform or law making" by "quietly and professionally using application reform" (Ian Bushnell 1992, 424–5). This case illustrates the sort of creative jurisprudence that justices can use in important areas of public policy. For the first time, the court had sanctioned broad federal economic regulation during peacetime (Snell and Vaughan 1985).

While Parliament had debated the court's docket and workload, some observers saw it as a chance to enforce rights and freedoms more strongly (McCormick 1994). Chief Justice Brian Dickson, Laskin's successor (1984–90), also viewed the act as changing the court's focus towards public law (Ian Bushnell 1992). Yet during his early years the court interpreted the Bill of Rights narrowly.

We can see one example of the narrow view in the court's decisions regarding abortion. In *Morgentaler v. The Queen* (1976), it ruled that an abortion doctor and associates could not raise a sufficient defence against their violation of the Criminal Code in performing abortions. Dickson, writing for the majority, opined that it was not the court's place to "decide or even to enter, the loud and continuous public debate on abortion" (*Morgentaler v. The Queen*,

1976). Dickson's view would change, however, with the Charter of Rights and Freedoms of 1982.

THE CHARTER ERA (1982–PRESENT)

The Charter of Rights and Freedoms

From the creation of the Supreme Court in 1875 until 1982, the court's role in Canadian governance was less prominent than that of other government institutions. We have seen above several factors responsible for this situation: the right of appeal (until 1949) to the Judicial Committee of the Privy Council (JCPC), the statutory Canadian Bill of Rights (1960) and its applicability only to federal legislation, and the tradition of parliamentary supremacy.

One scholar describes the court's use of judicial review as much less prominent than the US Supreme Court's is in American law, simply because Canadian courts are generally more deferential to Parliament than the US Supreme Court is to Congress (Vaughan 2001). Leeson (2001) describes judicial review by Canadian courts as "used sparingly" (298). The Canadian approach, he argues, rejects US-style judicial interpretation, yet does not fully embrace the British judicial model (Leeson 2001). Weiler (1974) criticizes the court's restraintist view of the role of law, arguing that justices are elitists who rarely connect with the public or Parliament. He finds the court much less responsive to the electorate than Parliament and that the appointment process makes justices beholden to the federal government (Weiler 1974). Both the Supreme Court and the JCPC had declared provincial acts *ultra vires*, and the early Supreme Court had often had the final say on whether a particular power was federal or provincial (Leeson 2001). However, the court could not declare laws in violation of fundamental rights and freedoms under the constitution (Leeson 2001).

The Charter of Rights and Freedoms (1982) changed all that. One view sees its creation and passage as a direct response to Canada's lack of uniform protection of civil liberties under the Canadian Bill of Rights. Vaughan (2001) suggests that the main critics of constitutional entrenchment believed that it would result in "judicial supremacy" and the "judicialization of politics" (Vaughan 2001, 13). However, it is precisely this protection of rights that proponents favoured. Others argue that the leadership of Prime Minister Trudeau in the 1970s and early 1980s was the main impetus for the Charter, focusing mostly on language rights. In 1971, Trudeau had proposed the Victoria Charter, which would have entrenched language rights, but it ultimately failed, and he continued his efforts.

Leeson (2001) describes the negotiations and compromises between the provinces and the Trudeau government in forging a constitutionally entrenched Charter of Rights and Freedoms. Many of the provinces were cautious because the Canadian Bill of Rights had not extended to provincial legislation. However, when the movement towards adoption of a Charter began in the late 1970s, provinces went to the table to negotiate (Ian Bushnell 1992; McWhinney 1987; Leeson 2001). In February 1979 at the First Ministers' conference, many provinces agreed to entrench a Charter but wanted to limit it to fundamental freedoms, democratic rights, and language rights, especially for francophones. Despite the proposal's safeguards for language rights, Quebec maintained its objections to entrenchment. The Parti Québécois (PQ) had gained power in the province in 1976 and had proposed a referendum on separation from Canada (Leeson 2001).

Hirschl (2004) describes the Charter's origins as the "culmination of a long and arduous political battle ... traced to the rise of Quebec nationalism in the 1960's" (75). He cites Trudeau's advocacy for civil liberties as one factor but calls his actions a "strategic response to the growing threat of Quebec separatism" (75). Earlier attempts at entrenchment failed because Parliament did not wish to cede supremacy to the constitution and hence the courts. Prior to the 1960s, parliamentary supremacy could survive with the status quo. However, rising Quebec nationalism, culminating with the PQ's election in 1976, led to the unsuccessful referendum on independence in 1980. In Hirschl's estimation, the Charter was Trudeau's response to this change in the status quo. There was an "expectation of national unity around the Charter" (Hirschl 2004, 75), and Parliament and the provinces embraced it.

Lebel-Grenier (2001) agrees that the motives for creating the Charter included devising a national symbol for all Canadians to rally around, but the country did so "against the express will of Quebec" (94). "PM Trudeau wanted to establish a mechanism that would make it possible for individuals to oppose the state" (95), to reinforce liberalism as a dominant ideology in Canada. However, "in selecting these means to meet his concerns, [Trudeau] gave the courts a free hand. These two motives for the establishment of the Charter could only mean increased judicial activism" (95). Hirschl finds "broad consensus among critical scholars ... that the enactment of the Charter was, at least in part, a self-interested maneuver initiated by elites" (Hirschl 2004, 77). Suddenly parliamentary sovereignty was not a difficult exchange for constitutional supremacy when separatism threatened the political status quo.

A seismic shift occurred with entrenchment of a Charter of Rights and Freedoms in Canada's Constitution Act, 1982, which patriated the British North America Act, 1867, ending Westminster's right to amend that founding legislation (Russell 1993). Most amendments to the new constitution would require approval by Parliament and seven provinces representing 50 per cent of the population (Constitution Act, 1982); others, such as changes to the composition of the Supreme Court and the amendment formula, would require unanimous provincial approval. With the principal exception of a notwithstanding (override) clause – see below – the Charter was virtually untouchable.

The Charter protects citizens from governmental encroachment in religion, freedom of expression, voting rights, mobility rights, criminal rights (principles of fundamental justice), equality rights regardless of race, religion, gender, age, or disability, language rights, and minority language education rights for English and French speakers. Unlike the US Bill of Rights, it recognizes both individual and communitarian conceptions of rights, including entrenched rights for linguistic communities (Sniderman et al. 1989).

The Supreme Court of Canada has the power to review acts of Parliament and provincial legislatures to see if they violate the Charter (Constitution Act, 1982). Cases involving civil rights and liberties have dominated the court's agenda since passage of the Charter, while private law appeals have virtually disappeared (Bushnell 1992). In entrenching judicial review, the Charter has "redefined the institutional balance of power among legislature, executive and judiciary" (Sniderman et al. 1989, 251).

Impact of the Charter

Most observers agree that the Charter greatly expanded the policymaking role of the Supreme Court. One scholar recognized long before its adoption that it "would alter the Canadian system of government by significantly expanding the policy-making role of the courts" (Fletcher 1999, 265). Another adds that the "Charter was designed to transform the Canadian legal system" (Weinrib 2001, 81). Hirschl (2004) considers the Charter's impact revolutionary. Although it passed in 1982, the Supreme Court did not decide its first Charter case until 1984. Before then, lower courts decided approximately 1,000 cases dealing with some aspect of the Charter (Snell and Vaughan 1985). Vaughan (2001) concludes that the Court "has not ... shied away from a vigorous application of the Charter" (14) and finds the court more activist under the Charter.

In its first Charter case, *Law Society of Upper Canada v. Skapinker* (1984), a unanimous court upheld a provision of Ontario's Law Society Act, which required that lawyers become Canadian citizens before the province would license them. Skapinker argued that the act violated the "mobility" provision of the Charter. However, the court held that that provision did not include a "right to work." In *Hunter v. Southam* (1984), the court's only other Charter case in 1984, the justices unanimously ruled that warrantless searches violated the Charter's protections, striking down sections of the Combines Investigation Act. Lebel-Grenier (2001) notes that judicial self-restraint was commonplace before the Charter but less so following its passage. Judges did not request the Charter, politicians imposed it on them, and it devolves responsibilities from the executive/legislative to the courts (and thereby helps governments avoid political backlash for unpopular decisions) (Lebel-Grenier 2001).

Ziegel (2001) believes that entrenchment of the Charter increased the court's role, although some Canadian judges disagree. For instance, in *Morgentaler v. The Queen* (1988), the abortionist whose case the court had decided in 1976 was again on trial. This time, the court held 5–2 that section 251 of the *Criminal Code*, which made abortion illegal except in rare instances, was unconstitutional because of section 7 of the Charter – government may not infringe on "life, liberty, or security of person" (Knopff 2001). Chief Justice Dickson indicated, and Justice Lamer concurred, that "in the pre-Charter days the court was to follow the values expressed by Parliament, but now the 'democratic values' expressed in the Charter as enforced by the judges was [*sic*] to govern" (*Morgentaler v. The Queen*, 1988). In this ruling and other Charter decisions, the court asserted itself as a policy-making body (Ian Bushnell 1992).

The *Morgentaler* (1988) decision may not have been a surprise to some commentators after passage of the Charter in 1982, but the court and Dickson had certainly changed their positions in a decade.

Scholars have noted decision-making patterns by the court since 1982. Vaughan (2001) finds that it decided more cases on legal rights than on equality rights between 1982 and 1992, with most Charter decisions dealing primarily with fundamental justice (section 7), search and seizure (section 8), the right to counsel (section 10b), and the right to an independent and impartial tribunal (section 11d). He suggests that these cases have been clearer in interpretation and less controversial than cases on equality and language rights (Vaughan 2001). However, Hirschl (2004) believes that the court has been a major decision maker regarding Quebec, "ruling that unilateral secession would be unconstitutional under domestic and international law" (81; referencing *Re: Secession of Quebec* 1998). According to Hiebert (2001), the Charter transformed the types of cases that the court decides; its enactment marked the "end of historic reluctance to enter into a sphere previously considered explicitly political" (165). As an example, she cites *R. v. Seaboyer* (1991) and Justice Claire L'Heureux-Dubé's forceful dissent questioning stereotypical views regarding sexual assault and relevant legal standards (Hiebert 2001, 184).

The Notwithstanding Clause

The majority of Canadian court scholars note the increased judicial activism of the Supreme Court of Canada and its more frequent exercise of judicial review since entrenchment in 1982 of the Charter of Rights and Freedoms. Experts had anticipated such a shift. Ian Bushnell explains the fear tactics that the press used after the earliest Charter rulings – for example, in the headline "Charter ruling worries legal experts: interpretation could open doors to US-style judicial intervention" (1992, 458). Perhaps fear of too much power for an unelected judiciary spawned "legislative review of judicial review" (Fletcher 1999, 266) – i.e., potential parliamentary oversight of the court's activities.

The Charter's "notwithstanding" or "override" clause "permits the legislature to set aside, for five years at a time, judicial enforcement of key sections of the Charter" (Fletcher 1999, 266). This check on judicial power is unique to Canada and stands in stark contrast to the unbridled judicial clout of its American counterpart. Pierre Trudeau was among the foremost proponents and advanced the proposal at the Victoria Conference in 1971, with Bill C-60 in 1978, and at First Ministers' conferences in the late 1970s and early 1980s (Russell 1993). There is a notwithstanding clause in section 2 of the Canadian Bill of Rights, but Leeson (2001) considers it "ultimately of little consequence" because of cautious interpretation of the statute.

Entrenchment of a Charter became a subject of serious debate among the provinces and the federal government, with Saskatchewan initiating its inclusion at the First Ministers' conference in September 1981 (Leeson 2001). Several provinces agreed that an override clause was necessary for some sections of the Charter and were willing to accept Ottawa's proposal for an amendment process in exchange for an override clause (Russell 1993; Leeson 2001). The Charter's notwithstanding clause allows provincial and federal governments to overturn rulings under sections 2 (fundamental freedoms, such as religion and speech) and sections 7–15 (due process and equality rights). Other rights are not subject to the notwithstanding provision: enforcement of the Charter, democratic rights, equality of the sexes, and rights vis-à-vis mobility, language, minority-language education, denomination schools, and multicultural heritage (Canadian Charter of Rights and Freedoms 1982; Johansen and Rosen 1997).

Some scholars suggest from the legislative history that the drafters intended "notwithstanding" as a check on the court that Parliament would use far more than the provincial legislatures. Most of the debates centred on the conflict between provincial power and Parliament's ability to legislate in emergencies. Some commentators argue that the framers did not anticipate provincial overrides to any extent. For several years Quebec's legislature invoked the clause in all bills as a protest of the Charter's imposition over its objection (Leeson 2001). Cairns (1998) and Hiebert (2002) both claim that the conflict between the court and the provinces is partly due to the fact that Canada's court system is unitary. All Charter rulings apply to all provinces without a federal question requirement, yet the provinces have always been able to determine their own means of applying federal law. Hiebert points out that the court has been sensitive to the provinces' traditional role (Hiebert 2002). The court has made special attempts in its judgments' wording to maintain provincial rights by interpreting the Charter loosely enough that it may mean different things to people depending on the province in which they reside. Still, the notwithstanding clause has been used, though rarely, by some provinces as a check on judicial supremacy. However, Quebec's blanket use of it was unpopular with many Canadians elsewhere, and many observers consider it a primary reason for the failure of the Meech Lake Accord.

The Charter, Meech Lake, and Charlottetown

When the Constitution Act went into effect in 1982, Quebec was the only province that did not give its assent – ratification of the Constitution Act and its Charter of Rights and Freedoms did not require unanimous consent. Brian Mulroney, who became prime minister in 1984, attempted to reach out to Quebec and fashion a constitutional scheme that it would accept (Russell 1993). The result was the Meech Lake Accord, which included five Quebec conditions for its acceptance of the constitution – recognition of Quebec as a "distinct society," a greater role in immigration, more say in selection of its three justices on the Supreme Court of Canada, the right to opt out of federal spending programs in areas of exclusive provincial jurisdiction, and a veto on constitutional amendments that would affect it (Meech Lake Accord, 1985).

The Meech Lake Accord was unpopular with much of the public outside Quebec. Russell explains, "the great majority of English-speaking Canadians simply did not accept that the 1982 Constitution was imposed on Quebec against its will" (Russell 1993, 142). Therefore public acceptance was slight, especially among interest groups that had pushed for the Charter (Dion 1992; Manfredi 1993; Leeson 2001). Yet the accord came close to adoption, its failure late in the process resulting ultimately from Quebec's misuse of the legislative override in the controversy over use of English in advertising signs.

In the negotiations for the accord, all provinces gained more power (equal to what Quebec demanded) in traditionally federal areas. One exception was that Quebec would receive special status to determine the existence and continuance of its distinct culture. The agreement had been reached through elite political compromise without consultation with the public or members of legislatures. Only Manitoba and New Brunswick had not yet signed the accord, but were close to doing so, when the Supreme Court of Canada overturned Act 101, the Quebec law that allowed French-only commercial signs outside public buildings (but permitted both languages indoors) (*Ford v. Quebec*, 1988). The court held that the measure violated the Charter's guarantee of freedom of expression (*Ford v. Quebec*, 1988). Quebec had argued that "liberty of expression concerns the substance of a communication, not the language used," and that the French-only requirement applied only to commercial public signs, not to "religious, political, or ideological ideas" (Dion 1992). Quebec immediately invoked "notwithstanding." Many Canadians elsewhere saw this move as illegitimate (Leeson 2001), and Meech Lake failed because many people saw it as a political deal with Quebec rather than as a document to benefit all Canadians.

Some scholars note that the 'distinct society' clause provided ammunition for failure to ratify the accord (Dion 1992). Further, constitutional scholars had disagreed about how the Supreme Court would interpret the clause, with some calling it meaningless and others saying that it would give Quebec more and more power until it finally became a sovereign state (Dion 1992). Still others argued that the Charter had made individual rights so central that any sort of provincial distinction was unacceptable. Russell explains, "It was not the substance of the Charter but the Charter as symbol, as icon, which in the heat and passion of mega constitutional politics became profoundly divisive. For a majority of English-speaking Canadians, Charter rights had displaced provincial rights as the fundamental constitutional rights" (Russell 1993, 146–7). According to Cairns, the Charter fortified the political power of previously marginal groups, such as women, seniors, the disabled, minorities, and Aboriginals (Cairns 1988).

Political tensions did not end with rejection of the Meech Lake Accord. While Quebec struggled over separation, politicians drew up another constitutional agreement that would satisfy Quebec and the other provinces. The sixty-provision Charlottetown Accord included several compromises. The Canada clause expressed "fundamental Canadian values that would guide the courts in future interpretations of the entire Constitution including the Charter of Rights and Freedoms" (Charlottetown Accord, 1992): commitment to a parliamentary and federal system, recognition of Aboriginal peoples' rights to promote their language and culture, recognition of Quebec as a distinct society, and guarantees of official-language minority communities throughout Canada, racial and ethnic equality, male and female equality, and provincial equality and diversity. The document also dealt with Aboriginal rights and self-government, including application of the Charter of Rights to Aboriginal governments. One section entrenched the Supreme Court of Canada and selection of justices, including the requirement that three be from Quebec. This section required Ottawa to name judges from lists submitted by the provincial and territorial governments.

On 26 October 1992, by national referendum, Canadians rejected the Charlottetown Accord: "It was perceived as giving Quebec too much, while inside Quebec it was perceived as not giving Quebec enough" (Russell 1993, 226). Constitutional politics are quiet in Canada these days. However, the history of the Supreme Court and of the constitution that it interprets suggests that the court's role as a national policy maker is far from being ultimately determined by the institutional structures that defines its powers.

CONCLUSION

To conclude this historical discussion, we observe that the Supreme Court did not always have status as a policy maker or, to put it another way, exist as an institution of the "judicialization of politics." Rather, the court's historical development as policy maker was slow but steady, culminating in 1982 when the Charter greatly expanded its power of judicial review. Factors in Canadian politics and society at large also affected the court's legitimacy and, in turn, its ability to play a prominent role in society. The political and social tensions that we examined in this chapter do not influence just society at large. They also shape judicial decision making, as we see below in chapter 7. Both the court's place in the institutional framework of government – at the federal level and as ultimate arbiter in provincial matters – and its composition increase the likelihood that justices will display signs of attitudinal decision making in their rulings.

3 Theories of Supreme Courts' Decision Making

As we saw in chapters 1 and 2, the Supreme Court of Canada has evolved dramatically from a relatively obscure institution to a high-profile body that helps resolve many of the most important issues of the day. Because of this major role, we should try to understand how and why justices reach their decisions. Questions about influences on judges' decisions have been the focus of many political scientists who have studied the courts during most of the past half-century. This chapter explores the relevance of such theories to the Canadian context.

As we see below, while no single theory completely explains judicial decision making, scholars increasingly use attitudinal explanations. After we examine existing scholarship on the three most prominent models – legal, attitudinal, and strategic – we turn to the attitudinal model and examine evidence for attitudinal approaches in both Canada and other democratic nations. Next we outline our interviews with justices to see whether they use such a model of decision making. Finally, we consider conceptual and theoretical issues in designing empirical research to assess the utility of the attitudinal approach.

Attitudinal theories of judicial behaviour focus on two questions. First, are the judges involved to an important extent in resolving salient political issues? And second, do their political values and ideologies shape the content of their decisions?

JUDICIAL POLICY MAKING

Judicial Policy Making around the World

To answer the first question, we explore the literature on the extent to which judges are actively involved in the resolution of important political issues. Scholarship on the making of judicial policy outside the United States has increased of late, with several national studies that note the substantial policy-making opportunity available to high courts (Tate and Vallinder 1995; Russell and O'Brien 2001; Hirschl 2004). Jackson and Tate (1992) show that expansion of judicial review in various countries has led to dramatic change in public policy. They note that European courts in practice are more likely than US courts to use judicial review.

Judicial review is also substantial in most of western Europe, Canada, and Japan, and extends to nations outside the industrialized world such as the Philippines and India. Hirschl (2004) notes the global spread of constitutionalism and focuses on judicial review in Australia, Canada, Israel, and New Zealand. He explains the theory of "juristocracy" as constitutional reform that "transferred an unprecedented amount of power from representative institutions to judiciaries" in over 80 countries (Hirschl 2004, 1). Tate and Vallinder (1995) refer to growth of judicial power around the world as the "judicialization of politics." In their analysis of the Philippines Supreme Court, they find that it was using its power to restrain executive power and governmental authority in general (Tate and Vallinder 1995).

Helmke (2002) provides evidence illustrating the way in which the Argentine Supreme Court attempted to build its power by providing evidence of justices' "strategic defections" at the end of a regime. Williams (2001) finds that in Australia judicial independence has led to perceived activism by the High Court with the court's decisions having "reshape[d] the social and political landscape" (Williams 2001, 122). In her study of the Italian courts in the 1950s and 1960s, Volcansek (1991) explains how they used strategies to show "judicial restraint" while they "declared a number of laws or acts having the force of law unconstitutional and invalid" (122). In Germany, Wallach (1995) suggests, the Constitutional Court has been only occasionally activist, yet disguises such decisions in legal principles of consistency. Similarly, in Canada, Baar (1991) concludes that Supreme Court justices were even more activist in their interpretations of the Charter of Rights and Freedoms than many experts originally expected. Finally, Toharia (1975) suggests that even in the authoritarian era in Spain from the mid-1930s into the 1970s, judicial power expanded.

Other scholars have noted that even with a growth of judicial independence, policy making by high court justices has not increased. According to O'Brien and Ohkoshi (2001), even though institutional independence of the judiciary has been preserved in Japan, individual judicial independence has been limited. Foglesong (2001) thinks Russian judges neither autonomous nor independent, with pressure coming from those who control their appointment and removal. Guarnieri (2001) examines France, Italy, Portugal, and Spain, countries with civil law, and concludes that greater institutional independence has not given judges more independence. In post-Communist central and eastern Europe, A.E. Dick Howard (2001) sees judicial independence only when there is a "constitutional culture," in which state officials recognize and accept judicial review (103). Finally, in England, Stevens (2001) describes a situation where judicial independence will expand only as the political culture accepts it.

This examination of the literature suggests that judicial policy making requires several conditions: judicial independence, judicial review, and general acceptance of judicial policy making.

Judicial Policy Making in Canada

Evidence of judicial policy making also exists in Canada. Much of the academic debate surrounding the Supreme Court in the Charter age has focused on the court's political impact. This debate has frequently overlapped with normative debate about what role the court *should* play. Commentaries on both the left and the right have attacked the court, often raising the key question of who wins and who loses.

The view from the left is that "legalization of politics" since 1982 has benefited primarily the social elites (Greene et al. 1998, 4). A prominent example is the argument of Mandel (1994) that the legal process tilts towards the rich and thus that any greater policy making by courts undermines democracy and further harms the underprivileged.

Critics from the centre-right have also characterized the Charter's effects as undemocratic, but with different consequences. One pair of them asserts that the Charter "is deeply and fundamentally undemocratic, not just in the simple and obvious sense of being antimajoritarian, but also in the more serious sense of eroding the habits and temperament of representative democracy" (Morton and Knopff 2000, 149). They see this new role as unfortunate, because the court may become the "pawn" of social activists (Knopff and Morton

1992). The court is now in the thrall of a group of leftist political forces that they dub the "court party," consisting of national-unity advocates, civil libertarians, equality seekers (most prominently, the Women's Legal Education and Action Fund, or LEAF), social engineers, and post-materialists (Morton and Knopff 2000, 59). They do not see the Charter as extending rights to minority groups; rather judicial activism and activist judges have applied it to benefit certain special interests.

First, Morton and Knopff (2000) argue that the Charter does not constrain judicial discretion and activism – Supreme Court justices had just as much discretion under the Canadian Bill of Rights of 1960 as they do under the Charter. The difference lies not in the legal power that the documents provide but in how justices interpret them. Morton and Knopff (2000) posit a generation gap between Bill of Rights and Charter justices, calling the former the "Parliamentary generation" (22). They assert that an explicit bill of rights (in whatever form) is neither a sufficient nor a necessary condition for judicial activism. It is judges who drive the Charter, they argue, not vice versa.

Morton and Knopff (2000) also write about the court party. Rights need a support structure to survive, which includes advocacy, government or foundation funding, and availability of sympathetic and competent lawyers. The writers show that recipients of funds are successful in the Supreme Court. The most frequent recipient of grants from the Court Challenges Program (CCP) – LEAF – also has the most success at the Supreme Court.

Others have been very critical of this view of the Charter, arguing that the document does introduce judicial activism and that the change is therefore institutional. Manfredi (1989) suggests that although judicial review has a basis in Canadian law, its increase with the Charter has led the court to a "very broad conception of its review powers" (1989, 319). One justice whom McCormick and Greene (1990) interviewed remarked that the "Charter of Rights has changed everything" (237). In a study of US citations in opinions of the Supreme Court of Canada, Manfredi (1990) finds support for an institutional effect, with citations to US cases substantially increasing after 1984, even by justices such as Brian Dickson, who served in both periods.

Epp (1998), also in contrast to Morton and Knopff (2000), suggests that a rights revolution presupposes widespread public support. While judicial activism plays a role, society matters more than the judicial institution. Morton and Knopff (2000) describe their approach as a "top–down, state-initiated interest group formation process" (89). While Epp too puts that argument in his account of how rights organizations, the legal profession, and federal policies help to create the rights revolution, the implication for democracy is different. Epp sees the expansion of rights as a democratic notion because the support for it is widespread. Morton and Knopff portray events in Canada as being elite-driven and lacking the widespread support needed for democratic legitimacy.

Some observers argue that rights cases had increased even before 1970, probably in response to the Canadian Bill of Rights (1960). Snell and Vaughan (1985) note that in the 1960s "Canadians began to look to the Supreme Court for leadership after John Diefenbaker's boast that their rights and freedoms were now judicially enforceable" (214). Many Canadians already considered the Supreme Court the body to enforce rights and freedoms. However, many saw its role there as much weaker and less effective than that of its US counterpart (Snell and Vaughan 1985). Epp argues that the court's obtaining docket control in 1975 expanded its activism vis-à-vis rights (Epp 1996), while its interest in economic matters waned. Other scholars have been critical of the court's role in expanding the rule of law up to 1982 as being outside the will of Parliament and the public (Weiler 1974).

Prior to 1975, the majority of cases before the court were appeals as of right (Hausegger et al. 2009). S.I. Bushnell (1982) reports a substantial shift from appeals as of right to appeals by leave after the 1975 term. According to Flemming (2004, 12), in the 1990s the court "grants leave to appeal to an average of 15 percent or one out of six or seven of the applications it receives while the United States Supreme Court grants certiorari to fewer than one out of a hundred of all the writs it receives." Since 1982 the Canadian court's agenda has certainly expanded into new areas, including judicial action to support rights claims (Greene et al. 1998).

One scholar proposes that the Charter did not in fact transfer much policy making to the courts (Russell 1995). After the initial decisions up to 1986, in which it upheld three-quarters of the Charter claims that it received, "the court settled down to a relatively moderate approach" (Russell 1995, 143). Other experts show that the justices are neither extremely liberal nor very conservative but rather political centrists (Morton et al. 1994; also Ostberg and Wetstein 1998; see Baar 1991 for a somewhat contradictory conclusion). But even centrist justices may behave politically, although they will choose differently from activist justices who are ideologically liberal or conservative. Thus the focus of the analysis below (see chapters 5–7) is not on whether to categorize a given justice as "liberal" or "conservative" in any absolute sense, nor on whether justices' political choices are normatively desirable or not. Instead, we concentrate on the empirical question of the extent to which their politically relevant attitudes (whether "liberal," "conservative," or "moderate") measurably affect their choices in the politically significant cases that they decide.

MODELS OF JUDICIAL DECISION MAKING

If judges and courts around the world are activist in interpreting their nations' laws and in shaping public policy, then it becomes important to ask the second question that we posed above in this chapter – namely, whether justices' personal ideology or policy preferences help shape their judicial decisions. Traditional accounts of courts – the legal model – present judges as skilled scholars who apply well-settled legal rules to settle concrete disputes. However, both social scientists and media writers wonder about the role of politics in those decisions. As one influential account puts it, "Many paths connect law and politics. The politics of selecting judges routinely screens out certain marginal voices and interests from the legal process ... [Moreover] the law does not consistently hear the voices of the poor" (Carter 1998, 3). Thus scholars examine both the court's political role, especially "who wins and who loses," and the potential significance of political factors for its decisions. The latter issue has spawned two approaches: the attitudinal model asserts that justices' political preferences influence their decisions, while the strategic model claims that institutional arrangements and the potential reaction of other political actors affects their propensity to make judicial policy that is consistent with their personal policy preferences. We explore each of these approaches – legal, attitudinal, and strategic – to understanding courts in the sections below.

The Legal Model

Because of the apparently competing views that various models promote, Lawrence Baum (1997) finds judicial behaviour still a "puzzle" after five decades of empirical analysis. The underlying assumptions, methods, and applications of the legal, attitudinal, and strategic approaches to judicial behavior differ greatly and yet are related.

The legal model offers the first piece of the puzzle. It is based on the view that judges are neutral arbiters of the law. They "find" the law, not "make" it (Hart 1960). They apply legal doctrine from previous cases to decide present cases. Adjudicating therefore allows both litigants and society predictable outcomes and continuity in the law (Carter 1998; Klein 2002). Central to this model, judges decide by analogy. After examining the law and its application in the prior case they assess how similar the present case is and apply the legal rule to it. In this model, the law applies itself (Carter 1998; see George and Epstein 1992). Judges carefully trained in the common law tradition can compare cases and apply the law accordingly (Dworkin 1986[8]).

Many scholars believe that such a pure, legalistic approach cannot exist in appellate courts. Few think that judges simply apply jurisprudence mechanically (Posner 1990), especially in appellate courts. Even in England, where law is deeply steeped in the tradition of mechanical jurisprudence (Horowitz 1977), political scientists question the use and utility of the pure legalistic approach (Robertson 1982; 1998).

A difficulty for the legal model is the distinction between "easy" and "hard" cases (Coffin 1980; 1994). In easy ones, the legal precedent and its application are clear. Typically the factual similarities are strong, and the legal community agrees about how the law applies, so that its application is relatively straightforward. Hard cases are those in which the law is unclear, so it is not easy to apply precedent in a straightforward, "objective" manner, and judges must interpret how existing law fits the case. Hard cases may include issues of "first instance," which courts have not previously addressed; cases where the language of the most relevant precedents is ambiguous; and cases in which competing precedents suggest different answers. The recognition that there are sometimes competing precedents is problematic for the legal model. For when precedent exists on both sides that could be used by justices to justify their decisions, one might argue that any decision is in accord with the legal model regardless of any evidence suggesting that the decision was politically motivated (George and Epstein 1992). Therefore a modified version of the legal model might hold that judges' actual behaviour fits with the legal model in easy cases, but that politics may intrude in hard cases.

The easy/hard distinction is crucial vis-à-vis discretionary docket control. Appellate courts with such power will take on few easy cases. However, a body such as the Supreme Court of Canada, which has a largely discretionary docket (see chapter 4) but still must decide some appeals that arrive "as of right," may see a mixture of easy and hard cases. In hard cases where the law is unclear, justices have a great deal of discretion. There, some scholars argue, they rely on their political preferences about what the law should be, whether in the outcome on the merits or in the legal rule that the court develops, or both. For this reason, a pure legal model may not explain all of the court's decisions completely. As one group of scholars argues, "The cases heard by the Supreme Court are likely to be more complex and to have no clear solution" (Hausegger et al. 2009, 116).

The Attitudinal Model

Unlike the legal model, which casts facts of case in the light of the constitution, statutes, and precedent, the attitudinal approach holds that justices base decisions on their own "ideological attitudes and values" (Segal and Spaeth 1993, 73) without the constraints of law and precedent. The attitudinal model assumes that their political preferences fully explain their votes in all cases. Even when the plain meanings of the text of the law or precedent are clear, "they are easily avoided" (Segal and Spaeth 1996, 973). Notwithstanding recent controversy, the attitudinal model is now the dominant paradigm among scholars who engage in empirical research on the US Supreme Court and has been found to be useful as an explanation of top appellate courts in a number of other countries. As one review states, "In scholarship on the [US] Supreme Court ... the view that policy considerations are dominant over legal considerations has been taken by the most prominent work" (Baum 1997, 22). Another assessment concludes that "the attitudinal model's systematic empirical shattering of the myth of mechanical jurisprudence permeates virtually all our work on judges and courts today" (Lawrence 1994, 3). Even critics of Segal and Spaeth concede that while judicial attitudes may not tell the whole story, "empirical scholarship has now firmly established that the ideological values ... of Supreme Court justices have a profound impact on their decisions" (Songer and Lindquist 1996, 1049). Even scholars in Canada not willing to go that far "will usually agree that policy preferences play some role in the [Canadian] justices' decisions" (Hausegger et al. 2009, 125).

Early in the twentieth century, legal realists, including US Supreme Court Justices Oliver Wendell Holmes and Louis Brandeis, began to argue that judicial decisions were "opinions as to policy which merely embody the preferences of a given body in a given time and place" (Robertson 1998, 7). According to a leading realist, "in any case doubtful enough to make litigation respectable the available authoritative premises are at least two and the two are mutually contradictory" (Kurt Llewellyn, quoted in G. Edward White 1994, 276). These realist premises began to receive systematic empirical study with the landmark work of Pritchett (1948), who postulated that justices' political ideology explained much of the voting on the US Supreme Court.

Glendon Schubert built on Pritchett's work in the 1960s and developed a well-delineated attitudinal theory of judicial decision making. He tested his psychometric model with scaling. By scaling justices' individual votes in prior cases, he predicts their likely voting in future cases (Schubert 1965). He aligns justices along several uni-dimensional ideological continua, assigning *i* points to represent the justices' ideology in multi-dimensional ideological space. *J* points stand for case stimuli, which he also measures in the same multi-dimensional space. "The decision of the Court in any case will depend upon whether the case dominates, or it is dominated by, a majority of *i-points*" (Schubert 1965, 38). That is, the basic intuition of Schubert was that if one examined the pattern of the justices' votes in a large number of cases there was a remarkably regular order that appeared time after time. Schubert argues that such a phenomenon is possible only if votes reflect justices' basic political preferences. Thus one could unambiguously identify the most liberal justice, then the second-most, and so on, down to the least liberal. The resulting prediction is that any time the "5th most liberal judge" casts a liberal vote, the four more liberal justices will do the same (e.g., the two most liberal justices will never team with the two most conservative). Schubert's extensive statistical analyses verified such predictions.

Schubert finds that votes form Guttman scales with high degrees of reproducibility. He concludes that this represents an attitudinal dimension in judicial votes. Simple statistical tests demonstrate that the scales' probability is so low that the ordering of the justices cannot flow from either chance or any effect that the legal model predicts. Schubert observes not one scale but two – the "E scale" for economic cases, and the "C" for civil liberties. The E scale includes virtually all cases dealing with government regulation of the economy, labour versus management, and private economic disputes pitting underdogs against corporate interests. A single ideological dimension very accurately predicts judges' votes on all these cases. The C scale includes virtually all cases involving criminal appeals, equal protection of the law, due process, freedom of expression, freedom of religion, and privacy. One can predict votes there using a single ideological dimension, but justices' positions on these two scales are not necessarily the same (e.g., a justice who is liberal on E may be conservative on C). With these two scales, one can accurately predict votes in more than 80 per cent of all non-unanimous decisions. Later research (e.g., Rohde and Spaeth 1976) has found that these two attitudinal scales have retained their predictive power for the US Supreme Court for many decades.

Schubert's approach has drawn two main criticisms. First, he uses votes to measure attitudes and then uses those attitudes to predict votes – a seeming tautology. Schubert might respond that the votes would not scale at all unless attitudes were in fact producing the votes. Second, there could be something besides ideology driving the pattern that Schubert finds. Attitudinalists ask in reply: "What would that something be?"

In response to the criticisms of scaling justices' votes, other scholars have sought to demonstrate the impact of judicial attitudes on votes. One approach is the attribute model (Ulmer 1973; Tate 1981; Tate and Handberg 1991), which uses judges' personal characteristics to predict their votes. This model certainly avoids the circularity inherent in scaling. Characteristics include race and gender, region, social class, religion, law school, and employment, as well as the political party of the appointing president. While this approach solves Schubert's problem of a priori independent variables, these demographic variables only imprecisely measure judicial attitudes. None the less this research has identified the most predictive characteristics. Additionally, the attribute model has been criticized for being time-bound (Ulmer 1986); the social meaning of attributes and thus their empirical associations with particular attitudes may change over time (Tate and Handberg 1991). The consensus from this body of work is that party and region seem the most significant factors in predicting votes, and race and gender are playing a larger role with increases in the number of women and members of minority groups on the bench (Tate 1981; Tate and Sittiwong 1989; Tate and Handberg 1991; Songer and Haire 1992; Songer et al. 1994; Brace and Hall 1997).

A third approach to determining judicial attitudes is through content analyses of newspaper articles. Segal and Cover (1989) measure US Supreme Court justices' attitudes prior to appointment by using newspaper editorials from four national newspapers (two liberal and two conservative). Defining judicial attitudes a priori, they argue, renders votes truly independent of ideology in a statistical sense, unlike using votes to predict votes. This approach also avoids imprecision because same-party, same-region justices still vary in their scores. Moreover, the results are quite robust, demonstrating a strong relationship between these media perceptions of attitudes and actual votes.

Despite the dominance of the attitudinal model and its impressive ability to predict US Supreme Court votes, substantial criticism of some of its claims continues. Songer and Lindquist (1996) and Brenner and Stier (1996) challenge its view of precedent. Looking at landmark decisions and their progeny, Songer and Lindquist find that justices in many cases use summary decisions rather than full opinions. Thus the court's upholding of landmark cases, even by dissenters in progeny cases, supports the norm of *stare decisis* as a guiding principle and a constraint on ideology. Although ideological preferences are significant, inclusion of summary dispositions in the model decreases their influence (Songer and Lindquist 1996). Brenner and Stier's (1996) similar results support judicial respect for precedent, especially among more moderate justices.

More recently, scholars have substantiated the joint effect of attitudes and the law on decisions by the US Supreme Court. In First Amendment freedoms, changing precedent in the form of "jurisprudential regimes" constrains votes even after researchers introduce controls for judicial ideology (Richards and Kritzer 2002). The intense debate between proponents of these models illustrates the importance of legal norms to the American judicial system.

In stark contrast to the generally attitudinal approach to decisions of the US Supreme Court, studies of other appellate courts suggest that judicial attitudes matter there, but the law constrains their expression, as do institutional and political contexts. Richardson and Vines (1970) conceptualize decisions of judges in federal district and appeals courts as resulting from conflicting demands from legal and democratic subcultures. Subsequently, many studies reach similar conclusions, including analyses of cases involving economic policy (Stidham and Carp 1982), job discrimination (Songer et al. 1994), labour and anti-trust (Songer 1987), libel (Gruhl 1980), obscenity (Songer and Haire 1992), patents (Baum 1980), review of agency decisions (Humphries and Songer 1999), and search and seizure (Songer et al. 1994). Reinforcing these results are admissions by a number of sitting federal judges (see Coffin 1980; J. Woodford Howard, Jr, 1981; Kozinski 1997; Posner 1997).

Thus there seems to be a consensus that in lower federal courts policy preferences influence at least some judicial decisions, but that precedent and other manifestations of the legal model do act as constraints on them. Even Segal and Spaeth concede that the "institutional rules and incentives that allow Supreme Court justices to engage in attitudinal decision making in votes on the merits do not apply in full to other courts" (1994, 11).

The contrast between these findings presents a conundrum: if justices' policy preferences appear so crucial on the US Supreme Court, why does the law still strongly influence other judges? Remarkably, there has been little research on this question. The analyses of decision making on the Supreme Court of Canada in the next three chapters will help to resolve this puzzle.

Several scholars (e.g., Rohde and Spaeth 1976; Segal and Spaeth 1993; Baum 1997) suggest that the answer to this puzzle involves a combination of institutional features thought to be unique to the Supreme Court in the United States context. Specifically, Segal and Spaeth propose, but do not test, the theory that justices are free to vote their policy preferences without constraint from precedent because "they lack electoral or political accountability, ambition for higher office, and comprise a court of last resort that controls its own jurisdiction" (1993, 69). According to their attitudinal model, *these* institutional factors set the court apart and allow justices to vote their policy preferences (Rohde and Spaeth 1976; Segal and Spaeth 1993; 2002). Furthermore, Segal and Spaeth state (1993, 69) that the absence of these factors in lower courts hinders attitudinal voting there. The implication of this view is that if other courts possessed these institutional features, judges would make their decisions based on their attitudes.

Strategic Models

Scholars have begun to develop strategic models recently, even though the seminal work appeared over 40 years ago. Murphy (1964) used a "rational actor model" to explain the behaviour of justices on the US Supreme Court, analysing individual members rather than looking at the court as a whole. He found them to be strategic actors who focus on policy. They pursue their policy goals within the constraints of the law but also with an eye to their colleagues and environment. Rohde (1972) and Rohde and Spaeth (1976), in their psychological approach, looked at assignment of opinions as well. However, strategic models then disappeared until the 1990s.

Two recent works have moved strategic models to the forefront. Epstein and Knight (1998) and Maltzman et al. (2000)[1] both use unique data sources to assess judicial behaviour in the Supreme Court. They argue that judges constrain each other – they strategically accommodate their colleagues' preferences without veering too far from their own. Maltzman et al. (2000) find them strategic in several stages. Chief justices choose colleagues to write majority opinions so as to influence the document's content. Justices use conference voting to gauge each other's preferences. Then opinion writers may bargain with and accommodate colleagues to expand their majority and maintain the majority coalition. Some justices may threaten to draft concurring opinions so as to influence the majority opinion. If bargaining fails, the dissenting opinion may become the majority opinion.

While less rigorous in method, Epstein and Knight (1998) describe a similar process. Using papers of Justices William Brennan, Thurgood Marshall, and Lewis Powell, they conclude that justices modify positions strategically to achieve their policy goals. One example is *Craig v. Boren*. Brennan's notes indicate that while he preferred a strict scrutiny approach to gender discrimination, he strategically modified his written opinion to secure a majority and avoid his least favourite position – a rational basis standard. The result was an opinion announcing the intermediate or heightened scrutiny approach. The authors provide additional examples of bargaining and compromise throughout the process, including the decision to grant certiorari[2] and illustrations of justices responding to congressional and public opinion.

The strategic model suggests that justices' anticipation of others' potential actions also influences their opinions. This approach acknowledges the human side of adjudication but goes further by emphasizing the constraining role of group interaction. Courts may also seek to maximize the impact of their policy preferences even while external forces constrain them.[3] A substantial literature suggests that state supreme courts in the United States are responsive to external political pressure, especially where justices face re-election. Langer (2002) shows that these courts set agendas so as to avoid salient political issues. They may fear retaliation by the governor and/or legislature, depending on the state's method of selecting them and the relative powers of its principal officials. Because systems of selection differ, judges must be strategically aware of their political environment.

One case study (Hall 1987) provides strong evidence that electoral incentives may at times compel judges to disregard personal preferences and go along with constituents. Institutional structures that influence behaviour have also been examined across states. Brace and Hall (1997) find that in death-penalty appeals the political environment and courts' features affect judges' pursuit of legal and policy goals (see also Brace and Hall 1993; 1995; Hall and Brace 1992; 1994). Similarly, in abortion cases such institutional features as retention of judges and whether the state has control by one party or is divided affect supreme court judges' freedom to follow their own preferences (Brace et al. 1998).

When scholars look outside North America, they develop strategic analyses that relate to political contexts and their effect on judicial independence. For example, Helmke (2002) finds that judges on the Supreme Court of Argentina often adopted a forward-looking strategic posture, reducing their support of the current government in anticipation of a likely regime change in the near future. She is not sure whether they do so to avoid sanction from a future government or whether the perception of the change in government frees them from past restraints (or possibly both). Nevertheless, judicial decision making seems highly responsive to perceptions of political change.

Authoritarian governments or emergency rule certainly constrain decision making by appellate judges. According to Toharia (1975), courts in Spain could operate independently under Francisco Franco (ruled 1936–75) only as long as they did not challenge the government in its core concerns or the authority of its special courts and courts martial. Similarly, Haynie (2003) discovered that in South Africa the courts inherited from the period of British rule were allowed to function with considerable independence on most cases under the Nationalist government (1948–94) as long as they did not attempt to challenge the basic tenets of Apartheid.

These examples may be symptomatic of a more widespread pattern. Tate argues that at least "crisis regimes" in Asia have kept traditional judicial systems "to maintain an *appearance of respect for constitutionality* ... Yet judges cannot be left free to challenge the power of the crisis regime. Consequently, ways are found to emasculate the power of judges without abolishing or directly attacking the judiciary" (Tate 1993, 317). Thus in Pakistan, after warnings from the new military "caretaker" government of President Zia al-Haq, the courts fairly quickly fell into line and declined to challenge the government directly (Tate 1993, 322). An analogous pattern appeared in the Philippines. Justices who had served under both Ferdinand Marcos's authoritarian regime and the presidency of Corazon Aquino agreed that Marcos had substantially restricted the Supreme Court's power, but most of them never received any pressure from the government to decide any case in a particular way (Tate and Haynie 1994). In contrast, during India's "Emergency" of 1975–7, Indira Gandhi's government suppressed any assertions of power by the Supreme Court; in much of common law (i.e., formerly British) Africa, revolutionary governments sought to substantially constrain or repress attempts to implement the rule of law (Widner 2001).[4]

Conclusion: Applying the Three Models

In the chapters that follow, we seek to apply these three approaches – legal, attitudinal, and strategic – to the decision making of the Supreme Court of Canada under the Charter of Rights and Freedoms. We consider in particular the impact of politics and of justices' political attitudes on the court's decisions. Before proceeding to our empirical analysis of the impact of judicial attitudes on the Supreme Court justices' decisions, we first describe evidence of attitudinal decision making in the courts of other democracies and then survey analyses of the Supreme Court of Canada.

ATTITUDINAL DECISION MAKING

Attitudinal Decision Making around the World

As we saw above, most of the early evidence for an attitudinal model of judicial decision making came from analysis of US courts. However, several quantitative studies have found attitudinal or ideological voting in appellate courts around the world. Attitudinal scholars examining US courts have argued that such institutional features as judicial independence, docket control, and lack of ambition for higher office enable judges to vote their attitudinal preferences.

But it is clear that similar institutional arrangements may be found in many top courts around the world. Thus it is no surprise that several quantitative studies have uncovered attitudinal or ideological voting in appellate courts of many nations. Following up on his pioneering work on the US Supreme court, Schubert (1968; 1969a; 1969b; 1985a and b; 1987) used scaling techniques and discovered ideological voting in the high courts of Australia, South Africa, and Switzerland. Scholars applying Schubert's methods have produced similar results in several other countries. For instance, scalogram analyses for supreme courts in India, Japan, and the Philippines found systematic ordering of the justices, which indicated attitudinal decision making (Danelski 1969; Gadbois 1969; Kawashima 1969; Samonte 1969; Becker 1970). And even in the face of a strong tradition of parliamentary supremacy and non-political courts, Robertson found political voting in the judicial decisions of the British House of Lords (Robertson 1998). These studies from around the world suggest that attitudinal voting often goes hand in hand with judicial policy making.

Other studies have used indicators of socialization or judges' personal attributes to investigate the impact of judicial attitudes on decisions in various countries. Two studies of the Philippines Supreme Court (Samonte 1969; Tate 1972) provide fresh evidence that at least some personal characteristics might reliably indicate that justices' attitudes affect their votes. A number of subsequent studies (e.g., Gadbois 1969; Kawashima 1969; Forsyth 1985) conclude that several characteristics – including political party, religion, region of birth, prior experience as a prosecutor or judge, and political party – as well as the identity of key actors in the appointment process, affect judges' votes on a wide spectrum of courts (including the Indian, Japanese, and South African supreme courts and Austrian and Swiss intermediate appellate courts). These exploratory studies suggest that attitudinal voting on courts is not a US phenomenon alone.

Studies of Attitudinal Decision Making in Canada

By 1983, the Supreme Court of Canada possessed all the institutional features that Segal and Spaeth believe make possible pure attitudinal voting. Thus the extent of attitudinal voting on the US Supreme Court would suggest a similar situation in Canada.

The Supreme Court of Canada appears to enjoy judicial independence comparable to that of its US counterpart. Canada too possesses a strong tradition of judicial independence (Manfredi 1993), and all the justices whom we interviewed stoutly maintain that that independence remains strong today. Supreme Court and provincial court judges may serve until the age of 75. Justices are difficult to remove. For that to happen, the Canadian Judicial Council must conduct an investigation, report to the federal minister of justice, and, if appropriate, request a joint address from both houses of Parliament (Dyck 2000). Like the United States, Canada has not removed a Supreme Court justice in the past century, and in interviews all justices stated that they never worry about sanctions from any source in response to their decisions. As a further indication of independence, the federal government loses 45 per cent of its appeals and loses 35 per cent of the time when it appears in the Supreme Court as the respondent.

The justices also evidence a lack of ambition for higher office. As in the US system, appointment to the Supreme Court represents the top rung on the career ladder. While in theory selection as prime minister might represent a "step up," no justice in memory has been a serious candidate for prime minister. No current justice has any recent experience in electoral politics, so such an eventuality remains extremely unlikely. As in the United States, in Canada there is no appeal possible to decisions of the Supreme Court. As we saw in chapter 2, the Judicial Committee of the Privy Council in London could review the court's decisions, but that route closed in 1949. Since that time, the justices have made the final decisions.[5]

Since 1975, the Supreme Court of Canada has largely controlled its own docket. Litigants generally must apply for leave to appeal. The court has the discretion to grant such leave, acting through three-judge panels. Of approximately 400 applications for leave to appeal each year, the court grants 15 per cent to 20 per cent. Once it does so, appellants may wait up to a year for a hearing. In a small number of cases, losing litigants in the courts of appeals retain an appeal as of right – primarily cases involving serious criminal offences in which the provincial court of appeal issued a non-unanimous decision regarding an important point of law and cases in which the trial court's decision to acquit a criminal defendant was reversed by the court of appeal.

Although the Supreme Court appears to possess the characteristics to support attitudinal voting, the few empirical studies disagree on whether political attitudes, especially those originating in the partisan selection system, affect justices' decisions. There have been many studies of the impact of justices' political preferences on their decision making, yet few look broadly at decisions in all areas of law and measure preferences in different ways. Roughly when scholars began applying scaling techniques to study voting in the US Supreme Court, their Canadian colleagues used similar techniques on the Supreme Court of Canada. Peck (1969) and Fouts (1969) uncover voting blocs on the court in the 1950s and 1960s, even before it obtained control of its docket and before introduction of the Charter of Rights and Freedoms. Specifically, Peck's analysis of the period 1958–67 reveals voting blocs across five dimensions: crime control, economic regulation, economic underdogs, taxpayers, and provincial authority. Fouts (1969) uncovers two scales for 1950–60: a criminal and civil liberties scale and a public law scale, similar to Schubert's (1965) for the US Supreme Court. Russell (1969) also reveals substantial evidence of attitudinal voting in this period.

Since the early scaling analysis, several scholars have improved scaling methods to detect ideological voting patterns. Looking at Brian Dickson's early court (1984–8), Wetstein et al. (1999) suggest two ideological dimensions underlying Charter decisions: liberal versus conservative (i.e., government versus Charter claimant) and regulation versus societal interest. These scales indicate that ideology in political elites may not be as straightforward in Canada as in the United States. The dimension of regulation versus societal interest is less likely in US Bill of Rights cases. In the later Dickson court (1989–90), according to Wetstein et al. (1999), the dimensionality of Charter decisions shifts, with justices choosing in terms of either crime control versus due process or ethic of care versus ethic of justice. By the beginning of Antonio Lamer's court (1991–5), ethic of care versus ethic of justice had replaced crime control versus due process (Wetstein and Ostberg 1999). The communitarian ethic-of-care dimension appears to relate to justices' gender rather than to their region.

Other scholars have assessed ideological decision making in Canada. Ostberg and Wetstein (1998) create newspaper ideology scores using editorial comments in the *Globe and Mail* concerning justices' ideological orientations prior to appointment. For two of the justices, Lamer and L'Heureux-Dubé, ideology and background characteristics predict voting consistencies more than legal variables in search-and-seizure cases. However, for the other justices' votes in search and seizure, legal factors seem more predictive.

A more recent exploration suggests that ideology's impact can vary in complex ways across a wide range of cases. Ostberg and Wetstein (2007a) modify their newspaper scores of judicial ideology to examine their ability to predict decisions in equality, free speech, labour disputes, right to counsel, search and seizure, and tax. Indicators of liberalism help predict voting in some areas, particularly criminal and economic issues, but not in civil rights and liberties. The authors conclude that the complex manifestations of ideological decision making flow probably from the less partisan appointments process and institutional norms that constrain ideological behaviour (Ostberg and Wetstein 2007a, 226).

Some scholars have used bloc analyses. McCormick (1998) uncovers voting blocs on Lamer's court but does not attempt to link them to ideological factors. In many studies the ideological patterns discovered through bloc analysis were not consistently tied to the judicial selection process. A more recent study reveals that for the years 1949–85 political affiliation deriving from appointment criteria did affect decision making (Tate and Sittiwong 1989). Several analyses of Charter decisions in the 1980s and 1990s have substantiated justices' ideological diversity, but the consensus is that attitudinal differences among judges are not a function of selection criteria or of a justice's party politics or gender (McCormick and Greene 1990; Ostberg and Wetstein 1998). Heard (1991) appears to agree. While he provides strong evidence that the outcome of many Charter cases depends on which justices hear the case, he notes substantial concurrence among justices on many issues. Moreover, he finds no evidence that differences among them flow from consistent partisan or ideological patterns in their selection (Heard 1991). As for selecting individual justices who are sympathetic to federal authority as opposed to provincial (or state) authority, Bzdera suggests that the "highly professionalized" appointment process achieves that goal (1993, 23).

Several studies explicitly deny any connection between justices' political preferences or ideology and their appointment. Morton et al. (1992) uncover little evidence that ideology guides appointments. However, because appointing officials assess appellate judges' writings, Bzdera (1993) suggests that – since high-court appointments in Canada, Germany, and the United States usually follow service on a lower appellate court, appointing officials are able to make appointments more in tune with their own ideological leanings (1993).

In earlier research, judges deny a connection between their appointments and political criteria. A leading recent study that uses interviews with Canadian Supreme Court justices finds that they do not believe that politics plays a large role in the appointment process (Greene et al. 1998). Several former Supreme Court clerks echo this view in interviews with one of this study's authors in 2001. For example, one who had served on the Supreme Court of Canada and the US Ninth Circuit Court of Appeals feels that ideology is more influential in the United States than in Canada; social issues and civil liberties do not appear to be political in Canada (Dodek 2001). One former Canadian clerk argues that although the court "exercises creative powers when interpreting the often vague phrases in the Charter ... this power is limited by the need to make good-faith interpretations of the text ... Judges cannot simply read their worldviews or political preferences into the Charter" (Roach 2001, 140). Roach also suggests that the court has consciously avoided extreme ideological positions, interpreting the Charter cautiously and seeking and reaching consensus when it can. Russell appears to agree. His statistical analysis of Charter cases uncovers "no clear ideological direction" (Russell 1993, 787); rather the court frequently adopts a middle-of-the-road perspective.

Yet Tate and Sittiwong (1989) suggest that partisan political differences affected voting in the period 1949–85. Judicial attributes could predict voting patterns in criminal and civil liberties cases and in economic cases. Specifically, region, religion, political experience, judicial experience, and party of the appointing prime minister could predict justices' votes. Updating their attribute model, Songer and

Johnson (2007) use judicial attributes to predict voting patterns in the period 1985–2000 in criminal, civil rights and liberties, and economic cases. Political affiliation, region, religion, and gender could predict justices' votes. McCormick and Greene (1990) also find social class a reliable predictor of Charter rulings.

Overall, the literature suggests attitudinal voting by justices of the Supreme Court of Canada, although some scholars disagree. Despite the court's policy-making role, many observers continue to believe that appointees' policy preferences play a much smaller role in Canada than in the United States. Still, none of the studies combines methods to link preferences with voting patterns. This study seeks to provide further evidence of attitudinal voting by the justices of the Supreme Court of Canada. By using diverse methods, it seeks to reassure readers that attitudinal voting on the Supreme Court is not just an artifact of the research method. As our first approach, we interviewed the justices themselves to determine their view of what relationship if any exists between their attitudinal preferences and their decisions.

Justices' Perspectives

Because of these different scholarly interpretations of judicial behaviour on the Supreme Court of Canada, we next investigated the perspectives of the justices themselves. One might assume that justices might repeat the expected line that they simply follow the law, period. For instance, former Justice Owen Roberts of the US Supreme Court explains: "When an act of Congress is appropriately challenged in the courts as not conforming to the constitutional mandate the judicial branch of government has only one duty – to lay the article of the Constitution which is invoked beside the statute which is challenged and to decide whether the latter squares with the former."[6] However, the Canadian justices whom we interview describe their behaviour without reliance on judicial mythology. Thus we feel considerable trust in the validity of their perspectives.

Some proponents of the attitudinal model might scoff at the justices' reports as self-serving, suggesting that they were just repeating the myths of a non-political judiciary in order to bolster their legitimacy. While we would not argue that by themselves these interview results provide conclusive "proof," we believe that they are well worth taking seriously. Our confidence rests on several considerations.

First, all scholars conducting elite interviews must assess the honesty and trustworthiness of respondents and their answers using the sorts of demeanour cues that all sorts of people apply in everyday life. Our judgment is that our respondents pass this test. Second, we guaranteed respondents anonymity in any accounts of the interviews, and they knew that we were foreigners and would probably publish the results outside Canada, thus reducing any potential gain they might receive from being less than honest. Third, justices do not describe their behaviour in a manner that one might expect of people trying to support the myths of a non-political judiciary. For example, they admit the influence of political attitudes in some cases and their engagement in activities such as bargaining, which are not part of stereotypical judicial behaviour. Their willingness to admit these activities makes their other comments more credible. Finally, the fact that they often describe specific behaviour vis-à-vis process, sometimes using examples from their cases rather than philosophizing about the bases of their decisions, also adds credibility to the findings.

Although we do not ask the justices to comment directly on our three models (i.e., legal, attitudinal, and strategic), their remarks about how they make decisions contain three basic themes. First, all of them believe that the legal model provides a partial explanation. Second, while no justice appears to accept the pure attitudinal model, many agree that for some cases their differences in judicial philosophy affect their decisions. Third, while none of them uses the term 'strategic,' the way most of them talk about their internal interactions is consistent with a strategic account. But they do not believe that they or their colleagues react strategically to external political pressure.

All the justices are comfortable with the basic tenets of the legal model. They all claim that law and precedent figure into their decision making. While social scientists might be sceptical about such statements, when we ask about *process*, all the justices describe specific actions of theirs that suggest that they take law seriously and that defy expectations from the pure attitudinal model. For example, every judge, without prompting, emphasizes that he spends a great deal of time preparing for oral argument so as to master the legal arguments in the factums. Moreover, all of them ask their clerks to do additional research on the primary legal issues that litigants raise, especially to analyse precedents in the factums with which they are unfamiliar. Finally, they all discuss the legal issues with their clerks prior to oral argument but rarely the policy aspects of the case. None of these approaches appears appropriate for a person who plans to base a decision solely on political considerations. Moreover, no justice indicates that he asks his clerk to prepare legal justifications for a position he has already reached (surely the rational way to use the clerk's talents for a purely political decision), and Justices B, C, and G state that they never tell their clerks their leanings before the clerk completes legal research because they want clerks to approach the legal issues with "a fresh mind."

All the justices remark that their writing about and grappling with the legal issues play a critical part in their deciding the case, but no one mentions political factors as being crucial. At least two observe that sometimes an initial dissenting position "just won't write," so that they accept the legal reasoning of the majority. And Justice E observes that two or three times a year the person writing the court's opinion changes his mind because the position that conference adopted "won't write" and therefore prepares an opinion in support of the opposite position (e.g., affirming rather than reversing), bringing a new majority along in the switch. Similarly, Justice B remarks, "Sometimes you think that justice requires X, but then after you get into the law trying to develop your reasons you conclude that you just can't support that position." In sum, then, the way the justices talk about decision making indicates that law and precedent affect their decisions substantially in many cases.

Yet justices' comments on decision making in conference and in opinion writing reveal that they often react strategically to their colleagues. That is, they clearly negotiate and bargain over the content of the court's opinion, and their ultimate positions reflect their calculations about their colleagues' reactions and probable reactions. However, their comments give little indication that they vote strategically in conference or that their general stance is a response to their calculations about outsiders' probable actions. These strategic interactions appear to help explain the court's many unanimous final decisions.

When we ask justices more generally about how they write decisions, both Justices C and D mention that there is quite a bit of fairly direct bargaining. Both say that everyone understands that most memos proposing changes in the opinion indicate the possibility of a bargain by which the responding justice joins the opinion in return for the change that he indicates. Moreover, he says, most of the time the opinion writer accepts such implicit bargains unless he has very strong feelings about his original position. Such bargaining, according to several justices, often limits the scope of the opinion in order to achieve unanimous support. This willingness to accept a narrower opinion appears to contradict what one might expect from justices focusing on policy concerns. Such a person would presumably agree to a narrower opinion only to achieve a minimum winning coalition (e.g., a 5–4 vote). To dilute an opinion or to narrow it in order to gain unanimity or to increase a majority beyond minimum winning would be irrational from the perspective of strategic accounts, which assume rational behaviour to maximize the influence of a justice's policy preferences.

Several justices indicate that, especially on complex cases, the give and take in conference and in opinion writing often lead justices to change positions; discussion of the legal issues often results in sincere agreement about the proper outcome, despite initial differences in conference. Justice D reports that his colleagues more often change his mind on the meaning of precedent than do the arguments of counsel. Justice A indicates that, even on hard cases, the court often reaches consensus to reverse the lower court after it carefully works through all the legal issues.

Justices are somewhat more ambivalent about strategic reactions to the external environment. Most appear to agree with Justice B, who observes that it would be naïve to think justices completely immune to politics and public opinion, but he adds that in large part their understanding of public opinion leads to concern with maintaining the legitimacy of the court and the legal system. Maintaining legitimacy is not the same as giving in to political pressure. Instead it depends on the selection of justices whom the public sees have superb legal qualifications. Also, impartiality is as crucial as judicial independence – appearing to cave in to political pressure might have some short-term benefits but might erode the court's legitimacy in the long run. The process must be open and transparent, and the outcome must appear to be the result of reasoned principle. According to Justice B, if such principles are firmly in place, then even if the outcome provokes strong disagreement the court can retain people's respect. And he believes that their court had remained popular despite issuing unpopular decisions. Nevertheless, he suspects that most of his colleagues understand that a long string of unpopular decisions might erode their legitimacy.

Justice B indicates that his comments on legitimacy have little to do with the possibility of Parliament or the legislatures' invoking the Charter's notwithstanding clause. Instead, he suggests that most common law courts have similar needs for legitimacy. Justice H agrees, stating flatly that he has never thought about the notwithstanding clause when deciding a case; so, he says, the clause provides no restraint at all. He views that provision as simply part of the system, and if a legislature invokes it that is its right. But the possibility of its use is not relevant to the court's job. Nevertheless, Justice H notes that, as a practical matter, all the justices realize that it would be very difficult politically for any legislature to invoke the clause.

When we ask justices how they handle external political pressure, all four who comment indicate that such pressure may affect the court's wording of its opinion, but none thinks that it ever affects which side "wins." For instance, Justice H suggests that political controversy might force him and his colleagues to be clearer about what they say, because they know that their language will receive close scrutiny. However, according to Justice C, if they perceive a tentative decision as likely to be highly unpopular, they sometimes search for narrower grounds to reach the same outcome. And Justice E indicates that on a very controversial issue there is more informal pressure to try to reach consensus, so justices may be more likely to compromise to allow the court to speak to the external world with one voice.

The justices readily concede attitudinal influence on decision making. All of them know about their differences in "judicial philosophy" and/or in "ideas about justice," and all appear to understand that such differences split the court on at least some issues. As Justice J comments, "Everyone knows there are policy or political or jurisprudential differences among us; the media write about them all the time, and although we don't like to admit it, they are usually approximately right. And when we split 5–4 or 7–2 usually no one who follows the court closely is surprised about who is on which side ... We are all public people – of course we have views on matters of public policy and especially with the Charter ... Many of the cases that are appealed to us raise issues on which we have opinions."

Justice I echoes these sentiments: "We are all political people to some degree – we all have our ideas about what constitutes 'justice' that have been formed from years of paying attention to public issues, and at conference you know that you aren't going to change those views with a couple of comments. But we all expect that whatever our differences in views, that ultimately one must be able to support your own preferences – they must be grounded in the law – and that takes place in the writing of the opinion."

Justice B agrees that all the justices have policy preferences and that "of course those influence the way we understand the law." But he adds that such attitudes do not completely explain their decisions. For example: "Sometimes I think before orals that justice requires X but then get into law and may decide that you can't support that outcome after all." To illustrate, he cites two Charter cases – one where he switched his support from the prosecution to the defence after reading the opinion draft, and another where he changed from opposing to supporting the equality claim after trying to write a dissent.

This perspective relates to the notion that the court's role is not to correct legal errors in a narrow sense, but to make legal policy. As Justice E notes, "Our focus is generally not so much the end result as the impact of the case; as a political scientist I suppose you would say on the 'policy' created by the decision – though we don't often use that word ... The conference often discusses collateral effects on other cases – we often go beyond who should win this case. We often discuss the impact a given decision will have on previous precedent ... We disagree less often on outcome than on impact and the line of reasoning to take."

One consistent theme among the justices was a belief that their attitudinal differences are more complex and multi-faceted than a simple "liberal–conservative" ideological spectrum would suggest. According to Justice F, their divisions often reflect different attitudinal perspectives, but these do not always fall neatly along liberal/conservative lines. For example, differences in "family values" often cut across liberal ideology for some of the justices. Similarly, Justice A thinks that ideology does not divide the Supreme Court of Canada as sharply as it does its US counterpart. He admits, however, that on hard cases the justices usually split along consistent lines that relate to their basic ideas about justice.

The justices fairly readily admit their variation in political perspectives and that these produce divisions in some cases. In fact, not a single one of them argues that political differences are irrelevant for their decision making. Justice E concurs with Justice A's view that political ideology divides them less than it does their colleagues on the US Supreme Court. Nevertheless, he thinks attitudinal differences evident in divisions in both criminal appeals (where justices give different weights to public order versus due process and fairness) and on many civil rights issues. Justice D, while not using the terms "attitudes" or "ideology," feels strongly that their disputes sometimes reflect differences in their "sense of justice" in a case and are apt to be sharpest vis-à-vis the meaning of the Charter. Similarly, Justice F: "Anyone who follows the court knows that there are jurisprudential splits among us – that we have different lenses through which we interpret the law – probably you political scientists would call those 'political' differences; but there is an important implicit rule that everyone will take seriously the views of colleagues and will try to accommodate."

Perhaps the best summary of the justices' general sense comes from Justice J.

> Do our opinions influence what we do? Of course! We are just people – how could our views not have some effect on how we decide? But that doesn't mean we are free to decide whatever we want. I think all of my colleagues take seriously the need to ground our opinions in our law and our traditions of interpretation – we seldom write on a clean slate. We are all judges and that is what judges do – *we interpret the LAW*. And just as important, we want to take stands that we can justify to our colleagues as legitimate approaches – we won't be fired if we don't, but maintaining the respect of your colleagues is important. And as I indicated earlier [when talking about unanimous decision] – we constantly have to remind ourselves of the need for some humility – that our colleagues' views are as legitimate as ours and we should take them seriously – so we try to find common ground even if it means the opinion doesn't say exactly what we would want if we were god and could just make the law.

Thus, while no justice speaks of the attitudinal model when discussing decision making, all of them appear comfortable with the idea that their attitudinal preferences affect their decisions in some cases. Therefore they freely admit that their political attitudes influence their decision making but agree that they do not focus on trying to shape the court's output to support their personal policy preferences. In both direct and indirect ways they indicate that law and precedent also matter and that unanimity is sometimes the result of agreement on what the law means. In addition, the justices are often willing to compromise their differences, not just to produce a "minimum winning coalition" but more frequently to achieve a unanimous court.

Testing an Attitudinal Explanation

Overall the review above of the literature suggests considerable disagreement about the extent of attitudinal decision making on the Supreme Court of Canada. Still, none of these authors combine methods to link preferences with voting patterns. The justices themselves take something of a middle position: their political attitudes seem definitely to affect their decisions, particularly in hard cases, where law and precedent are unclear, but legal norms and the preferences and expectations of their colleagues on the bench constrain their translation of these political preferences into outcomes. In chapters 5–7 we analyse voting on the court to see if there is evidence of attitudinal voting under the Charter. By using diverse methods, we seek to obviate the criticism that attitudinal voting is an artefact of the research method

A test of the attitudinal model might answer the basic question, "Do the political values of the justices exert a measurable impact on a substantial number of their decisions?" The first answer, from the justices themselves, appears to be "Yes," but attitudes are not a complete explanation of judicial voting. In chapters 5–7, we examine this question comprehensively, using a series of quantitative analyses of judicial votes. That is, we ask whether the justices' actual behaviour is consistent with their explanations of that behaviour. In addition, we explore the cleavages on the court and their relationship to Canadian political conflict more generally.

Measuring Judicial Ideology

The most immediate problem one encounters in designing a test of the attitudinal model is how to measure justices' attitudes or political preferences. Three approaches have dominated attitudinal studies of both the US Supreme Court and the top courts of other countries. As we saw above, early quantitative scholarship used votes on the US Supreme Court to infer justices' ideological voting patterns (Pritchett 1941; Schubert 1965; 1974). While Pritchett's bloc analysis began the behavioural study of courts, many early empirical studies relied instead on scalogram analysis. The finding that a large proportion of the votes form one, or a small number of, unidimensional, ordinal scales appeared to offer evidence of the votes' attitudinal derivation. The basic argument is that the very high levels of consistency have no logical explanation except attitudinal voting (see Schubert 1965; Robertson 1998). Subsequent critics point to problems with circular reasoning and propose use of other measures independent of votes to assess judicial ideology (see Segal and Spaeth 1993, 221–9, 361–2).

An alternative to the scalogram analyses that also analyses justices' votes to uncover ideological preferences is factor analysis. Unlike scalogram analysis, it does not presuppose a liberal/conservative ideological divide on the court. It allows actual voting behaviour to guide determination of attitudinal conflicts. Its power lies in its blend of quantitative and qualitative analysis to determine the fulcrums of attitudinal conflict (Ostberg et al. 2002, 240). The underlying dimensions that emerge from this research strategy will provide valuable evidence to either support or refute the relevance of the attitudinal model outside the US context. This strategy forms the basis for our first inquiry into whether voting on the Supreme Court of Canada is consistent with the attitudinal model. We present the results in chapter 5.

Critics of methods that rely on justices' votes to infer their attitudes suggest looking for indicators independent of and prior to justices' voting behaviour. In studies of the US Supreme Court, this criticism led to at least two alternative strategies. The first derives independent assessments of judicial attitudes prior to confirmation by analysing the content of newspaper editorials. Segal and Cover (1989) find substantial correlations between these measures of justices' attitudes and their votes on the court. They analyse the content of editorials regarding nominees in four major newspapers: the *Chicago Tribune*, the *Los Angeles Times*, the *New York Times*, and the *Washington Post*. In essence, their indicator ranks nominees along a liberal-conservative continuum on civil rights and liberties. The beauty of this measure lies not only in its independence from a justice's voting record, but also in its powerful ability to predict subsequent decisions vis-à-vis civil rights and liberties. However, some scholars have demonstrated the measure's limited viability outside this area of law (see Epstein and Mershon 1996, 261–94). None the less it has strong predictive power and has received wide use in the United States.

Recognizing this success, scholars have set out to develop a similar, more general measure of ideology in the Canadian context. An initial effort by Wetstein and Ostberg (1999) relies on newspaper coverage of nominations to the Supreme Court of Canada in the country's leading newspaper (Toronto's *Globe and Mail*) to help predict over 77 per cent of the votes in search-and-seizure cases under the Charter. Despite this measure's success, some observers question its utility because it uses only one newspaper's account.

This study builds on their effort by creating a newspaper ideology score using commentary in news articles and editorials in nine regional papers. We believe this a far more rigorous indicator of ideology because it necessarily takes into account the possibility that journalists from different regional newspapers may cast the appointments in a different light. As such, it provides a more comprehensive and subtle picture of nominees' ideological proclivities. Chapter 6 uses this new measure of judicial ideology as a further test of the attitudinal model.

One of the discipline's most obvious a priori measures is the party affiliation of the appointing official (for US examples, see Tate and Handberg 1991; Wasby 1993; for Canadian, see Tate and Sittiwong 1989; Ostberg and Wetstein 1998; Wetstein and Ostberg 1999; Songer and Johnson 2007). The presumption here is that appointing officials will choose candidates who mirror their own ideological beliefs. In general, judgments on this score in the United States have been fairly accurate, with few exceptions (for example, President Dwight Eisenhower, in office 1953–61), and so this measure has served as a reliable and convenient indirect indicator of a justice's ideological tendencies. In line with research in this area, we include a measure of the party of the prime minister in our analysis, which we code as a dichotomous variable (1 = Conservative appointee, 2 = Liberal appointee). If ideological voting patterns occur under the Charter, we expect a strong coefficient when party of prime minister acts as an independent variable to explain the justices' ideological voting record.

The logic of this second approach soon expanded to include other judicial attributes (e.g., region, religion, professional experience) as measures of attitudes and values, and studies employing these attributes uncover statistically significant relationships between these attitudinal measures and voting patterns in the US Supreme Court (Tate 1981; Tate and Handberg 1991), US courts of appeals (Goldman 1975; Songer et al. 2000), US state supreme courts (Hall and Brace 1992; 1994), and a number of appellate courts outside North America (Schubert 1969b; Tate 1972). In chapter 7 we develop an attribute model of judicial attitudes and use it to analyse the votes on the Supreme Court of Canada as an alternative test of the attitudinal model.

None of these measures provides a perfect indicator of judicial attitudes; all may contain non-trivial amounts of error. Consequently, to understand more fully the extent and nature of attitudinal voting in the Supreme Court of Canada, we employ all three approaches in turn. Thus the analyses in chapters 5, 6, and 7 provide independent but complementary strategies for assessing the extent of attitudinal voting on the Supreme Court of Canada.

Before proceeding to our empirical analyses we first describe, in the next chapter, the process of decision making on the Supreme Court of Canada. We then proceed to the three empirical chapters, each of which provides the analysis using one of the three approaches discussed above.

4 The Process of Decision Making

As we noted in the last chapter, the role of the Supreme Court of Canada in the era of the Charter of Rights and Freedoms has provoked considerable debate. One of the most prolific commentators argues that the Charter has changed the degree, but not the nature, of judicial power (Russell 1983). While not everyone agrees, there seems to be a consensus that the court has played an important role in Canadian public policy since 1982. As we detailed above, this situation does not please everyone. Both the left and the right have attacked the court's role under the Charter.

Despite the wide variety of perspectives, most observers agree that the court's role is important (e.g., see Hausegger et al. 2009). In contrast with the extensive literature on the court's impact, we know less about its operations. In fact, one prominent scholar maintains that the "internal decision making process of the Supreme Court of Canada has been shrouded in secrecy" (Baar 1988, 70). In this chapter we attempt to lift that shroud and illuminate the main features of the court's decision-making process in the Charter period. To do so we rely on in-depth interviews with the court's justices (see Appendix A), an analysis of trends in recent decisions, and other recent commentary.[1]

The Supreme Court of Canada is composed of nine justices, all appointed by the prime minister in consultation with the cabinet but without the need for formal confirmation by Parliament (Hausegger et al. 2009). Justices serve during good behaviour until they reach the mandatory retirement age of 75 (McCormick 1994). While Parliament can in theory remove them by a simple majority vote, it has never done so. When asked about the possibility of removal from office, the justices all believed that, as a practical matter, there was no threat to their independence – it would be "unheard of" for any government to attempt to remove a justice for political reasons. As Justice H puts it, while the court's decisions sometimes upset the government, "they have no access to us," and it would be political suicide for it to be too heavy-handed. Or as Justice C put it, "Sometimes you just have to put your head down and take the abuse [from government officials or the public] ... but no one is worried about their job."

Geographical representation strongly affects appointments to the court – far more than for its US counterpart. By law three justices must be from Quebec, and by convention three are from Ontario. Generally two are from the western provinces and one from the Atlantic provinces (Snell and Vaughan 1985; McCormick 1994; Hausegger et al. 2009). There appears to be an unwritten rule that no western province will have two justices. For example, when discussing the retirement of Justice John Major (from Alberta), justices on the Court of Appeal of British Columbia all agree that as long as Chief Justice Beverly McLachlin (a former justice of the BC Court of Appeal) remains on the Supreme Court of Canada, none of them will be candidates – rather it is now either Manitoba or Saskatchewan's turn.[2]

Justices on the Supreme Court in the Charter period have ranged in age from 53 to 74 years of age. The average age has generally been in the 60s (e.g., Greene et al. 1998 report that it was 63 in 1989 and 65 in 1996). Currently there are four women, including the chief justice; there has been at least one female justice on the court throughout the Charter period. Most of the justices served on provincial courts of appeal immediately before joining the Supreme Court, although in recent decades one justice is usually appointed directly from private law practice and one from the Federal Court (Greene et al., 1998, 101).

SETTING THE AGENDA

The procedures that set a court's agenda can have far-reaching effects. Which cases a court hears directs and moulds development of law and creates winners and losers in society (Flemming 2000, 40). Most cases must receive leave to appeal to be heard by the Supreme Court. However, review of some criminal cases is mandatory, and each year the court decides a small number of reference questions from either the federal or a provincial government. Reference cases are essentially requests by the government for an advisory opinion, usually on the constitutionality of some potential course of action. But reference questions make up a negligible part of the court's docket, averaging less than one per year since 1982. Those criminal appeals that reached the Supreme Court as of right during most of the Charter period include cases in which an acquittal was overturned by a provincial appellate court and those in which there was a dissent on a point of law. Similarly, the crown has a right of appeal when an appellate court overturns a conviction. For most of the Charter period, the Supreme Court used to decide 25 to 30 appeals per year as of right, but the number dropped to "just a handful" each year after an amendment to the *Criminal Code* in 1997 substantially narrowed the circumstances for such an appeal (Monahan 2000, 4).[3]

As the result of the Supreme Court Act, 1975, and amendments in 1997, the Supreme Court now largely controls its own agenda (Snell and Vaughan 1985). With the exceptions we noted above, no case reaches it unless the court itself grants the appellant leave to appeal. The court's power to determine which cases it will hear is both broad and vague. Section 40(1) of the act states that leave is to be granted if "the Supreme Court is of the opinion "that any question involved therein is, by reason of its public importance or the importance of any issue of law or any issue of mixed law and fact involved in such question, one that ought to be decided by the Supreme Court or is, for any other reason, of such a nature or significance as to warrant decision by it."

The statute does not define "public importance," and the court has not published any guidelines to clarify its meaning. Most commentators have interpreted this criterion to mean "national" importance, but there has been widespread agreement that the court has left the standard deliberately vague (Baar 1988; Greene et al. 1998; Flemming 2000; 2004). One former clerk for the court confirms that the justices are centrally concerned with the national importance of issues and that examples might include matters on which provincial courts of appeal have split or where the law is uncertain (Sossin 1996, 289). Several justices who served during the Lamer court (1990–9) explained what justices look for in leave petitions – questions of general importance in the whole country, preferably only after several courts of appeal had had a chance to rule on the issue. Leave was most likely when lawyers filing petitions describe the central issue clearly and succinctly (Greene et al. 1998, 109–12). Justice John Sopinka elaborated that the public importance criterion includes constitutional challenges, issues that involve conflict among provincial appellate courts, and appeals raising a new point of law (Hausegger et al. 2009, 109)

Only one study attempted to discover indicators in the nature of the actual cases that the court accepted or denied leave to. Flemming (2004) concludes that the nature of neither the litigants nor the lawyers significantly affects the likelihood of a petition's acceptance. Instead chances increase if the appeal comes from a divided court of appeal or if courts of appeal in several provinces disagree.[4] In addition, petitions raising novel issues or issues with potential for a major impact on federal interests have a greater chance for review. In contrast, petitions seeking primarily correction of errors in the courts below and fact-intensive issues have less chance.

To increase our understanding of the agenda-setting stage, we asked justices on the McLachlin court (2000–present) what they look for in petitions for review. Although we made no specific mention of the official court criteria, every single justice agreed with Justice G's succinct summary: "National importance is the key." Justice E admitted the truth of the widespread complaint about the absence of specific guidance on leave criteria: "Essentially there are no formal guidelines – it is just a matter of what is a major issue." And he added, "It is a lot like what your justices [i.e., US Supreme Court] say about obscenity – we know it when we see it." Despite the absence of specific guidelines, Justice E argued that in "the vast majority of the cases" the decision to deny leave is easy, and all the justices agreed that in most petitions the court's decision is unanimous. When we prodded him about important versus non-important issues, he replied that what interests all the justices is law development, especially in new fields with few precedents to guide lawyers and lower-court judges. "We won't take cases on which the law is well settled," he said, "and we are generally not interested in cases that are 'fact driven' – 'Who done it?' is a question for the lower courts."[5] He said that generally the Supreme Court was not interested in error correction – that was for courts of appeal. As a result, the justices were not concerned primarily with whether the court below "got it right or wrong" (pause), "unless something went *really* wrong and you just have to fix it."

This ambivalence about error correction was a theme that appeared in almost all the interviews. The justices would first indicate that they didn't see their job as correcting mistakes in the courts below, but then almost always qualified that initial remark by indicating that on relatively infrequent occasions the errors were so egregious that the Supreme Court had to intervene. With slightly varying language, all the justices appeared to agree with the assessment of Justice C: "In theory, just because the case was wrongly decided below you won't necessarily hear it. Instead there must be some indication of national importance; that is, some point of law that has national significance. But sometimes the decision is so far off track that you just can't let it stand."

In contrast, uniformity of law looms large in their minds. They appeared unanimous in their assessment that it was important for federal law to mean the same thing throughout a quite diverse country. Interestingly, the importance of maintaining national uniformity applies to both the common law and for statutory law in each province – not just for cases raising questions of federal law or constitutional interpretation. Justice A asserted that national uniformity was "especially" important in interpretation of the common law. Since judges make the common law, they must speak with one voice, so that there is not a perception that justice depends on the "luck of the draw," with rules varying from case to case, depending on the judge. Consequently, conflict among provincial courts of appeal over interpretation of some question of law is usually a significant indicator of the issue's national importance. However, like their colleagues on the US Supreme Court, they indicated a clear preference for waiting until an issue was "ripe" for review. That is, when a new issue arises, if it seems likely to surface in many contexts, the court will probably deny leave on the first petition raising the issue and wait until after extensive vetting in lower courts.

US studies of case selection speculate that the identity of the petitioner's lawyer may affect chances for review, as the reputations of lawyers in the small "Supreme Court bar" serve as cues for the justices. While the justices we interviewed agreed that the lawyer's skill in framing issues for appeal probably affected chances for review, they doubted that the lawyer's reputation influenced the decision to grant leave. As Justice D pointed out, there is not a small, identifiable "Supreme Court bar" in Canada that might familiarize justices with individuals' reputations, and the summary of leave petitions that justices receive from staff lawyers does not name counsel. Consequently, at the leave stage most justices do not know who the lawyers on each side are. Similarly, justices denied that the standing or reputation of the judge who wrote the opinion below would noticeably affect the leave decision. However, several indicated that dissent in the court of appeal often suggested an unresolved question of law, and if a particularly well respected judge wrote it, it would carry some weight.

Finally, in stark contrast to US practice, justices do not perceive any pressure to deny petitions for leave to appeal. Whereas US participants frequently assert that when they examine cert petitions they are looking for reasons to deny the petitions (see Perry 1991), Canadian justices look for reasons to grant leave. Justice F was most emphatic: to his knowledge, the court had never turned away a case just because its docket was full. When we asked about the national differences, several justices suggested that they were probably simply a function of numbers. Both federal Supreme Courts hear approximately the same number of cases each year, but the US court receives roughly ten times as many petitions for review.

The formal process for evaluating leave petitions in Canada appears straightforward. Requests that meet formal requirements go to staff lawyers in the Law Branch of the Supreme Court.[6] These personnel prepare objective summaries of each case, with a history of the case, an outline of the facts, and a succinct statement of the issues that the petitioner raises (see Flemming 2004). This summary then goes to all nine justices.

Each full petition, with supporting material,[7] goes to one of the three special three-judge panels that the chief justice appoints each year. Each panel receives about the same number of cases per year. These panels have the formal authority to decide by majority vote whether to grant or deny leave. However, despite this decentralization, the justices maintain that any or all of them can participate in the decision making on any petition. In practice, before a panel makes a formal decision to grant or deny leave, it circulates a memo to colleagues saying that it will deny or grant leave unless someone objects. If a single justice objects, the petition will be placed on the agenda of the next meeting of the court's conference.

At the conference, everyone can discuss whether to grant leave to appeal. The justices stressed that these deliberations are literally "discussions" and make no formal decision, although at the end of the session someone will sometimes ask for a show of hands. Justice G stated, "There is no absolute rule on the number required to grant leave ... nor is it a matter of deference [to a colleague who wants to hear the case] – it is a matter of persuasion." When we asked about similarities to the US "rule of four,"[8] justices seemed to agree with Justice G that, even though that number is no guarantee, "there would be a much better than even chance that the panel would grant leave." Ultimately the panel decides, but most justices expect that it will give great weight to colleagues' opinions. According to Justice D, the panel "almost always" follows the sentiment of the conference, except "possibly two or three times a year."

A panel's recommendations tend to carry significant weight in conference discussions, because all the justices recognize that its members have examined the petition most closely. Moreover, as we saw in other aspects of the court's work, the McLachlin court appears highly collegial. While the justices do not automatically defer to their colleagues' decisions, most seem to think that they all share a common conception, at least in general terms, of what constitutes an issue of "national importance" and that they can trust each other to make decisions according to professional standards. It appears, for example, that no justice worries that some faction will use majority status on a leave panel to advance its private policy goals. Thus, if a panel's initial decisions are unanimous, colleagues rarely challenge them in conference. Several of the justices admitted that they usually gave only cursory attention to objective summaries of leave petitions going to other panels unless either the issue was of particular interest to them or another non-panel member had already asked for a conference discussion.

On the whole, the leave process appears less political or ideological than the US cert process (see Hausegger et al. 2009 for more on this point). A large majority of decisions appear to be unanimous, and while several justices noted that some colleagues had one or two favourite issues, none perceived stable "blocs" that consistently aligned on leave decisions. Since the justices hear a much higher proportion of petitions than is possible in the United States, it is easier for them to accommodate the interests of even one or two colleagues. The potential for political conflict on leave petitions is probably also less because only direct parties to each case participate in leave decisions. Interest groups may not submit briefs in support of or opposition to leave petitions, and government actors rarely attempt to intervene at the leave stage. Provincial governments appear frequently as interveners, especially in cases involving other provinces, but usually just at the merits stage; other provinces rarely file briefs in support of leave petitions.

Finally, the Canadian government has no office directly analogous to that of the US solicitor general and so some observers believe that no one national official appears to regularly monitor leave petitions. In fact, Justice G indicated that Ottawa appeared not to be very selective in which cases it sought leave to appeal and speculated that there was no centralized process to co-ordinate leave decisions. Despite this speculation, some recent research by Hennigar (2004) suggests that the Justice Department does have a decision-making process to review possible leave applications from across the country.

WHO DECIDES?

Once a case has been placed on the Supreme Court's agenda (either as an appeal as of right or after granting of the leave petition), the first decision is about who will hear the appeal. Cases will be heard either by panels of five or seven justices or by all nine justices sitting *en banc*.[9] The decision on the size of the court to hear the case and the members of the panel if it is to be less than the whole court is at the discretion of the chief justice. During the Charter period, there have been a substantial number of cases of each of the three sizes.

No formal rules constrain the choice of the chief justice on panel size, and other justices are typically not consulted in advance (except about scheduling conflicts that would prevent their participation). Nevertheless, the other justices seem quite content with Beverly McLachlin's pattern of choices. Most important for a political analysis of the court's role, no justices complained that she has ever "stacked" a panel to advance her own or any other policy agenda. However, despite these consistent disclaimers, one empirical examination found several interesting patterns. First, in both the Dickson court and the Lamer court, justices who frequently voted with the chief justice were significantly more likely to be on panels

Table 1
Variations in panel size by indicators of case importance, Supreme Court of Canada, 1982–2003*

	Panel size			
Issue?	*5*	*7*	*9*	*Total*
A. Presence or absence of a Charter issue?				
No	30.8%	45.5%	23.8%	
	(447)	(660)	(345)	1,452
Yes	15.8	39.9	44.3	
	(57)	(144)	(160)	361
Total	504	804	505	1,813
B. Presence or absence of a statutory interpretation issue?				
No	32.7%	43.5%	23.8%	
	(428)	(568)	(311)	1,307
Yes	16.5	47.5	36.0	
	(75)	(216)	(164)	455
Total	503	784	475	1,762

*Data are original analyses of the author's data.

than justices who disagreed with him. Second, in both courts, female justices were on panels proportionately more often than their male colleagues (Hausegger 2000; Hausegger and Haynie 2003).

Panels of five justices are typically used for two quite different purposes. First, cases from the Court of Appeal of Quebec that involve interpretation of civil law traditionally merit a five-judge panel that includes all three justices from Quebec.[10] This arrangement appears to reflect justices' own beliefs and their understanding of the legal community's expectations that common law judges should not decide on civil law. However, just a case's origin in Quebec will not guarantee a five-judge panel. Appeals from Quebec involving interpretation of the Charter or federal law are as likely to go to seven or nine justices because they raise similar issues to other provinces.

Five-judge panels can be a labour-saving device in appeals as of right when the chief justice thinks that they do not raise issues of national importance, for which justices would normally expect the full court to sit (see Table 1). Specifically, our data show that cases dealing with either a Charter issue or statutory interpretation are much more likely to go to the whole court.

Chief Justice Lamer indicated that he would strike a five-justice panel "if it is an as-of-right case that we would not have granted

Table 2
Number of justices participating in decisions, 1982–2003

Size of panel	*Percentage of cases*
4	01.4
5	25.1
6	04.8
7	41.4
8	01.9
9	25.3

leave to, and where it appears that we are practically unanimous" (quoted in Greene et al. 1998, 115). If his practice has continued, we would expect that most criminal cases decided with five-judge panels would be unanimous. Our data indicate that Chief Justice Lamer's approach to striking five-judge panels appears to have been followed by all three chief justices during the Charter period. Of the more than 500 cases decided by five-judge panels, 87.3 per cent had unanimous outcomes, 5.6 percent were decided by 4–1 votes, and only 7.1 per cent split 3–2.

If a case does not fall into one of the categories that usually triggers a five-judges panel, there is usually a presumption that it will be heard by all nine justices *if possible*. But that qualifier is important. It appears to be relatively common for at least one justice to recuse himself because of a conflict of interest, illness, or other official obligations. In such instances, the chief justice usually strikes a panel of seven, rather than eight, to avoid a tie vote. In practice, seven-judge panels have in recent years decided more cases than the court *en banc* (see Table 2).

Our data reveal that seven is the most common panel size (roughly two-fifths of all cases). The full court sits in only a quarter of cases, and five justices in a similar proportion. Panels with an even number of justices decide a very few cases, probably when one member had to leave before the final decision.

The desire for all nine justices to hear the case appears especially strong for the most important issues. Hausegger (2000) and Hausegger and Haynie (2003) find some support for this norm. According to Hausegger, in the 1990s two indicators of case importance – a Charter issue, and participation by interveners – increased the probability of a full court. Our data (Table 1) provide a similar picture.

Table 3
Levels of agreement (%) among justices on decisions in the Dickson, Lamer, and McLachlin courts in three policy areas

Issue	*5-judge panel*		*7-judge panel*		*Full court*	
	Unanimous	*3–2*	*Unanimous*	*4–3*	*Unanimous*	*5–4*
A. Dickson court						
Criminal	91	6	75	7	64	4
Civil liberties	–	–*	67	17	50	50
Private law	80	20	81	12	50	16
B. Lamer court						
Criminal	82	8	69	10	65	11
Civil liberties	–	–	55	15	60	13
Private law	86	9	71	11	74	09
C. McLachlin court						
Criminal	88	6	81	7	70	10
Civil liberties	–	–	72	0	67	22
Private law	100	0	75	11	68	10

*When there were five or fewer cases decided, percentages are not displayed.

Our interviewees expected the chief justice to avoid a five- or seven-judge panel for issues likely to divide the court. This norm apparently has characterized much of the Charter period. Chief Justice Lamer explained his approach, which continues to have at least tacit support from most current justices: "If there is the possibility that the outcome of a case might be different with fewer than nine judges, I'll do my best to strike a panel of nine judges. How do I know if there will be a division? First, my executive legal officer helps me flag these cases. Also, I know my colleagues and I have a fairly good idea about what they are thinking on particular issues" (quoted in Greene et al. 1998, 115).

Despite wide agreement that an *en banc* decision is preferable in a closely divided case, there has been little analysis of recent chief justices' ability to achieve this goal. To examine this question, we compute the simple percentage of decisions with 4–3 and 5–4 majorities versus those with higher rates of agreement in the major areas of law during the tenure of each chief justice since 1982 (see Table 3).

The data in Table 3 provide the percentage of votes for each size of panel that was unanimous and for those with a minimum winning coalition (i.e., 3–2, 4–3, or 5–4).[11] One might worry that if a five-

or seven-judge panel produces a minimum winning coalition, the outcome might have been different with a larger panel. Overall, the data suggest that none of the three chief justices in the Charter period reserved all the most controversial cases for *en banc* consideration. Most noticeable, under all three, the proportion of seven-judge panels that produced 4–3 splits was between 10 per cent and 17 per cent for both civil liberties and private law. For all three, there were fewer 4–3 splits in criminal appeals. Over 80 per cent of decisions by five judges were unanimous for all three case types.

ARGUMENT BEFORE THE COURT

Once a case has been accepted for review and a panel struck to decide the case, detailed consideration begins. Every case granted leave to appeal or appealed as of right is scheduled for oral argument, and the justices designated to decide a case typically receive their case materials about a month in advance of the hearing date. The materials include the factums (i.e., the written legal arguments from the lawyers) from each side, the "book of authorities" (copies of all precedent decisions and academic articles that counsel wish to cite), and the trial transcripts (Greene et al. 1998). Increasingly, the case materials going to the justices also include factums from one or more interest groups or non-party government officials who request to participate as an "intervener" in the case.[12]

During each of the three sessions per year, the justices typically have two "sitting weeks," followed by two weeks for writing opinions and preparing for the next set of cases, two for sittings, and two for writing and preparing, and so on. During sitting weeks, justices typically hear one case in the morning and one in the afternoon. Each justice develops his own style and pace in preparation for oral argument, but several features stand out. First, the norm is that the chamber of each justice prepares for oral argument independently – there is virtually no contact between chambers before oral argument. Memos and research findings are not shared, and there is virtually no discussion either among justices or between clerks from different chambers. Consequently, all justices commented that they often approach oral argument without having a very good idea about where their colleagues stand.

Possibly most surprising to people more acquainted with the work habits of top officials in the other branches of government (e.g., committee chairs in Parliament and cabinet ministers), all justices, including the chief, do a surprisingly large proportion of the actual work required to make effective decisions. Compared to most officials in government and the private sector with comparable authority, the justices have surprisingly small staffs. Each justice is limited to three law clerks and a few secretarial assistants. The law clerks typically serve for a single year and are chosen from among the very top recent graduates of Canada's law schools. Because of the prestige of the position, the twenty-seven clerks represent the "cream of the crop" of the annual law school graduates (Greene et al. 1998, 114). Nevertheless the justices must analyse a large volume of dense legal argumentation each week assisted only by three inexperienced professional staffers. The consequence is that each justice must spend a substantial amount of time examining original case materials.

Each of the justices makes extensive use of his clerks, although the actual division of labour varies. The typical practice is for the justice to first divide the cases more or less equally among the three clerks. Justice H tells his clerks to read the case summaries and then divide responsibilities among themselves, but other justices simply assign cases, either randomly or taking into account the special interests of each clerk. The clerk assigned to a given case is usually asked to prepare a "bench memo" – a ten- to fifty-page essay that provides an overview of the facts and issues, with particular emphasis on recent case law that seems relevant to possible dispositions. Bench memos usually synthesize and summarize the arguments of both sides and analyse their strengths and weaknesses. Some justices reported that they ask their clerks to include a suggested disposition of the case, while others prefer an objective analysis of each issue. The justices frequently ask for additional research, beyond that presented in the factums, on points they think key to the resolution of a particular case.

While their clerks are preparing their bench memos, all the justices indicated that they read extensively from the case materials. However, most reported that, except for particularly simple cases, they could not read all the case material before oral argument. Justice E said that he typically first reads the objective summary from staff lawyers and then instructs his clerks about the legal points on which to concentrate their research. He then starts with the opinion of the lower court, reading concurring and dissenting opinions as well as the opinion of the court. Next, he typically turns to the jury instructions at trial and then carefully reads the factums of each litigant. Finally, he reads his clerk's bench memo a day or two before the hearing and then usually sits down with the clerk to talk informally about ideas for disposition of the case and remaining questions that need further clarification at oral argument.

In contrast, Justice F waits until he receives his clerk's bench memo, which he expects at least a week prior to the hearing, before he begins serious preparation. After he has digested the memo, he turns to the opinion of the court below and then to the factums. His preference is next to look at all the cited precedents that appear central to resolution of the key issues and reread them completely. However, he admitted that in the majority of cases he doesn't have time to read all these precedents in their original form and thus must rely on the analysis of his clerk.

Justice D follows a slightly modified version of this approach. He stressed that he initially assigns cases to his clerks without indicating what he considers the key issues or his initial inclinations of how the case might be decided. He then analyses each factum in turn, referring back to the opinions below and to cited portions of the record only as they become relevant to deciding whether the argument in the factum is well supported. He approaches each factum as if he were cross-examining it, trying to find ways to tear down the crucial elements of the argument. Once he has completed his own analysis he reads his clerk's memo and then schedules a meeting with his clerk, typically one or two days before the hearing. He wants his clerks to debate him vigorously on all the key issues, both acting as a sounding board for his tentative ideas about approaches to the resolution of the case and vigorously defending their own, alternative solutions.

One striking pattern: all the justices prefer that their clerks write their bench memos from a fresh perspective. Thus, while some suggest issues to focus on, none indicate their own ideas about resolving those issues.

At the hearing for a case before the Supreme Court, the lawyers of record are typically granted one hour for each side to present arguments to the justices. Counsel may petition the court for additional time, but such requests are infrequently granted. The time limits are enforced by small lights on the lecterns used by counsel (Greene et al. 1998). Counsel for interveners frequently receive less time to present their arguments orally. As in most common law countries, in Canada oral argument is a very interactive process. The justices frequently interrupt counsel with questions, sometimes before counsel are more than a few minutes into their presentation. Both justices' questions and counsels' answers count towards the one-hour time limit. The hearings are now recorded and broadcast on the Canadian parliamentary channel (both video and audio).

The justices disagree about how much impact the hearing has on the ultimate decision of the court. All find the questions and answers sometimes very useful in exposing the strengths and weaknesses of counsels' positions. A couple indicated that the hearings allow them to test out tentative theories about how to resolve the case without having to commit themselves to a position before they are sure of it themselves. So a justice may take a tentative position on a key issue and pose it as a hypothetical to counsel for one or both sides. Then if the answers or the reactions from other justices indicate that the position is not viable, they never have to go "on record" with the position.

While clarification of positions and gathering information may be the focus of oral argument, the hearing may serve other functions as well. At one time or another, all the justices have apparently used their questions addressed formally to counsel to make a point to their colleagues. They note a strong norm that they not make "speeches" or "arguments" during the hearing; they should speak in the form of a question.[13] Nevertheless, Justice F suggested that a question may in reality be pointing out (to the other justices or perhaps to a single justice perceived to be undecided) the weakness in counsels' position or that of another justice. For example, if counsel has struggled with a question from a justice, another justice might propose their own answer to the question just asked by saying something such as, "But isn't it also true that our decision in XYZ case could be interpreted to mean ..." and then providing a plausible answer. Such a strategy, Justice F said, is particularly attractive for more senior justices – who, by tradition, will be the last to speak at conference. Both Justices B and D suggested that using questions to "feel out" colleagues or to attempt to influence them is often useful, because the near-absence of communication before oral argument means that a justice often enters a hearing without a very good idea of where colleagues stand. According to Justice A, this informal exchange at the hearing sometimes helps the court to coalesce around a given position.

There is no clear consensus among justices as to how often minds change because of oral argument. Justice C said that his mind was pretty well made up before the hearing in 70–80 per cent of cases. In contrast, Justice F made up his mind no more than half the time before oral argument, and Justice D forced himself not to make a decision before oral argument. Justice E indicated that the effects are less about changing sides than about changing the way of thinking about an issue. Similarly, according to Justice H, one doesn't often change sides as a result of argument but may develop a more nuanced position and begin to flesh out reasons to support a position or rethink an initial view about the scope of the solution.

A WORD ABOUT INTERVENERS

While the primary focus of this study is not the role or impact of outside groups vis-à-vis the court's decisions, the work of the court increasingly attracts the interest of many actors besides the formal litigants. Since 1982, the number of applications to intervene has varied dramatically from year to year, without any clear pattern. The total number of applications has ranged from a high of 139 in 1996 to a low of 11 in 1985 (Brodie 2002, 37). Changes in the court's rules have meant that the success rate of applicants (i.e., whether they actually participate) has increased substantially since 1987 and has usually been over 90 per cent since 1991. The most frequent intervener has been the attorney general of Canada, followed closely by the attorney general of Ontario. Other frequent interveners have been the Women's Legal Education and Action Fund (LEAF), the Canadian Civil Liberties Association, bar associations, and the attorney generals of other provinces. There have been approximately equal numbers of interveners from three broad categories: governments, economic interests, and citizen groups. Among citizen groups, rights groups have been most common, followed by representatives of indigenous peoples. Among economic groups, professional societies have appeared more frequently than either business associations or individual corporations (Brodie 2002, 38–9).

Charter cases have most frequently attracted interveners, drawing the interest of both governments and rights-oriented groups – participation has become the norm in recent years. During the 1990s, interveners participated in more than half of Charter cases in all but one year,[14] and the median was one or more interveners in 61 per cent of all such cases (Brodie 2002, 43). The actual impact of interveners is very much in dispute. Overwhelmingly, attorney generals have intervened to oppose the rights claim; in contrast, non-governmental interveners have supported the rights claim by more than two to one (Brodie 2002, 46). Despite the clear pattern of support, there is less agreement about whether support translates into victory.

Unfortunately, our interviews shed little light on the impact of interveners. Only three justices mentioned interveners vis-à-vis decision making on the court. Justice D felt that they usually were not at all useful because they tended to be "too political." In contrast, Justice A thought their contribution "often valuable" because they tended to bring quite different perspectives from formal litigants. Justice F took a middle ground, saying that their utility "varies enormously" – some just want to make a political statement for the newspapers – and he quoted counsel for one group: "If you can't make law, you can at least make headlines." In contrast, some interveners make a valuable contribution because some have considerably more expertise in a particular area than counsel for the litigants.

THE CONFERENCE AND OPINION WRITING

Immediately at the end of most hearings, all the justices go into the conference room. They sit around a large round table in order of seniority. With the chief justice presiding, they speak about their views of the case. They speak in reverse order of seniority, from the most junior to the chief (opposite of the US practice). Each provides a brief summary of their view about how the case and the major issues should be resolved. Thus, without a formal vote, it is usually obvious by the time the chief justice speaks how the case will be decided (see Greene et al. 1998, 119–20).

Implicitly, the first decision for the conference is whether the court should announce an oral judgment shortly after it reconvenes in the courtroom. During the period we studied, from 1982 to 2003, the court did so in 22 per cent of hearings. An oral judgment generally indicates that the justices quickly discovered unanimity and realized that resolution of the case would not require any significant change in precedent. In interviews, justices generally agreed that this occurred mostly in cases that reach the court as of right in criminal appeals that probably would not have been granted leave to appeal. This view is consistent with our finding that as the proportion of as-of-right cases on the docket has declined in recent years so has the proportion of oral dispositions.

The conference discussion among justices rarely resembles a debate. In many cases the justices simply go around the table giving their brief view without responding to each other. As Justice H remarked, there is often only a clarification of positions, with little or no give and take. But Justice D noted that after it seems from the first three or four justices that the court is divided on the resolution, subsequent speakers tend to focus on why they agree or disagree with the earlier statements, and more junior justices may speak again. Justice E concurred that usually they simply "go around the table" but that more complex cases often generate more free-flowing discussion. Both Justices B and C summarized their view of the conferences by concluding that there is "a fair degree of actual discussion," usually after a more senior justice responds directly to an earlier remark rather than simply stating their own position. And according to Justice A, while the justices are always polite towards each other, quite frequently one justice will break into another's statement with an observation or question, which sets off more responses and may necessitate the chief's becoming a referee.

At the end of the discussion, the chief justice will often summarize how the court is aligned as to outcome and the main issues that still need resolution. While the formal power to assign the writing of the court's reasons[15] ultimately resides with the chief justice, the actual practice is more informal. It appears to involve interplay between suggestions by the chief and requests from volunteers.

Under some previous chief justices it appears that seniority was the main determinant of who was assigned the court's opinion, but in the McLachlin court, while seniority still counts when two or more justices volunteer, the most senior justice does not automatically write the opinion. Most justices apparently feel that there are no hard and fast rules to determine who will write the reasons of the court; instead there is a sense that three crucial factors – the seniority, special expertise, or intense interest of a particular justice; justices' other writing assignments; and the chief's sense of who might best unite the court – all play a role. While the justices' comments on selection of the opinion writer were noticeably vaguer than those about most aspects of court procedure, there seems a consensus that the present system works well and is fairer than some earlier practices.

While there is often little give and take before or during the conference, that is decidedly *not* the case during opinion writing, which all the justices view as the key stage in decision making. With slight variation in phrasing, all felt that lawyers, journalists, and academics all tended to put too much emphasis on the outcome – often conceived too narrowly as simply who won and who lost – and to ignore the nuances of the reasons. The justices view their opinion-writing chores as both their most time-consuming and their most important activity. And as one simply listens to the justices one can easily form the conclusion that it is also the most satisfying part of their jobs.

Writing the reasons of the court is a time-consuming, intensive task that may take a couple of weeks or a couple of months. While there is considerable variation in individual styles, all the justices take very seriously the details of the actual writing. In writing opinions in important cases, justices do a great deal of research about the issues. Most feel no reluctance to go beyond the materials presented by counsel and often do extensive supplementary investigation of precedent and scholarly writing in law reviews and other sources. Justices will on occasion also investigate the way other common law courts (especially those in England, Australia, and the United States) have resolved similar legal issues, although of course none of these precedents is binding on Canadian courts. The justices typically make heavy use of their clerks to provide this supplemental research, but the justices also indicated that they did some of the research themselves.

An earlier study found that two justices typically had their clerks write a first draft of the judgment after a detailed post-conference discussion with them, while the others produced the first draft and then asked their clerks to comment on and criticize their work (Greene et al. 1998, 120). Our interviews suggest that a similar pattern remains the norm. Whether justices will ask a clerk to write all or write a portion of a first draft varies among them (and even with the nature of the issue), but four generalizations appear to apply to all the justices. First, in some form, the clerks are heavily involved in meaningful work on the reasons written by their justice. Second, the justices are always intensely involved in the detailed crafting of the reasons, and the final product always reflects the position and priorities of the justice rather than of the clerk. Third, the final product is always the product of considerable collegial interaction unless the case is so simple and straightforward that the conference revealed that there was a clear consensus from the beginning. Fourth, after the lawyers have had their say at the hearing, there is no influence or input on the reasons from anyone outside the small community of the court and its staff.

The specific way that clerks are used varies considerably among the justices. For example, one justice said that he does not involve his clerks at all in the writing of opinions in French because he is quite comfortable with his own style. But he asks for extensive critiques for drafts of an opinion or a memo in English and will sometimes ask a clerk to write a first draft of an opinion in English. Justice F, in contrast, always writes the first draft himself but usually writes in a whole series of questions in boldface throughout the draft and asks his clerk to make specific responses or to do additional research to respond to each query. He also asks his clerks to critique the overall thrust of the opinion and indicates that he often gets responses such as, "I don't agree with your conclusions in paragraph 36 because they ignore X precedent." Justice G often divides the initial writing into segments dealing with different issues and writes some segments himself and assign others to a clerk. Each clerk then critiques the initial draft of the other. Justice B usually asks a clerk to write up the "preliminary stuff" that has to go into the opinion (e.g., a summary of the facts, the history of the case in the courts, and an explanation of the issues raised by the appellant), while he writes a draft of the reasoning section. He then asks his clerk to write a "comment memo" on his first draft and discusses that memo with the clerk before beginning on revisions and polishing.

The justices we interviewed were in remarkable agreement on the way opinion writing works in practice. In most important respects, the ten interviews produced only minor variation on a set of common themes. When the assignment of the opinion writer is made, the chief justice lays out a time line, which depends on the perceived difficulty of the case, but that time line is flexible. When the reasons are officially announced depends on how quickly the author works and how much negotiation is needed to reach agreement.

Once the author has worked with his clerks to polish the opinion draft, the author will circulate the draft to all the other justices on the panel that heard the case. The draft goes to all the justices simultaneously, and they all feel quite free to comment on what everyone understands to be only a first draft. Most justices first ask one of their clerks to write a "comment memo" analysing the strengths and weaknesses of the draft. This memo usually is for the eyes only of their own justice, and clerks are admonished to be completely frank in their analysis. Typically clerks have quite a short time to complete these memos. When a justice decides to respond to a draft of the reasons, the comments are typically in writing and go simultaneously to all the justices on the panel. On occasion, however, a justice phones the author or informally drops by his office.

After justices receive the first draft, there is an informal rule that they wait for at least two weeks before formally "signing on" to the reasons. This convention is designed to give other justices a chance to raise objections to some aspect of the opinion or to suggest revisions. Similarly, even if it is clear from conference that one or more justices disagree with the majority, a dissenting opinion is never circulated until two weeks after the draft of the majority reasons is received. However, a dissenter usually circulates a brief memo in those first two weeks after receiving the draft of the majority reasons indicating that there will be a dissent and usually presenting an outline of the basis of the forthcoming dissent.

Extensive comments on the draft opinions, with a good bit of give and take among everyone concerned, appear to be the norm. As a result, many opinions go through multiple drafts before release. On occasion, perhaps two or three times a year according to the justices, the original draft is completely rewritten, and about as often the court holds a second conference after comments on a couple of drafts to try to work out an agreement. Most of the positions that justices announce at conference on whether they support a ruling for the petitioner or for the respondent remain constant throughout the negotiations, but some may change in response to the exchange of views. Justice E estimated that on perhaps 10 per cent of cases at least one justice switches sides and that two or three times a year the majority changes, so that the published opinion provides a ruling opposite to the tentative judgment arrived at in conference.

Several justices indicated that the current chief justice prefers to have the court speak with one voice and encourages justices who express initial differences to try to work them out if possible. Justices E, F, and H suggested that there is more "pressure" from the chief to eliminate concurrences[16] than there is to eliminate dissents, because when the majority is divided it tends to confuse the legal community in its attempts to understand the meaning of the new precedent.

Other justices (especially Justices A, B, C, and D) did not like a characterization of "pressure" to reach agreement but instead talked of widespread willingness to "compromise" or to "accommodate" the views of others when one could do so without doing violence to one's deeply held principles.

Often the attempt to avoid concurrences comes in the form of a suggestion to drop from the opinion discussion of some of the issues initially included as not essential to resolving the litigants' dispute, and so the final judgment rests on narrower grounds than the opinion writer initially preferred. It is also common, according to most of the justices, to search for possible changes in wording that do not change the basic substance of the opinion but allow everyone to "live with" the final opinion. This may involve switching to a deliberately more ambiguous statement of the precedent. In the words of justice G, "Opinions are sometimes '*fudgier*' ... or more limited than the opinion writer initially preferred in order to obtain a unanimous decision."

Justice C maintained that the justices often make implicit bargains about the wording or content of the opinion, but that each always tries to approach a colleague tactfully. Justices rarely use the word "bargain" when proposing changes in the draft of an opinion. Instead, they may say something such as this: "I think it would strengthen the opinion if the approach to the second issue was such and such." Or a justice may write, "Subject to the following reservations, I agree with your excellent analysis" (followed by details of the "reservations").[17] In partial contrast, two justices said that the bargains are sometimes fairly explicit. For example, according to Justice D, a justice may write a memo in response to a draft of the opinion that says something such as, "If you could see your way to change section III of the opinion in the following way (and sometimes then several alternative paragraphs would be included), then I would be comfortable joining the opinion of the court; otherwise I am inclined to write separately."

While some of the justices appeared comfortable characterizing the interactions during opinion writing as "bargaining," all three of the justices who used that term immediately explained (without any prompting) that such bargaining is only a form of reaching compromise within the context of a single case. They were emphatic that there is absolutely no trading of votes on one case for consideration on another case. Nor are there any "side payments" of any kind; i.e., no justice expects any future benefits from the chief justice or anyone else as a reward for support on a case.

Finally, analysis of the actual results of this opinion-writing process reveals how frequently the court rules unanimously. In the Charter period, the final vote has been unanimous in slightly over 76 per cent of judgments. We address this tendency and its implications for an attitudinal account of decision making below in chapter 8.

CONCLUSION

In conclusion, opinion writing on the Supreme Court of Canada appears to be marked by strong collegial norms. While the justices feel free to vote their individual preferences when they perceive important principles to be at stake, they take the general approach of first looking to see if compromise is possible. Most of them appear to respect the views of their colleagues and to admit the legitimacy of alternative ways of approaching many legal problems. As a result, they are often willing to accept either compromise language or a judgment based on a less expansive interpretation of the law than what they might have privately preferred if such compromise will help the court speak with a unified voice.

In the following chapter we begin our analysis of the actual patterns of votes on the Supreme Court of Canada to discover what empirical support there is for the theories of decision making reflected in perceptions of the justices or proposed in the earlier studies discussed in chapter 3.

5 The Dimensionality of Voting

The previous chapters suggested that ideological differences may lie at the heart of decision making on the Supreme Court of Canada, especially in high-profile disputes. However, other forces, such as strategic interaction between justices and disagreements over legal doctrines, may dampen the relevance of ideology. Moreover, the fact that the Canadian appointment process lacks the ideological orientation of its American counterpart leads one to question whether ideological considerations will drive decision making in Canada to the degree that they do in the United States. Given these considerations, our study features a research strategy that tests the applicability of the attitudinal model in the Supreme Court of Canada and provides data to either confirm or refute its claims. In chapter 3 we discussed three ways to assess the impact of ideology or political preferences on the decisions of appellate judges: factor analysis, independent assessments of judicial ideology, and the personal attributes of the justices. In this chapter we use a factor-analytic strategy to assess the degree to which ideology explains judicial conflict on the Charter-era court of Antonio Lamer, chief justice from 1990 to 2000 – specifically in the period 1992–7, when its membership was stable. This statistical technique sets the stage for further multivariate analysis of the attitudinal model in subsequent chapters.

FACTOR ANALYSIS AND JUDICIAL BEHAVIOUR

Establishing the Continuum

Before we begin, a caveat: the focus of the analysis is to discover the bases of disagreements among the justices. However, in approximately three-quarters of the cases, the Supreme Court reaches consensus and produces a unanimous decision. We consider the implications of such a high degree of unanimity in chapter 8. For the present, our focus is explaining patterns of decisions in those cases in which the justices disagree.

We apply factor analysis to examine judicial voting behaviour because, unlike standard attitudinal studies, it does not presuppose a liberal/conservative ideological divide on the court. This effort echoes the approach pioneered by Flango and Ducat (1977) and Ducat and Dudley (Dudley and Ducat 1986; Ducat and Dudley 1987) for analysing US Supreme Court decisions, and subsequently applied by Ostberg, Wetstein, and Ducat (Ostberg and Wetstein 1998; Wetstein and Ostberg 1999; Wetstein et al. 1999; Ostberg et al. 2002) to Canadian rulings in the Supreme Court under Chief Justices Brian Dickson (1984–90) and Antonio Lamer. This strategy allows actual voting behaviour to guide us in the determination of attitudinal conflicts on the Lamer court.

Factor analysis works something like this: imagine sorting all the cases of the Lamer court where there is disagreement along a continuum running from closely divided cases (say, 5–4 or 4–3 splits) featuring one bloc of justices at one end of the continuum voting against the other bloc at the other end, where the same kind of 5–4 or 4–3 splits exist, but with the same blocs of justices on the other sides of the outcome. In between those two poles, there might be other kinds of vote splits: 6–3, 5–2, 4-1, and so on. When looking at that list of votes across the cases, we might see one extreme end of the list with cases where, for example, Justices L'Heureux-Dubé and LaForest are part of the five-member majority, but the other end might find these two justices aligned together in a four-member dissent. These opposing distributions of justices (5–4 on one end of the list of cases, and 4–5 on the other) are the building blocks of the mathematical technique of factor analysis.

Put simply, the largest number of disagreements helps identify the most significant factor of dispute between the justices. One can "transform" votes into either +1 or −1 scores, depending on their presence in the majority or dissent. As a first step, this arrangement of the decisions of individual justices helps to identify mathematically the matrix of the most significant disagreements between them. Once one identifies the most frequent pattern of 5–4 and 4–5 vote splits, a second sorting of the cases would apply the same technique to isolate the second most frequent patterns of voting disagreement among particular justices.

The mathematical sorting of patterns of disagreement was only the first step in our factor analysis. Once we identified the two primary sources of conflict, we computed mathematical values associated with each case to rank them from high to low on each dimension and then read the actual opinions of the justices to try to determine what it was that was driving their disagreement so frequently. The second stage involved a detailed analysis of the cases in order to tease out the underlying dimensions that generated disagreement. Unlike the attitudinal model pioneered by Segal and Spaeth (1993; 2002), our approach does not superimpose any liberal/conservative dimension on voting patterns but rather relies on the written reasons for judgment to identify the underlying dimensions of attitudinal conflict, which may or may not be aligned along a liberal–conservative continuum. The beauty of this method lies in its blending of quantitative and qualitative analysis to determine the fulcrums of attitudinal conflict that emerge on a court (Ostberg et al. 2002, 240). All told, the underlying dimensions that emerge from this strategy will either support or refute the relevance of the attitudinal model outside the US context.

Data and Methods

Data for this chapter are derived from non-unanimous cases in three fields – economic, criminal, and civil rights and liberties – argued before the Supreme Court of Canada between 1992 and 1997 and published in the *Supreme Court Reports*. There are several qualifications about our method that we need to mention. First, factor analysis requires the examination of voting during a period of uninterrupted court membership because it is based on analysis of variance in voting alignments that appear within a given court. In the light of the court's high turnover, we chose to examine decisions between 13 November 1992 and 30 September 1997, because they were handed down during the longest span of stable membership in the Charter era.[1] The period also featured a substantial number of dissents in the three areas of law. Second, we focused on non-unanimous cases because they constitute a large portion of the court's docket and represent arguably its most significant decisions during this period. We further limited our analysis to cases featuring written reasons for judgment, because they necessarily highlight the rationale for attitudinal conflict on the court. Collectively, there were a total of 42 economic, 75 criminal, and 26 civil rights and liberties cases in our analysis.[2]

Since factor analysis involves an examination of correlations between the justices' voting patterns across a particular set of cases, it is ideally based on cases featuring participation by all the justices. However, since the court often sits with fewer than nine justices, it was necessary to introduce non-participation scores for justices who did not take part in the hearing for a given case. Consequently, the factor analysis was based on the votes of the justices, which we scored as +1 for a majority vote, 0 for non-participation, and –[minus]1 for a dissenting vote (we provide extensive commentary on our method in a footnote).[3]

Factor analysis of judicial votes is more of an art form than an exact science.[4] Since we are simply using the technique as a heuristic device for identifying the most prominent cases featuring attitudinal conflicts, we are confident that our analysis of the top-scoring cases on the positive and negative poles of each factor enabled us to accurately characterize the underlying dimensions of disagreement.

The classification of the decisions in each area of law was based on whether the case featured an economic, criminal, or civil rights and liberties concern. Some of the cases appeared in more than one legal area if they addressed multiple issues. For example, *Symes v. Canada* appeared in both the economic and civil rights analysis because it addressed whether the denial of childcare tax deductions as a business expense violated equality provisions in the Charter.[5] Cases were categorized into the three areas in the following ways: civil liberties included civil rights, both constitutional and statutory (such as those relating to minority and gender discrimination), and the standard set of civil liberties claims (i.e., those relating to freedom of expression, religion, privacy, language education, and aboriginal rights). The economic category included labour relations, government regulation of the economy, tax cases, and private economic disputes. Criminal cases involved disputes where criminal charges were filed. Some of the more prominent criminal cases featured issues pertaining to principles of fundamental justice and other Charter rights such as guarantees against unreasonable search and seizure, arbitrary detention, right to counsel, and ensuring a fair and speedy trial by an impartial jury. Collectively, the cases that were factor analysed in these three legal areas represented 133 of the 135 non-unanimous cases featuring written reasons for judgment handed down by the Lamer natural court. As such, the analysis presented here provides a robust account of the sources of conflict that divided justices of that court.

DIMENSIONS OF CONFLICT IN NON-UNANIMOUS CASES

Economic Cases

In economic disputes, attitudinal disagreement can be driven by a host of concerns, including disputes over federal or provincial authority, deference to an agency's regulatory power, union–management relations, favouritism towards economic elites, creditors' interests versus economic underdogs and debtors, and claims engaging fairness and due process rights. Ultimately, these concerns may be subsumed under a larger judicial rubric pertaining to economic liberalism or conservatism, yet we did not presuppose that this would emerge as the dominant attitudinal dimension at work in this area on the Lamer court. Even though it is often difficult to determine which side prevails in economic disputes because individuals are sometimes pitted against other individuals, corporations frequently oppose each other, and the government may be serving the interests of the elite or of the have-nots, depending on the opposing party in the case, we were able to classify outcomes by paying careful attention to which party represented the economic underdog in each dispute. We "scored" outcomes favouring an underdog as liberal, and those favouring economic elites as conservative (see Schubert 1965; 1974; Ducat and Dudley 1987). While we did not use these as a guiding force in our determination of the underlying factors that emerged in the economic realm, the identification of underdog wins or losses did serve as one component in our analysis of the cases. This identification, in conjunction with prevailing issue patterns, notions of federalism, activist–restraintist tendencies, considerations about regulatory power, and principles of procedural fairness, collectively helped to identify the dimensions that animated the conflicts underlying the two principal factors. Consequently, we considered numerous potential factors during our reading of the cases in an effort to find the consistent themes that tied the cases and votes together.

Table 4
Factor-analytic matrix loadings (varimax rotation) for non-unanimous economic decisions of the Lamer natural court, November 1992–September 1997

Justice	*Factor 1*	*Factor 2*
L'Heureux-Dubé	**.610**	–.347
LaForest	**.601**	.055
Gonthier	.533	.438
Cory	.295	.421
McLachlin	.123	**–.782**
Lamer	–.056	.536
Iacobucci	–.219	**.654**
Major	**–.645**	.065
Sopinka	**–.830**	.212
Eigen value	2.28	1.87
Proportion of variance	25.3%	20.7%

While the first factor in the two-factor solution in the economic area featured economic liberal/conservative themes in private law and business regulation disputes, the second pertained to a non-ideological disagreement over deference to agency and regulatory power, whether at the federal, provincial, or local level. Overall, the two-factor model accounts for 46 per cent of the total variance of judicial voting in these non-unanimous cases (see Table 4).[6] The mathematical sorting of the cases and votes identified two factors that accounted for the largest set of disagreements among the justices in economic disputes, covering roughly half of all the patterns of disagreement.

The sorting of the cases and judicial votes allowed us to assign "factor scores" to each justice on each of the dimensions of conflict. Those scores can range from roughly +1 to –1 when disagreements are most extreme. In other words, when one is looking at the scores for justices on each factor, those scoring near +1 are most often in conflict with those scoring near –1. We then calculated loadings for each case based on the justices' scores. We subsequently read the five cases scoring most positively and negatively in order to help identify the underlying factor or content of the disagreement between the justices. In the economic disputes, the factor loadings on the first dimension featured an attitudinal conflict between Justices L'Heureux-Dubé (.610) and LaForest (.601), who anchored the positive end of the dimension, and Justices Sopinka and Major, who occupied the negative side (–.830 and –.645, respectively; see the first column of Table 4). This sorting implies that the most common 5–4 and 4–3 splits featured regular appearances of Justices L'Heureux-Dubé and LaForest pitted against Justices Sopinka and Major at both ends of the continuum. The second factor featured the other female on the court, namely Justice McLachlin (–.782), who was juxtaposed to Justice Iacobucci (.654) in her voting behaviour (see the second column of Table 4). The factor analysis in this area highlights the distinctive voting patterns of Justices L'Heureux-Dubé and McLachlin, the two most prominent dissenters on the Lamer court (see McCormick 2000; Ostberg et al. 2004). In addition, the two principal factors collectively featured strong loadings for six of the nine justices, suggesting that two-thirds of the Lamer court's justices disagreed with each other because of the underlying dimensions that emerged in these cases.

After our in-depth reading of the cases scoring most extremely on the first factor, we could see relatively clearly that the factor should be labelled economic liberalism in private law and business regulation disputes. The issues in the cases pertained to a constellation of private law concerns, namely tort, contracts, labour relations, and bankruptcy claims, with seven of the ten cases scoring most extremely on this factor drawn from these areas of law (see Appendix B for a list of cases that score strongly on each factor). Two additional cases addressed governmental regulation of business in the areas of pollution and commercial advertising. Moreover, this factor featured a clear ideological cleavage, with economic underdogs winning all five of the highest-scoring disputes on the positive side of the factor, while economic elites won victories in four of the five lowest-scoring cases on the factor.

Examples of this economic liberalism can be seen most readily in the three tort cases scoring on the positive side of factor 1, where the court favoured the underprivileged party. In *Hodgkinson v. Simms* (1994), the court ruled that an investment adviser owed damages to his client because he failed to provide information about his own connections to the investment vehicles he recommended. Likewise, in *Galaske v. O'Donnell* (1994), the court determined a driver involved in an accident owed damages to an injured minor for failing to require him to wear a seat belt. Additionally, in *Winnipeg Child and Family Services (Northwest Area) v. G. (D.F.)* (1997), the court ruled that the government could not detain a pregnant woman addicted to drugs in a health facility until she gave birth. Although one could argue that protection of an unborn fetus might represent the underdog argument in this case, as the majority pointed out it ultimately involved government encroachment on the individual liberty of the woman and, if allowed, would have represented an exceptional expansion of the common law doctrine of *parens patriae* (*Winnipeg Child and Family Services (Northwest Area) v. G. (D.F.)* [1997] 3 SCR 925, at 959–60).[7]

The court majority's liberal bent on this side of the factor can also be seen in its clear endorsement of Parliament's power to impose criminal penalties on companies releasing toxic chemicals into the environment in *R v. Hydro-Québec* (1997). The liberal tenor of this side of the dimension is further illustrated by the fact that Justices L'Heureux-Dubé, LaForest, and Gonthier cast a cumulative total of 14 out of 14 possible liberal votes in all five cases scoring most positively on factor 1. As the dominant justices on this dimension, their consistent pattern of liberal votes amplifies the conclusion that traditional notions of economic liberalism versus conservatism highlight the justices' stance in these disputes.

As for the negative side of the first factor, examples of conservatism on the part of the court are found in four of the five most extremely scoring cases. For example, in *Finlay v. Canada (Minister of Finance)* (1993), the court ruled that a disabled person must return welfare overpayments to the government, while in *Béliveau St-Jacques v. FEESP* (1996), it ruled that a woman was barred from filing a sexual-harassment civil suit because she had already collected workers' compensation benefits. Clearly these two cases represent significant losses for the economic underdogs. This conservative trend is further illustrated in *RJR-MacDonald Inc. v. Canada (Attorney General)* (1995) and *Royal Bank of Canada v. Sparrow Electric Corp.* (1997), where the government lost to elite corporate interests that were defending the right to advertise tobacco products freely and the rights of creditors to be on equal footing with tax authorities when pursuing bankruptcy claims. Overall, the cases on the first factor leave the unmistakable impression that conflicting values regarding economic liberalism drive the primary dimension of conflict in the economic decisions of the Lamer natural court.

A review of the ten cases scoring most positively and negatively on the second economic factor led us to conclude that its fulcrum of conflict centred on attitudinal disagreement over deference to agencies and regulatory power, whether at the federal, provincial, or local level. Unlike in the first dimension, here we could glean no clear liberal–conservative pattern in the decisions on the second factor because the most extremely scoring cases on both sides featured predominantly conservative rulings (nine out of ten decisions). Thus the cases at the two extremes of the second factor did not reflect opposite ideological voting patterns. However, since fully eight of the ten disputes dealt with questions of deference to policy and regulatory decisions of government agencies, it was clear that this was the thread that tied these cases together. Moreover, the cases are replete with voting conflicts between Justices McLachlin and Justice Iacobucci. The principal dispute on this factor is demonstrated by Justice Iacobucci's tendency to defer to federal and agency regulatory power in six of the eight cases on which he participated: *Canadian Broadcasting Corp. v. Canada (Labour Relations Board)*; *Friesen v. Canada*; *Hickman Motors Ltd. v. Canada*; *Hy and Zel's Inc. v. Ontario (Attorney General)*; *Slattery (Trustee of) v. Slattery*; and *Symes v. Canada*. In the majority of these cases, the stance taken by Justice Iacobucci is juxtaposed against a less deferential position taken by Justice McLachlin. Two other cases that scored most strongly on the second economic factor did not fit the agency deference pattern. Yet they appeared on this second factor because they also involved a disagreement between Justices Iacobucci and McLachlin over the scope of tort and common law principles (*Gold v. Rosenberg* and *Wallace v. United Grain Growers Ltd.*). Taken together, these cases demonstrate that the underlying dimension of conflict on this second economic factor pivots on differing notions of deference to agency rulings, especially pertaining to the interpretation of tax provisions.

The overall impression that we drew from the two principal dimensions of conflict in the economic area is that the court was locked in two overarching debates: 1) a liberal/conservative split over private and regulatory law matters and 2) a struggle over the reach of government regulatory power. Ironically, the two dimensions of conflict that appear on the Lamer court in the 1990s bear striking resemblance to two of the underlying dimensions fuelling economic disputes on Warren Burger's US Supreme Court in the early 1970s. In their earlier research, Ducat and Dudley (1987, 534) found that liberalism–conservatism and deference to administrative agencies were two of the three dimensions accounting for 51 per cent of the variance during the early Burger court. Although federalism provoked much more prominent debate in the late-twentieth-century US Supreme court (Ducat and Dudley 1987; Hagle and Spaeth 1992; 1993), we believe that notions of liberalism and conservatism are still prominent features in both the US and Canadian courts of the modern era.

Our finding of a strong ideological factor also parallels the conclusions of Hagle and Spaeth (1992, 131), who characterize the strongest variable explaining the pro- or anti-business decisions of the Burger court as a form of economic libertarianism. Their understanding of the court's treatment of business interests squares with our view of the Lamer natural court justices' treatment of economic elites and underdogs. They found agency power to be the fourth-strongest predictor of the Burger court's rulings (Hagle and Spaeth 1992, 131), ranking behind variables tapping the exercise of judicial power and federalism.

While the slight differences in the results explaining attitudinal conflicts in economic cases can be chalked up to different levels of measurement and different methods, it is clear that there is a significant ideological divide at work within both the US and Canadian courts when these cases are decided. Moreover, concerns about federal and state or provincial regulatory power occupy an important position in the minds of the justices in both modern courts. The parallel nature of these concerns makes intuitive sense in high courts that are situated in advanced industrial societies that increasingly face similar economic challenges and regulatory environments. Questions of agency power and government treatment of business interests are bound to remain significant in both countries, even if the New Deal–era understandings of economic liberalism and conservatism have shifted to a more nuanced web of interpretations (see Ducat and Dudley 1987).

CRIMINAL CASES

The analysis of non-unanimous criminal decisions by the Supreme Court of Canada between November 1992 and September 1997 accounted for 50 per cent of the total variance in the justices' voting (Table 5).[8] The fact that coalitions of justices are found at the two ends of the first factor suggests that the first criminal dimension

Table 5
Factor-analytic matrix loadings (varimax rotation) for non-unanimous criminal decisions of the Lamer natural court, November 1992–September 1997

Justice	*Factor 1*	*Factor 2*
Sopinka	**.819**	.081
Major	**.723**	.241
Lamer	**.642**	–.100
Cory	.116	**.654**
Iacobucci	–.104	**.781**
McLachlin	–.151	**–.615**
LaForest	**–.578**	–.010
Gonthier	**–.624**	–.186
L'Heureux-Dubé	**–.796**	–.060
Eigen value	3.01	1.53
Proportion of variance	33.4%	17.0%

is based on a struggle between two opposing blocs of the Lamer natural court. While one wing was dominated by Justices Sopinka, Major, and Lamer (.819, .723, and .642, respectively), the other was led by Justices L'Heureux-Dubé and Gonthier, with Justice LaForest as a more moderate affiliate (–.796, –.624, and –.578, respectively). The voting behaviour of the three remaining justices was featured on the second factor, with Justices Iacobucci and Cory (.781 and .654) facing off against Justice McLachlin (–.615).

A detailed reading of the cases scoring most extremely on factor 1 led us to identify this factor as liberalism/conservatism towards treatment of the criminally accused (see Appendix B for a list of cases and factor scores). The second factor featured a conflict over fair trial and due process, pertaining principally to non-ideological questions surrounding the admission of evidence. The assertion that ideological differences drive the first factor is demonstrated by the fact that the majority ruled in favour of the accused in nine of the ten most positively scoring cases, yet sided with the crown in four of the five scoring most negatively.[9] One of the salient issues running through many of the cases on the first factor pertains to the approach towards sexual offenders and dangerous criminals. In eleven of the fifteen cases scoring most extremely on this factor, the court seemed to be grappling with how to balance these defendants' due process rights with the community's interest in protecting the public from some of the most heinous criminal elements of society, such as rapists, murderers, and pedophiles. Anyone reading the cases would immediately equate the ideological divide on the court as one in concert with Packer's (1968) crime control and due process models of criminal procedure.

Prime examples of the communitarian bent of the wing led by Justice L'Heureux-Dubé towards the criminally accused are highlighted in three dissents on the positive side of factor 1. In *R. v. Heywood*, the majority bloc, led by Justice Cory, struck down a law that prevented sexual offenders from loitering near parks and schoolyards because it was overbroad and violated an individual's fundamental right to liberty (section 7 of the Charter). Justice L'Heureux-Dubé, along with others in the minority, emphasized that the legislative intent behind the law was to protect vulnerable members of society, particularly children, from individuals who posed a threat to reoffend (*R. v. Heywood* [1994] 3 SCR 761, at 807). While the same majority of the court ruled in *R. v. McDonnell* that deference must be afforded to a trial judge who made no obvious error in handing down light sentences for sexual offences, the same dissenting bloc highlighted the need to impose a harsher punishment for such an egregious crime, and one more in line with previous sentences. Likewise, in *R. v. P. (M.B.)*, the majority bloc found that the trial judge committed a critical due process error when he allowed the crown to reopen its case and amend the dates in the indictment. The dissent, in contrast, would have upheld the conviction on the grounds that the amendment of the indictment did not prejudice the defendant or prevent him from providing a defence against the charges (*R. v. P. (M.B.)* [1994] 1 SCR 555, at 589).

The communitarian approach of Justice L'Heureux-Dubé's bloc can also be found in several of the cases scoring most negatively on factor 1 – most notably, *R. v. E. (A.W.)*, *R. v. Jones*, and *R. v. O'Connor*. In *R. v. Jones*, this majority coalition determined that the accused's pre-trial statements to a psychologist could subsequently be used to classify him as a dangerous sex offender in the sentencing phase of his trial. In *R. v. O'Connor*, the same bloc determined that the defendant's right to a fair trial was not violated when the prosecution failed to disclose private therapeutic records in a high-profile case of sexual assault involving a Catholic priest. Our overriding impression from the cases loading on factor 1 is that there was an underlying conflict between the more liberal bloc, which wanted to ensure fundamental due process rights of the accused, and the more conservative bloc, which sought to protect society from dangerous offenders.

The ten cases scoring most extremely on the second criminal factor led us to label this dimension as fair trial/due process concerns, particularly in relation to the treatment of evidence. Remarkably, errors pertaining to the admission of evidence dominated over half of the cases loading on the second factor (6 of 10), while other due process errors appeared in two additional cases. Cases on this factor featured Justice McLachlin at odds with Justices Iacobucci and Cory in a series of disputes involving the admissibility of evidence, the credibility of testimony by witnesses and the accused, the sufficiency of jury instructions on evidence, and the possibility of drawing erroneous inferences from evidence. Although these issues have important ramifications for procedural due process and the conduct of a fair trial, what distinguishes this factor from the first is that it was *not ideologically driven* by opposing camps on the Lamer natural court, but rather seemed more narrowly focused on the technicalities of trial procedure. Indeed, while Justice McLachlin ruled in favour of the accused in 60 per cent of the cases, Justices Cory and Iacobucci voted for the accused 40 per cent of the time across both sides of the factor. None of these tallies is indicative of the pure ideological voting that appeared so readily on the first factor.

Our impression of the evidentiary locus of this dimension of conflict is derived from a collection of cases on each side of the factor. One of the most positive-scoring cases on the factor was *R. v. Noble*, where Justices Cory and Iacobucci were juxtaposed against Justice McLachlin in a debate over whether the trial judge could legitimately infer guilt from the accused's failure to testify in the case. While Justice McLachlin and the other dissenters said that it was a legitimate inference to make as part of a web of inculpatory evidence, Justices Cory and Iacobucci in the majority claimed that such an inference violated the accused's presumption of innocence and necessarily shifted the crown's burden away from proving facts beyond a reasonable doubt (see *R. v. Noble* [1997] 1 SCR 874, at 946–7 and 911, respectively). Likewise, in *R. v. Feeney* these same justices disagreed over whether evidence should be excluded in a case where police conducted a warrantless arrest after forcibly entering a home, and whether serious violations of the right to counsel and search and seizure protection had occurred. Justices Cory and Iacobucci believed that the evidence should be excluded because police had engaged in egregious violations of sections 8 and 10(b) of the Charter (*R. v. Feeney* [1997] 2 SCR 13, at 25). However, Justice McLachlin signed on to a dissent that maintained that the evidence should be admitted because the initial unlawful entry was necessary to prevent the destruction of evidence. Moreover, since police eventually obtained a warrant while the accused was in custody, no Charter breaches had occurred (*R. v. Feeney* [1997] 2 SCR 13, at 115–16). Taken together, the *Feeney* and *Noble* cases highlight the underlying evidentiary disputes that seemed to characterize this dimension.

Four of the five cases on the negative side of factor 2 also address the evidentiary conflict between these justices, although there were instances of agreement between Justices McLachlin and Cory in two of the cases (*R. v. Swietlinski* and *R. v. Belnavis*). Yet the Iacobucci/McLachlin divide remained consistent in all four of the rulings addressing the treatment of evidence. For example, in *R. v. Swietlinksi,* Justices McLachlin and Iacobucci disagreed over whether inflammatory comments by a crown attorney constituted testimonial evidence that jeopardized the fairness of a parole hearing. While Justice McLachlin agreed with the majority that the comments might have negatively influenced the jury in its deliberations, Justice Iacobucci, along with other dissenters, claimed that the comments had little impact because the judge had subsequently provided sufficient jury instructions (see *R. v. Swietlinksi* [1994] 3 SCR 481, at 513 and 506–10, respectively). Similarly, in the complex case of *R. v. R. (D.)*, Justices Iacobucci and McLachlin accorded different relative weight to a trial judge's treatment of testimonial evidence by young victims of sexual assault and the psychiatric and medical evidence entered at trial. While Justice McLachlin believed that the trial judge's errors required an acquittal for two of the defendants, Justices Iacobucci and Cory thought that a new trial was necessary for one of the defendants, given the potential strength of the children's testimony (see *R. v. R. (D.)* [1996] 2 SCR 291, at 341). Our general conclusion from the discussion of these cases on the second criminal factor is that it involved a debate between Justices Cory and Iacobucci on the one hand and Justice McLachlin on the other, in a procedural battle focusing on admissibility of evidence and its impact on the fairness of criminal proceedings.

The analysis of non-unanimous cases in the criminal area suggests that two critical approaches emerged on the Lamer natural court in the resolution of criminal controversies. The first involved a much broader ideological debate between two blocs over the maintenance of procedural due process rights and the community's interests in protecting citizens from dangerous offenders. Although the second factor can be seen through the same prism of procedural fairness, the approach to criminal disputes here was much narrower in scope, with the justices focusing on technical details involving evidentiary rulings and their impact on fair trial proceedings. However, unlike the first factor, the debate between the key justices on the second factor was not driven by any consistent liberal–conservative pattern.

There is a striking parallel between the underlying dimensions found in the criminal area and some of those uncovered by Ostberg et al. (2002) in their factor analysis of Charter disputes in the Lamer natural court. The first dimension uncovered here mirrors the criminal cases loading on their first dimension in the sense that both involve an ideological communitarian-versus-libertarian debate. In both sets of analysis, Justices L'Heureux-Dubé and Sopinka anchored the two ends of this ideological divide, with Justice L'Heureux-Dubé promoting communitarian values that were juxtaposed to Justice Sopinka's libertarian vision (see Ostberg et al. 2002, 242–4). Similarly, both of the criminal factors identified in our study touch on themes of fairness and due process, which matches up nicely with their second factor (Ostberg et al. 2002). Yet their findings dealt with a whole host of fairness concerns, while our second factor focuses more narrowly on its evidentiary orientation (Ostberg et al. 2002, 245). In general, Canadian court watchers will not be surprised that both studies found that criminal issues produced an ideological split on the Lamer natural court, since both communitarian and individual values are prominently featured in the text of the Charter.

CIVIL RIGHTS AND LIBERTIES CASES

The Lamer natural court handed down only 26 non-unanimous cases relating to civil rights and liberties. A principal-components analysis featuring a two-factor solution accounted for a total of 47 per cent of the variance in voting behaviour, with the first factor capturing 25 per cent of that variance and the second factor the remainder (Eigen value = 2.27 and 1.97, respectively; see Table 6). The first factor featured a debate between both Justices LaForest (–.767) and Gonthier (–.763) on the one hand and Justice McLachlin (.781) on the other, with Justice L'Heureux-Dubé aligning with her on nine of

Table 6
Factor-analytic matrix loadings (varimax rotation) for non-unanimous civil rights and liberties decisions of the Lamer natural court, November 1992–September 1997

Justice	*Factor 1*	*Factor 2*
McLachlin	**.781**	–.314
Cory	.233	.234
L'Heureux-Dubé	.213	**–.614**
Iacobucci	.158	**.805**
Sopinka	.021	**.731**
Lamer	–.176	.472
Major	–.576	–.096
Gonthier	**–.763**	.010
LaForest	**–.767**	.158
Eigen value	2.27	1.97
Proportion of variance	25.2%	21.9%

the ten most positively scoring cases (.213). Meanwhile, the second factor highlighted a debate between Justice L'Heureux-Dubé and two of her male colleagues, namely Justices Iacobucci (.805) and Sopinka (.731).

The cases scoring most extremely on the first factor indicate a consistent liberal/conservative divide over discrimination and liberty claims, while the second featured a debate over the degree to which justices should defer to agency power. Our conclusion regarding the first factor is illustrated by the fact that in nine of the ten positively loading cases the majority rejected the constitutional claims of disadvantaged groups, while in all five of the most negatively scoring cases, the majority favoured the liberty and equality interests that were advanced (a list of the cases appears in Appendix B).[10] One of the distinguishing features of the positive side of the factor is the extent to which the two female justices (McLachlin and L'Heureux-Dubé) stand in stark contrast to their male counterparts on discrimination and aboriginal rights. In fact, they comprised the only two dissenters in seven of the ten cases on this side of the factor, and in six of those rulings they overwhelmingly endorsed the constitutional claims of disadvantaged groups such as native people, religious minorities, gays, and women (*R. v. Nikal* is the exception to this rule).

In contrast, the court's male majority, led by Justices Gonthier and LaForest, rejected the bulk of the liberty and discrimination arguments of these groups in favour of governmental regulation or the maintenance of traditional community values. For example, in *Egan v. Canada*, the court addressed the question of whether the government's requirement that only opposite-sex couples could qualify for old age benefits violated the right to equality (section 15) under the Charter. The two female justices, along with Justices Cory and Iacobucci in dissent, argued that the definition of a spouse discriminated against gay couples and was based on stereotypes of homosexuals that furthered the marginalization of an already disadvantaged group (*Egan v. Canada* [1995] 2 SCR 513, at 566–7 and 599–603). While the majority bloc of justices recognized that sexual orientation should be read into section 15 of the Charter, they argued that Parliament was justified in determining that only opposite-sex couples could receive benefits because this definition of marriage furthers the promotion of strong and stable family units (*Egan v. Canada* [1995] 2 SCR 513, at 535–40). In another set of equality cases found on the positive side of this factor, the court addressed whether government licensing requirements for the catching and selling of fish violated aboriginal treaty rights enshrined in the Charter (section 35; see *R. v. Van der Peet* and *R. v. N.T.C. Smokehouse Ltd.*). While the majority argued that no historical legacy of commercial exchange of fish existed, the female justices in dissent took a more liberal reading of the historical record and endorsed the rights of the aboriginal groups. Their sympathy for the rights claimants is also illustrated in *Symes v. Canada*, where they endorsed the proposition that working women should be entitled to claim childcare deductions on their taxes and that a denial of such deductions represented a violation of their equality rights.

While the overarching theme of the negative side of this factor pertained to liberty interests in the areas of free press and access to information, two discrimination claims were found on this side of the factor that represent mirror images of the equality cases that we discussed above. In *University of British Columbia v. Berg*, the court addressed the issue of discrimination when examining the denial of services usually available to the public at large. Ultimately, the majority ruled that a university's denial of keys and application documents to a mentally disabled graduate student fell within the ambit of public services that could not be denied on the basis of disability. In the other discrimination suit (*Miron v. Trudel*), Justice McLachlin, writing for the majority, ruled that common law couples, like their married counterparts, deserved equal access to spousal insurance benefits. Ironically, she criticized the dissent for abiding by the same circular logic that Justice LaForest had employed in *Egan v. Canada*, namely that the law was not discriminatory just because the legislature had favoured married couples and traditional notions of family (see *Miron v. Trudel* [1995] 2 SCR 418, at 478–81). Clearly, the fact that equality rights prevailed in both *Berg* and *Miron* stands in direct contrast to the communitarian interests that succeeded in *Egan* and *Symes* on the positive side of the factor.

In the three remaining cases on the negative side of the factor, the majority also ruled in favour of liberty interests, although the focus of these disputes pertained to free press, commercial advertising, and access to government information; see *Dagenais v. Canadian Broadcasting Corp.*; *Dagg v. Canada (Minister of Finance)*; and *RJR-MacDonald Inc. v. Canada (Attorney General)*. These cases counterbalance the positive side of the factor in the sense that Justice McLachlin's libertarian emphasis is pitted against Justice Gonthier and LaForest's proclivity to support conservative communitarian arguments advanced by government officials.

The most extreme scoring cases on the second factor involved principally questions of the extent to which justices should defer to agency power. Nine of the thirteen cases scoring strongly on factor 2 pertained to deference to government agencies such as the Department of Fisheries and Oceans, the minister of national revenue, the Yukon Human Rights Commission, the Ontario Labour Board, and the Matsqui Indian Band Tax Assessment Board. All the cases on the positive side of factor 2 pitted Justice L'Heureux-Dubé against Justices Iacobucci and Sopinka on these issues. Although the pattern of judicial disagreement is less clear on the negative side of the factor, Justice L'Heureux-Dubé disagreed with one of these same two justices in four of the five most extremely loading cases. We did not believe that the second factor was ideologically driven because the two male justices did not exhibit a consistent pattern of liberal/conservative voting across the two sides of the factor. Indeed, while Justice Iacobucci cast liberal votes in 46 per cent of the cases, Justice Sopinka did so in only 23 per cent of the most extremely scoring cases. Additionally, Justice L'Heureux-Dubé exhibited strong liberal patterns on both sides of factor 2, providing further evidence that the cases on opposite poles of the dimension are not mirror images of an ideological divide.

Two cases on the positive side of the factor that epitomize the debate over deference to agency power are *Gould v. Yukon Order of Pioneers* and *Dagg v. Canada (Minister of Finance)*. In the first case, Justices Sopinka and Iacobucci joined the all-male majority in ruling that a male-only membership policy for a fraternal organization did not represent discrimination because membership in the organization did not amount to a service offered to the public. In dissent, Justices L'Heureux-Dubé and McLachlin chastised their male colleagues for failing to defer to the expertise of the members of the Human Rights Tribunal, who had declared the policy discriminatory towards women (*Gould v. Yukon Order of Pioneers* [1996] 1 SCR 571, at 626–7). Subsequently, in *Dagg v. Canada (Minister of Finance)*, the court addressed the issue of whether the minister of finance could refuse to disclose personal information contained in employees' work logs. The majority ruled that the minister could disclose such information because it dealt with generic responsibilities of workers and did not divulge personal details about them, only the hours that they worked. In dissent, Justice L'Heureux-Dubé, along with three other colleagues, agreed that the minister could reject the request for information because it touched on privacy rights (*Dagg v. Canada (Minister of Finance)* [1997] 2 SCR 403 at 458–9). These two cases, along with four others found on the positive side of this factor, highlight an ongoing debate between Justice L'Heureux-Dubé and Justices Iacobucci and Sopinka over the degree to which the court should defer to government agency rulings.

The debate over agency deference is also illustrated by three prominent cases on the negative side of the factor, two of which are particularly noteworthy (see *Weber v. Ontario Hydro*, *Haig v. Canada*, and *Canadian Pacific Ltd. v. Matsqui Indian Band*). In *Weber v. Ontario Hydro*, the justices split over the power of a labour arbitration board to hand down Charter rulings and award damages in relation to a dispute over the alleged abuse of sick-leave benefits. Justice L'Heureux-Dubé and others in the majority sided with the board, arguing that it could serve as a court of competent jurisdiction to decide such issues and hand down Charter remedies. In dissent, Justices Iacobucci and Sopinka would not have extended such broad Charter powers to the labour board (*Weber v. Ontario Hydro* [1995] 2 SCR 929, at 942–8). In *Haig v. Canada*, the court dealt with the discretion of the chief electoral officer to disqualify a voter who had failed to meet provincial residency requirements prior to a federal referendum. Justice L'Heureux-Dubé, writing for the majority, claimed that the officer properly disqualified the voter given the residency guidelines in the Canadian Elections Act. Justice Iacobucci, in dissent, believed that the voter's right to free expression was violated under the *Charter*, and therefore the elections official should have allowed him to vote (*Haig v. Canada* [1993] 2 SCR 995, at 1066–7). Collectively, the theme of the cases on factor 2 provides a classic illustration of a judicial conflict on the Lamer natural court over the extent to which justices should defer to decisions by government agencies, with Justices L'Heureux-Dubé, Sopinka, and Iacobucci serving as the principal protagonists on this issue.

CONCLUSION

This chapter set out to examine the nature of attitudinal conflicts on the Lamer natural court in three pivotal areas – economic, criminal, and civil rights and liberties. Moreover, it sought to examine the extent to which the attitudinal model, so dominant in the US literature, accounts for the principal dimensions of conflict on the court between November 1992 and September 1997. This portion of the book was guided by the belief that justices of the Canadian court, like their US counterparts, possess many of the same institutional reasons for casting votes in line with their policy preferences. Since they occupy powerful positions on the highest court of the land and are not interested in seeking higher office, they are not beholden to others in the government structure to rule a certain way. Therefore the Canadian justices could be expected to exhibit the same ideological divides that are found in the US Supreme Court in these three issue areas. We also sought to advance the theoretical markers in the attitudinal literature by assessing whether any substantive differences exist between how the two Supreme Courts address conflicts in these advanced post-industrial societies. In an effort to address these questions, we employed factor analysis, which does not presuppose any ideological dimensions on the Canadian court, but rather allows the justices' votes and the issue content of the cases to guide our analysis of the attitudinal disagreements that emerged on the Lamer natural court.

The findings reveal ideological divides between members of the Lamer court in all three areas of the study. Indeed, the most prominent factor in the non-unanimous cases in each of these areas is dominated by ideological conflict, which confirms the applicability of the attitudinal model in the Canadian context. While the first factor in the economic area pertained to liberalism in private law and business regulation, in the criminal area it dealt with a liberal-conservative struggle over the treatment of the criminally accused, and in civil rights and liberties cases the first factor was dominated by a similar divide over discrimination and liberty claims. Although ideological conflict is not prominent on the second factors in the three areas of law, it is clear that when attitudinal conflicts emerged they were driven principally by ideological discord. Although publicly expressed disagreement occurs less often on the highly collegial Charter-era Canadian court (28 per cent of the time in the Lamer natural court) than on the US Supreme Court, it seems that the justices, when they did disagree, were indeed influenced by their ideological proclivities in a manner similar to their US counterparts.

There is an underlying theme that seems to unite the second factors across all three areas in the Lamer natural court. While factor 2 in economic and civil rights and liberties areas pertained to judicial deference to agency power, the second factor in the criminal area dealt with judicial deference to lower courts' evidentiary rulings. In short, the tie that binds these three dimensions of conflict is characterized by the Supreme Court's exercise of either *lateral deference* to other branches of government or *hierarchical deference* to the procedural rulings of lower-court judges. The factor-analytic results on this second dimension nicely parallel some prior research on the US Supreme Court's economic cases that demonstrates patterns of conflict over deference to agency power in the Burger court (see Ducat and Dudley 1987; Hagle and Spaeth 1992). From a comparative perspective, these findings suggest that disagreements over judicial intervention and deference may be a common theme in high courts around the world that increasingly face politicized regulatory disputes.

Despite the fact that both the US and Canadian high courts exhibit ideological discord in the three areas analysed, an underlying complexity to the way that Canadian justices approach these cases provides an important theoretical contribution to the attitudinal model. Scholars of public opinion argue that elites in democratic societies will be consistent in their ideological beliefs across different issue areas (see Campbell et al. 1960; Sniderman et al. 1996). This research suggests that a politically sophisticated individual is

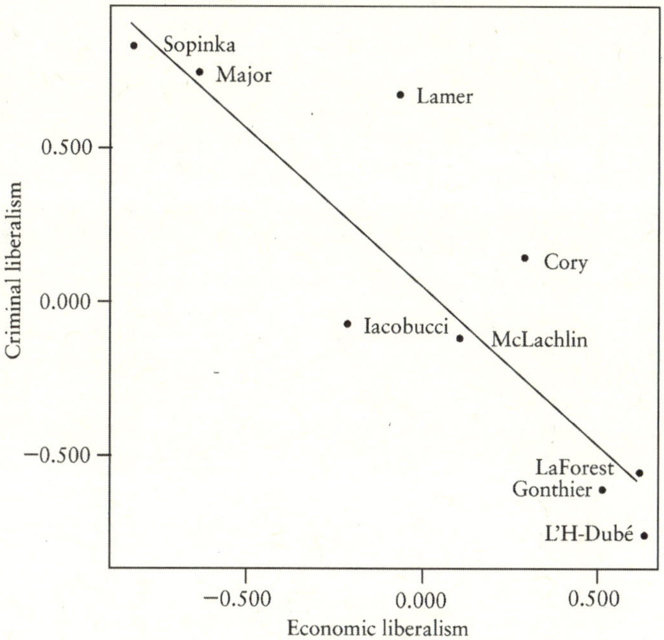

Figure 1
Ideological loadings for economic and criminal cases, Lamer natural court, 1992–1997

one who has ideologically consistent and stable attitudes and values over time and across different issue domains. What is striking about several members of the political elites who occupied the Lamer natural court is the lack of ideological consistency apparent in their decisions in contested economic, criminal, and civil rights and liberties cases. In fact, the voting patterns of members of the Lamer natural court in such cases reflect more ideological complexity than is found in the US Supreme Court. This complexity is grounded in the fact that more than half of the Canadian justices scoring most extremely on the factors take far more nuanced ideological positions than their US counterparts. We illustrate this in Figures 1, 2, and 3, which provide a visual representation of each justice's liberalism score, or factor loading, on the first factor in each issue area, in two of the three areas of law studied.[11]

For example, Figure 1 compares the justices' economic liberalism (on the x axis) with their criminal liberalism (on the y axis), while Figure 2 plots civil rights with criminal liberalism, and Figure 3

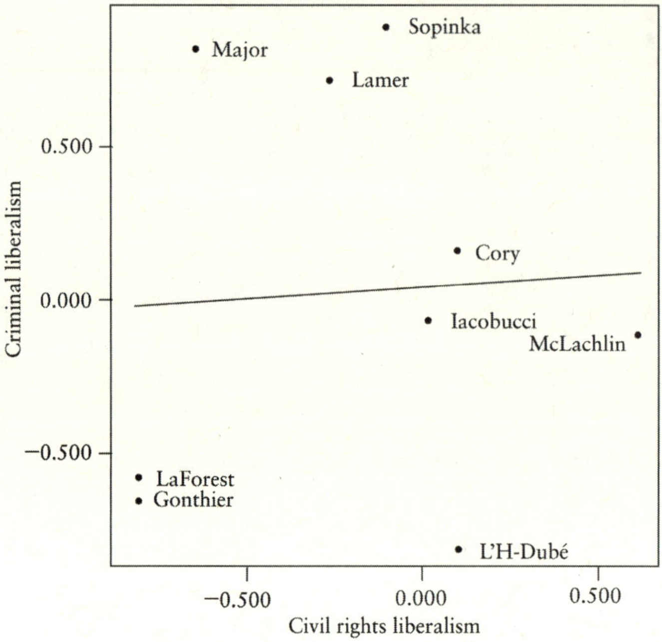

Figure 2
Ideological loadings for civil rights and criminal cases, Lamer natural court, 1992–1997

assesses ideological proclivities in economics and civil rights. Figure 1 reveals a clear inverse relationship between economic liberalism and criminal liberalism. For example, Justices L'Heureux-Dubé, LaForest, and Gonthier, who were found at the most liberal extreme of the economic ideological dimension, turned out to be the least liberal justices on the criminal factor (see the bottom right quadrant of Figure 1). In contrast, Justices Major and Sopinka, who occupied the most conservative position on economic cases, turned out to be the most liberal justices on criminal decisions that scored strongly on the ideological factor (see the top left quadrant of Figure 1). When a line of best fit was superimposed to reflect the relationship between these two indicators of ideological voting, two-thirds of the justices clustered closely around the line, indicating a pretty strong 1-to-1 inverse relationship between the economic and criminal liberalism dimensions in non-unanimous cases.

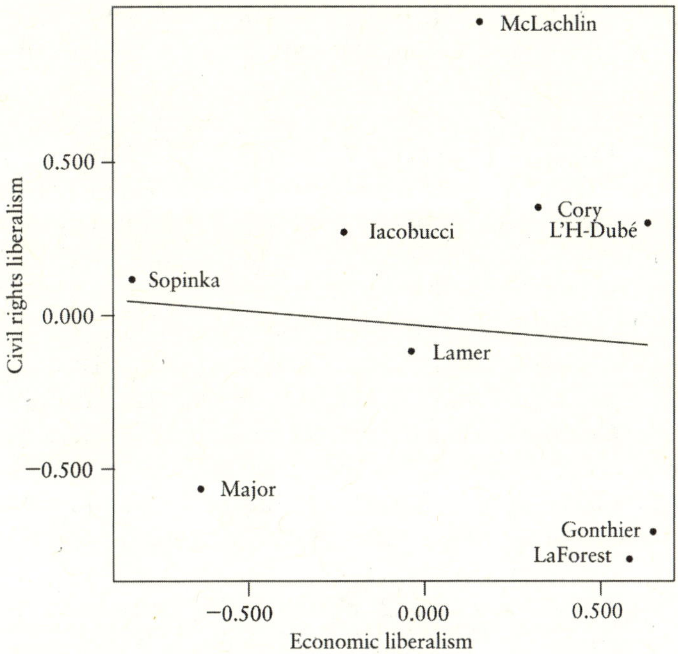

Figure 3
Ideological loadings for civil rights and liberties and economic cases, Lamer natural court, 1992–1997

Figure 2 shows little evidence of any strong connection between the justices' liberalism in the civil rights and criminal areas of law, which is highlighted by the relatively flat slope of the regression line in the plot. The individuals closest to this line of best fit are Justices Cory and Iacobucci, who staked out consistent moderate ideological positions in these two areas of law. Justices Gonthier and LaForest showed strong and consistent conservative tendencies in these cases (see the bottom left quadrant of Figure 2). However, the five remaining justices did not show any clear pattern of liberalism across civil rights and criminal law cases.

Figure 3, which compares ideological factor loadings in the economic and civil rights areas, also features a relatively flat slope for the line of best fit, suggesting little ideological consistency among the justices in these fields of law. This is surprising, because one would expect that a liberal justice in the economic area would also be liberal in civil rights and liberties cases. Only Justice Major fit the classic definition of a consistent ideologue in these two domains (see the bottom left quadrant of Figure 3). Justices Gonthier and LaForest, in contrast, demonstrated an ideologically inverse voting pattern in these two areas of law. In other words, they were the most conservative in civil rights and liberties cases, which matched their tendency in criminal cases, yet were at the other end of the ideological spectrum in economic decisions (see the bottom right quadrant of Figure 3).

If one were to compare the voting behaviour of justices across all three ideological factors, only Justices Cory and Iacobucci exhibited consistent ideological stances, and ironically it was characterized by their staking out a relatively centrist position across all three areas of law. With the exception of Justices Cory and Iacobucci, these findings indicate that, unlike most US Supreme Court justices today, Canadian justices of the Lamer natural court did not adhere to rote liberal or conservative stances across multiple issue dimensions. Rather, their voting behaviour reflected a more nuanced ideological approach to the contested cases in these three distinct legal areas. This is a surprising and intriguing finding, because one would expect that members of the political elite who have risen to the top of the legal profession would be likely to adhere to consistent ideological positions across various issue domains.

The fact that over half of the justices on the Lamer natural court displayed more complex voting behaviour than is typical of their US counterparts has important theoretical ramifications for attitudinal scholars. Too often, US scholars equate attitudinal voting with ideological consistency across a broad swath of issues, but the evidence from Canada poignantly demonstrates that this assumption deserves serious scrutiny. Indeed, we believe that the results from the factor analysis in this chapter suggest that attitudinal theorists should posit only that justices will take positions in accordance with their attitudes and values and recognize that a justice's ideological views may frequently diverge in different categories of law. The results of this chapter suggest that attitudinal theorists must devote more attention to the fundamental complexity of attitudinal decision making by justices on high courts outside the United States.

One critical qualification regarding the use of factor analysis to identify ideological dimensions of conflict: some scholars have suggested that the method suffers from circularity (see Segal and Spaeth

1993; 2002). The concern here is that since judicial factor scores are derived from the votes of the justices in Supreme Court rulings, one is using the very case outcomes to label the alleged dimensions that drive the conflict in the cases. As a result, one of the inherent problems with factor analysis is that it does not apply an a priori measure of judicial attitudes to predict future voting behaviour (see Segal and Spaeth 1993; 2002). Despite this shortcoming, the underlying utility of factor analysis lies in its reliance on the opinions of the justices to identify the dimensions of attitudinal conflict, rather than simply presupposing that a liberal/conservative divide will dominate the rulings of the court. Since our analysis has demonstrated that the primary factor in three key issue areas of the Lamer natural court is ideological in nature, we can now employ other statistical techniques to combat the apparent circularity inherent in the approach. The next chapter discusses the importance of developing an a priori measure of judicial ideology to use as a predictor for analysing subsequent voting patterns. More important, it sets the stage for a sophisticated logistic-regression analysis of the forces that shape judicial decisions on the Supreme Court of Canada under the Charter.

6 Measuring Ideology and Justices' Votes

The factor-analytic results in chapter 5 revealed that liberal/conservative differences between the justices on the Lamer natural court (13 November 1992–30 September 1997) constituted the primary dimension of conflict in all three areas of law that we analysed: economic, criminal, and civil liberties. Although some members of this court were less rote than others in their attitudinal stances across the three areas, a clear liberal/conservative cleavage existed in the court's contested rulings. The primacy of ideological divisions uncovered in the factor-analysis chapter leads us to the next stage of our study – namely, a holistic assessment of the relevance of attitudinal decision making across the Charter-era Supreme Court (1984–2002) in economic, criminal, and civil liberties cases.

While chapter 5 relied solely on the votes and the written decisions of the justices over a five-year period to provide an accounting of the ideological tenor of their decisions in non-unanimous cases, this chapter moves beyond that approach to examine the connections between two a priori measures of ideology – the party affiliation of the prime minister appointing the justice to the court and newspaper assessments of their ideology – and justices' subsequent behaviour. This approach allows us to evade the circular reasoning criticism that is sometimes levelled against scholarship based solely on the votes cast by the justices once they reach the high court. Instead, if significant links are found between these two distinct prior indicators of judicial attitudes and long-term voting trends, the results will further validate the attitudinal patterns found in chapter 5.

DATA AND METHODS

Before conducting bivariate regression tests of attitudinal decision making in the Charter-era court (1984–2002) in economic, criminal, and civil liberties cases, we explain how we operationalized the two a priori measures of ideology. In other words, we describe how we coded liberal judicial votes and the types of cases we included in the study. The logic of our approach is that indirect measures of a justice's purported ideology before reaching the Supreme Court will be reflected in his voting on the court. This approach makes intuitive sense: by the time justices are appointed to high-level judicial positions, their approach to resolving cases is fairly settled because of their prior life experience and years of grappling with legal questions. Since the party-of-prime-minister/president variable has been effective in prior attitudinal studies on appellate courts in both the Canadian and US settings, respectively, we decided to include it in our analysis and coded it as a dichotomous variable (1 = Conservative Party appointee, 2 = Liberal Party appointee). If ideological voting patterns occur on the Charter-era Canadian court, we expect a strong coefficient to appear when party of prime minister is used as a separate independent variable to explain the ideological voting record of the justices examined in the study. To the extent that partisanship does capture liberal/conservative differences, we also expect it to be strongly correlated with a second set of independent variables – namely, the newspaper measures of ideology.

One of the fundamental goals of this chapter is to apply Wetstein and Ostberg's (1999; 2007a) measures of judicial ideology in the Canadian context because they represent a more sophisticated and nuanced measure of ideology than a single measure would. We base our measures here on commentary in news articles and editorials in nine regional papers in Canada: Toronto's *Globe and Mail*, the *Ottawa Citizen*, the *Halifax Chronicle-Herald*, the *Montreal Gazette*, the *Toronto Star*, the *Winnipeg Free Press*, the *Calgary Herald*, the *Edmonton Journal*, and the *Vancouver Sun*.[1] Clearly, this more comprehensive approach provides a far more rigorous indicator of newspaper ideology than a measure based on one newspaper's commentary, because journalists in different regions may view the ideology of the appointees from different vantage points. Therefore the aggregation of these various perspectives can provide a more complex and layered account of the ideological tendencies of nominees (for a similar discussion, see Ostberg et al. 2004; Ostberg and Wetstein 2007a).

Similar to the earlier work of Ostberg and Wetstein (2007a), the scoring for this measure is found on an ideological continuum that ranges from +2, for references that were demonstrably liberal, to –[negative]2 for very conservative comments, while moderate references were scored as a zero (Ostberg et al. 2004; Ostberg and Wetstein 2007a). The goal here was to create a kind of ideological predictor at the time of a justice's nomination, using comments about nominees in newspapers. The comments come from court watchers, legal professionals, and journalists who cover the court beat. Commentary that received the highest liberal score of +2 included statements such as ones that Judge X is a "strong believer in the Charter," "champion of the rights of the criminally accused," "noted civil libertarian," " great democrat," " liberal judge," " liberal feminist." Comments that received a more moderate, but still liberal code of +1 included statements such as ones that Judge Y has "liberal leanings," is "a moderate liberal," "a small-l Liberal," "willing to invoke the Charter," "quietly activist," or "hinted at a liberal interpretation of the Charter." Scores at the other end of the ideological continuum (-2) tended to highlight restraintist tendencies: "follows the letter of the law," "committed follower of precedents," "conservative justice," and "strict constructionist – takes words literally." Scores of –1 featured comments describing judges such as "mildly conservative," a "cautious interpreter of the Charter," "small-c conservative," or "shies from legislative interference." As for justices who scored zero, they were characterized as "middle of the road," "resisting labels," "can't be categorized as either left- or right-wing," "won't bring an agenda to the court," or "straight down the middle."

Although some judgment calls were necessary, particularly when deciding between a +1 or +2 and –1 and –2 scores, when these comments were read in the larger context of the article, a relatively clear ideological pattern emerged for a particular nominee. Since our research includes a separate party indicator, and an exclusive measure of ideology should be the only indicator in the model that takes into consideration ideological references, any newspaper comments that referred to a nominee's party ties or service to a particular government were omitted from the ideological scoring of the justices (Ostberg and Wetstein 2007a, 56–9; Ostberg et al. 2004).

JUSTICES' IDEOLOGICAL SCORES

Table 7 provides a summary listing of each justice's ideological score from four perspectives that we thought would be relevant: 1) a *Globe and Mail* score, 2) an *Ottawa Citizen* score, 3) a score based on the seven remaining regional papers, and 4) a cumulative score based on equal treatment of individual comments found across all the papers. We also list the party of the appointing prime minister in the first column as a point of reference for each justice. We provide separate ideological scores for the first two papers because of the national prominence of the *Globe and Mail* and the fact that the *Ottawa Citizen* is published in the country's capital. Moreover, both papers tend to have more commentary on Supreme Court appointees than the others. We create a separate score by grouping the remaining seven together because they frequently publish the same wire-service story, or a slight variation of it, especially for justices appointed from outside their region.

As can be seen in Table 7, for most of the justices we have full information across all three news sources, despite three notable exceptions. First, where a news source simply comments on a nominee's party connections without any ideological reference, we enter "party" in the table (see, for example, Justice Deschamps's entry under the *Globe and Mail* column). Second, where no party or ideological commentary appears, we list "not applicable" (see, for example, the row highlighting Justice Dickson). Third, as the table indicates, neither Justice Dickson nor Justice Beetz received any ideological commentary in any paper. Consequently, we label them moderates and give them zero on the cumulative index. We believe that this will introduce a "conservative" bias into the data results: it will be more difficult for the cumulative newspaper variable to achieve statistical significance in any model predicting the votes of the justices (our discussion here parallels Ostberg and Wetstein 2007a, 59–60).

We divide the ideological score for Justices L'Heureux-Dubé and Charron into separate components for criminal and for civil rights and liberties issues. Justice L'Heureux-Dubé was one of the only justices singled out by commentators as straddling the ideological divide in these two areas of law (conservative in criminal law and liberal in civil rights and liberties). The comments about her conservative approach to criminal cases in the lower court were drawn exclusively from reports in the *Globe and Mail*, because other papers did

Table 7
Ideology scores for justices based on newspaper commentary at the time of appointment, 1984–2002*

Justice	*Party of prime minister*	*Globe and Mail*	*Ottawa Citizen*	*Seven other regional newspapers*	*Cumulative score*
Wilson	Lib	1.800	1.636	1.556	1.618
Abella	Lib	1.696	1.750	1.409	1.571
LaForest	Cons	1.000	party	1.667	1.500
Lamer	Lib	1.667	party	1.167	1.417
Bastarache	Lib	1.000	1.167	1.556	1.333
L'H-Dubé (C.L.)	Cons	1.125	1.667	1.125	1.320
Estey	Lib	1.333	.500	1.500	1.273
Fish	Lib	1.200	1.000	1.100	1.105
Cory	Cons	party	1.250	.923	.967
Charron (C.L.)	Lib	.231	.875	1.625	.793
LeDain	Lib	.714	.750	.737	.733
Arbour	Lib	.467	.769	1.400	.727
McLachlin	Cons	1.000	.000	.625	.667
Stevenson	Cons	1.000	.600	.333	.500
McIntyre	Lib	.600	.000	.333	.444
Binnie	Lib	.000	.667	.400	.211
Sopinka	Cons	.000	.000	.273	.150
Deschamps	Lib	party	.000	0.000	.000
Iacobucci	Cons	–1.000	.000	.250	.000
Dickson	Lib	na	na	na	.000
Beetz	Lib	party	na	na	.000
Gonthier	Cons	party	–1.000	.000	–.182
Charron (Crim.)	Lib	–1.286	2.000	1.333	–.273
LeBel	Lib	–.300	–.727	–1.333	–.704
Rothstein	Cons	–.571	–.643	–.929	–.768
Major	Cons	–1.167	–1.143	–1.500	–1.320
Chouinard	Cons	–1.375	party	party	–1.375
L'H-Dubé (Crim.)	Cons	–2.000	na	na	–2.000

* Scores on the table reflect only ideological commentary from newspaper articles. In other words, we removed all commentary related to party affiliation or ties from the calculation of scores. If one of the three news sources published comments based solely on a nominee's party ties, we omitted a score and inserted "party" in the respective column of the table. If the news source did not publish any political or ideological comments, we entered "na" in the table. We assigned Justices Dickson and Beetz a middle score of zero because they received no ideological commentary in any of the newspapers. Justices L'Heureux-Dubé and Charron feature scores divided into separate civil liberties (C.L.) and criminal (Crim.) scores because they received commentary on these two components at the opposite ends of the ideological spectrum.

not offer commentary on her criminal ideological leanings. Yet we believe that the *Globe and Mail* comments reflect a highly accurate assessment of her ideological leanings in this area. Justice Charron also receives separate scores of her ideological tenor in these two areas of law (moderately conservative in criminal law, but liberal in civil rights and liberties), but the commentary on her ideology in the criminal area was more mixed. The *Globe and Mail* characterized her as a conservative on criminal issues, while the other papers tended to classify her as more liberal. Since the commentary in the *Globe and Mail* tended to be more extensive, the cumulative score characterizes Justice Charron as a moderate-conservative on criminal issues, while there is a clear notation of her as an expected liberal on civil rights and liberties issues across all the papers.

In Table 7, the most important score for each justice's ideological proclivities is the cumulative score in the last column, because it is based on the most information. The scoring for this indicator is not an average of the averages reported in the prior three columns, but rather an average based on all the unique references found across all newspapers in the study. The scores in Table 7 indicate that the cumulative ideological rankings range from a liberal high of 1.618 for Justice Wilson to a conservative low of –2.0 for Justice L'Heureux-Dubé in the criminal area (see column 4). Other justices at the liberal end of the spectrum include Justices Abella (1.571), LaForest (1.500), Lamer (1.417), Bastarache (1.333), and, intriguingly, L'Heureux-Dubé (1.320) for civil rights and liberties. Justices categorized as the most conservative include Justices Chouniard (-1.375) and Major (-1.320). 'Moderates' are Justices Iacobucci and Deschamps (0.00), Sopinka (.150), and Gonthier (-.182). In general, observers familiar with the voting patterns of the court would not be surprised with how the journalists categorized most of the justices and thus would confirm the face validity of most of the scores (see Ostberg and Wetstein 2007a, 60–1).

PARTY OF PRIME MINISTER

A correlation matrix was subsequently created to assess the degree to which the four newspaper measures actually tap the same concept and to determine whether party of prime minister is highly correlated with them as well (see Table 8).[2] Values can range from 0 to 1.0, with 1.0 indicating perfect agreement between the two measures and

Table 8
Correlation matrix for party of prime minister and ideology measures

Variable	*Party of prime minister*	*Globe and Mail*	*Ottawa Citizen*	*Seven other regional newspapers*	*Cumulative score*
Party of PM	1.000				
	(28)				
Globe and Mail	.092	1.000			
	(23)	(23)			
Ottawa Citizen	.113	.496*	1.000		
	(22)	(19)	(22)		
Seven other papers	–.001	.616**	.847***	1.000	
	(24)	(21)	(22)	(24)	
Cumulative score	.016	.933***	.755***	.879***	1.000
	(28)	(23)	(22)	(24)	(28)

* Significant at $p < .05$ or better (one-tailed).
** Significant at $p < .01$ or better.
*** Significant at $p < .001$ or better.
The number of justices in the correlation analysis is reported below the Pearson's *r* statistic.

0 meaning no correlation at all. As a rule of thumb, if the newspaper and party measures are all tapping the same concept, they should have a correlation coefficient greater than or equal to .50.

Overall, the results indicate a high degree of agreement between the four newspaper measures. Indeed, the lowest correlation in the table occurs between the *Globe and Mail* and *Ottawa Citizen* measures, with a Pearson's r value of .496 (statistically significant at the 95-per-cent confidence level). Not surprising, Table 8 indicates that the other three newspaper indicators are significantly correlated with each other, at .616 or higher. Overall, these statistics provide compelling evidence that the four newspaper measures are all tapping the same concept – namely, what we label "ideology." None of the newspaper indicators is significantly correlated with party of prime minister (the highest r = .113 with the *Ottawa Citizen* measure, although it is not statistically significant). Since party of prime minister is not correlated with any of the three newspaper scores, it is clear that it is tapping a latent variable that is distinct from ideology. We believe that this separate variable is really tapping the concept of party patronage. For present purposes, it seems that the four newspaper indicators are valid measures of the latent concept of ideology, while party of prime minister is not. This exercise points to the importance of developing multiple indicators of ideology in an effort to tap this concept as accurately as possible. Yet only subsequent regression analysis will confirm or dispel this claim about political party's usefulness as a predictor of ideological voting patterns.

As we indicated above, the attitudinal model presumes that institutional arrangements in the US and Canadian Supreme Courts enable justices to vote their policy preferences once they are elevated to the high court. One of the easiest tests of this neo-institutional assumption is to analyse the bivariate correlation between measures of ideology and the long-term voting trends of the Charter-era justices. Our analysis here parallels the work of Segal and Cover (1989; see also Segal and Spaeth 2002, 321–3), who conducted ordinary least-squares regression to examine the relationship between the attitudes of US justices, as measured by newspaper ideology scores, and their votes in civil liberties cases between 1953 and 1999. The presumption is that preconceived notions of ideology will influence how justices decide cases on the highest bench, and the newspaper scores of ideology serve as the ideological "predictor" of how justices will vote. Segal and Spaeth (2002, 321–3) found a high correlation between newspaper ideology scores and the percentage of liberal votes cast by US justices.

In order to conduct a similar, but more extensive analysis of the Canadian high court, we code all the decisions of the court published in the *Supreme Court Reports* and decided in the calendar years 1984–2002. This period was chosen for analysis because it encompasses the first year when Charter claims reached the court through to the first three years of the McLachlin court. Cases are included in the analysis if the primary legal issue pertains to economic issues, criminal appeals, or civil liberties. The economic category covers government regulation of the economy, labour–management relations, and private economic disputes in which a clear economic underdog can be identified. The civil liberties category includes cases pertaining to civil rights, both constitutional and statutory (such as minority and gender discrimination), and the standard set of civil liberties claims (including those relating to freedom of expression, religion, privacy, and education). Following the coding of Schubert (1965; 1974), as well as Tate and Sittiwong (1989), we classify a vote as liberal if it supported the government in an economic regulation case, unions or workers in a labour case, or the economic underdog in a private economic dispute; the defendant in a criminal case; or the party asserting the denial of a civil right or liberty.

The dependent variable is measured by computing the percentage of cases in which justices voted in support of the liberal position in each of three policy areas. Since the dependent variable is continuous (measured as a percentage), we estimate the effects of judicial ideology scores using weighted least-squares regression (weighting by the number of votes that comprised each justice's career score).[3] Assuming that ideology influences votes, we expect the coefficients for newspaper and party of prime minister measures of ideology to be positive and statistically significant[4] in our bivariate regression equations across the three areas of law.

We include votes from both unanimous and non-unanimous decisions for several reasons. First, given the high proportion of cases decided by unanimous votes during the 1984–2002 time frame (76 per cent), counting only non-unanimous cases would miss the ideological direction of votes in three-fourths of the cases. Second, since the court frequently sits in panels of five and seven, rather than nine justices, there is a possibility that the composition of a five- or seven-member panel will reach a unanimous outcome while a nine-member panel might have harboured one or two dissents. Therefore unanimity in the Canadian context necessarily takes on a different flavour from that in the US setting simply because the absence of a justice or two may have altered the voting outcome in the case. Third, as we discussed above, there is a norm of consensus pervasive in the Supreme Court of Canada. Indeed, interviews with the justices indicate that many unanimous opinions initially included disagreements about outcome and/or reasoning. Intensive negotiation, persuasion, mutual accommodation, and sometimes even overt bargaining often resolve these disagreements. Thus, on the Supreme Court of Canada, at least, informal norms appear to encourage compromise as long as no one feels that he or she is sacrificing a strongly held principle. This implies that decisions reached through compromise and bargaining are presumably influenced by the attitudinal preferences of justices on the panel. Consequently, even some of the unanimous decisions may reflect justices' policy preferences. Collectively, these unique features of the Canadian court influenced our decision to include both unanimous and non-unanimous cases in the data analysis.

Table 9
OLS regression analysis of the relationship between newspaper ideology scores and the liberalism of justices, by issue area, 1984–2002

	b	*Std error*	*Adj. R sq.*	N
Civil liberties				
Ottawa Citizen ideology	.071***	.012	.691	16
Globe and Mail ideology	.032	.022	.070	18
Cumulative newspaper index	.036*	.020	.087	21
Party of prime minister	.054#	.035	.063	21
Criminal cases				
Ottawa Citizen ideology	.047**	.015	.364	17
Globe and Mail ideology	.037***	.013	.263	18
Cumulative newspaper index	.038**	.013	.250	22
Party of prime minister	.064*	.032	.123	23
Economic cases				
Ottawa Citizen ideology	.035**	.011	.373	17
Globe and Mail ideology	.031*	.015	.159	18
Cumulative newspaper index	.036**	.013	.241	22
Party of prime minister	.044	.045	.002	22

* $p < .05$.
** $p < .01$.
*** $p < .001$.
\# $.05 < p < .10$.
The results for each justice are weighted by the number of cases that they decided.

IDEOLOGY AND CAREER VOTING PATTERNS

In Table 9 we present data from four distinct regression equations in each of the issue areas. The equations separately examine the relationship between liberal voting and the following independent variables: 1) the *Ottawa Citizen*'s newspaper ideology score; 2) the *Globe and Mail*'s indicator; 3) the cumulative newspaper index of ideology; and 4) party of prime minister. The inclusion of all the regression results in one table allows one to assess the relative strength of each of the newspaper ideology measures in relation to each other and to assess their predictive power in relation to party of prime minister. Overall, the results provide substantial support for the general proposition that the political preferences of the justices are related to their overall pattern of support for liberal versus conservative outcomes in the cases before them. Both the cumulative ideology measure and the score from the *Ottawa Citizen* relate to voting behaviour to a statistically significant extent in all three policy areas. That is, the tendency of justices categorized as liberals at the time of their appointment to support liberal outcomes more frequently than justices categorized as conservative is so strong that we can be very confident[5] that it did not occur by chance and that it is not simply a result of the particular cases analysed. The *Globe and Mail* score has a significant relationship to justices' career voting scores in both private economic and criminal cases, but not to their scores on civil liberties (although the coefficient is in the expected direction).

For an example of the impact of the various measures, look at the results for the *Ottawa Citizen* indicator in criminal law in the middle of Table 9. The coefficient suggests that for every one-unit increase in the ideology score of a justice (which ranges from +2 to −2), there is a 5-per-cent increase in support for liberal rulings in civil rights and liberties (b = .047). That is, the difference in the proportion of votes supporting a liberal outcome between a justice scored as +2 (the most liberal category) versus a justice scored as −2 (one of the most conservative justices) would be approximately 20 percentage points. The adjusted r square value (.364) indicates that almost 37 per cent of the variance in career liberalism for 1984–2002 can be explained by this single newspaper measure.

Closer examination of the data reveals some interesting differences between the results for Canadian justices and those reported earlier for members of the US Supreme Court by Segal and Cover (1989). First, for eight of the nine newspaper ideology ratings in Table 9, the strength of the relationships and the amount of the variance in voting behaviour explained are considerably more muted in Canada than Segal and Cover's (1989) findings for civil liberties for the US court (for data for 1953–89 they reported an $r = .79$, adjusted r square = .60; see also Segal and Spaeth 1993, 228). Table 9 reveals that only the *Ottawa Citizen*'s ideology measure in civil liberties outperforms Segal and Cover's (1989) explained variance, but the *Globe and Mail* and cumulative index are not even close.

Disregarding the unique predictive power of the *Ottawa Citizen*, for the moment, we suggest that one explanation for the lower levels of variance explained in the Canadian context may stem from the smaller panels in many of the cases and our inclusion of both unanimous and non-unanimous decisions. Put another way, the overwhelming norms of collegiality and consensus that pervade the Canadian court make it difficult for the newspaper ideology measures to perform as strongly as the ones used in the US context. Thus the newspaper ideology measures may not hold the same predictive power in Canada simply because the Canadian justices agree to agree more frequently. Even though we include unanimous rulings, the disparity between the *Ottawa Citizen* and the other two newspaper measures in civil liberties is more puzzling. Perhaps journalists for the *Ottawa Citizen,* who cover the capital beat, have the best opportunity and are the most aware of the ideological proclivities of the justices in civil rights and liberties, which tend to be revealed and covered more readily than judicial tendencies in criminal and economic disputes.

Another distinctive finding in our study is that the correspondence between the ideology of justices and their votes in economic cases appears to be nearly as strong in Canada as the relationship of ideology to votes in criminal and civil liberties cases. The evidence for this point can be seen in the roughly equal size in the newspaper ideology coefficients across the three areas of law. An interesting correlate of this ability of the newspaper ideology indicators to predict the voting choices of the justices across issue areas is that the long-term vote scores of the justices in these three areas are not highly correlated with each other. Most notably, the simple Pearson correlation between the criminal and civil rights vote scores is actually negative ($r = -.261$). Thus the fact that at least two newspaper scores are positively and significantly correlated in both criminal appeals and civil liberties records of the justices suggests that these assessments appear to pick up multiple dimensions of the justices' attitudes.

A further indication that these newspaper ideology scores are doing just that rather than simply presenting a reflection of the traditional liberal/conservative ideology that has been found in analyses of attitudinal voting on US courts is the relatively poor performance of the indicator party of prime minister. In sharp contrast to findings on voting by US appellate court judges (e.g., Goldman 1975; Tate 1981), party of prime minister does not provide a very satisfactory prediction of the career voting patterns of the Canadian justices. Partisan appointment is related to judicial voting patterns (to a statistically significant degree) in only one of the three issue areas, and even for those criminal appeals party appears to have a smaller impact on judicial voting than the three ideology measures drawn from newspaper stories. Perhaps most surprising, partisan appointment has virtually no relationship to the patterns of judicial voting in economic cases. In contrast, in US appellate courts, there have been continuing links between partisan appointment and the economic liberalism of the judges for nearly three-quarters of a century.

Overall, these results reinforce the conclusion that the ideology of Canadian justices does have a measurable impact on the general trend of their support for liberal versus conservative outcomes in most cases in the Charter era. As we noted above, another explanation for the muted results in Table 9 is that they are based on all decisions of the Supreme Court, not just the non-unanimous ones (used by Segal and Cover 1989) or some other subgroup of cases for which ideology is predicted to be especially salient. Moreover, the three separate newspaper measures of ideology relate to voting patterns of the justices in three distinct issue areas, which points to the importance of ideology, albeit in a more muted tone in the Canadian context.

CONCLUSION

This chapter set out to highlight the value of new a priori measures of judicial ideology for Charter-era justices based on newspaper accounts at the time of their nomination and to examine the extent to which these measures, along with party of prime minister, account for ideological voting differences among the justices. Following the lead of Segal and Cover (1989), we develop a set of newspaper ideology indicators that are drawn from content analysis of coverage in the *Ottawa Citizen*, the *Globe and Mail*, seven other regional papers, and a cumulative index across all the papers in the study. Subsequent bivariate analysis demonstrates that these measures have overwhelming predictive validity for the voting patterns of the justices in economic, criminal, and civil rights and liberties cases during the period 1984–2002. In every instance, the newspaper measures perform better than party identification, leading us to conclude that they, like the US measures developed by Segal and Cover (1989), provide a more exacting account of a justice's long-term ideological proclivities, even when we include both unanimous and non-unanimous cases. Clearly the bivariate analysis at the end of the chapter demonstrates that the Charter-era Canadian justices, despite their frequent claims to the contrary, are indeed influenced by their ideological predispositions in these three areas of law.

The results of our bivariate analyses reinforce the factor-analytic results in chapter 5 and collectively suggest that on the Canadian court, as on the US Supreme Court, clear patterns of attitudinal decision making exist in the Charter era. Even though comments from the justices suggest that on the whole members of the high court believe that attitudinal expression is largely constrained by legal, strategic, and institutional norms, our quantitative analysis paints a clearer picture of attitudinal forces at work. In short, the application of two different methods to date reinforces the notion that ideological decision making plays an important role in the Canadian context.

However, the justices' assertions are not without merit. Given that fully three-quarters of the decisions in the Supreme Court of Canada are unanimous, it is not surprising that the regression coefficients in our bivariate analysis are much smaller than those in attitudinal studies of the US Supreme Court. The results also indicate that ideological factors are far more muted in the Canadian court and suggest that other factors, such as building consensus and writing good law, are prominent in the minds of the Canadian justices as well. So, while different methods turn up evidence of attitudinal judicial behaviour, the weaker strength of the Canadian evidence relative to US studies implies that legal and strategic models of behaviour are surely relevant as well. This aligns well with the statements of the Canadian justices, who recognize that attitudinal differences will emerge from time to time but do not overwhelmingly drive the court's decision making.

The question remains how powerful these measures of ideology will be when other independent variables are accounted for in a more sophisticated regression equation. This is the question we turn to in the next chapter, using a third method to examine attitudinal decision making by applying a multivariate model to test the influence of social attributes and ideology on Charter-era judicial voting patterns.

The results of this chapter also suggest that while conflicts among justices appear to reflect stable attitudinal differences, they do not seem to derive from an ideologically polarized system of judicial selection. Overall, these results are consistent with the belief of both the justices themselves and many other Canadians that judicial selection has not become part of a partisan battle over the direction that judicial policy should take. But partisanship is only one of a multitude of sources that drive cleavages in recent Canadian politics. In the next chapter, we explore the extent to which judicial decisional trends reflect divisions based on region, religion, and gender.

7 The Socio-political Bases of Attitudinal Voting

Our first assessment of attitudinal voting, in chapter 5 above, examined patterns of voting by the justices on the Supreme Court of Canada between 1992 and 1997 in cases where there was a divided ruling. That analysis demonstrated that ideological factors are at work in the first dimension of conflict in the three main issue areas of the Lamer natural court. The findings also revealed that these justices displayed more complex voting behaviour than that typical of their US counterparts, suggesting ideological divergence in different categories of law. The results imply that attitudinal theorists must recognize the complexity of attitudinal decision making on non-US high courts.

As we mentioned above (chapter 5), critics have observed that factor analysis of ideological dimensions of conflict suffers from circularity (see Segal and Spaeth 1993; 2002). None the less it relies on the opinions of justices to identify dimensions of conflict rather than simply presupposing a liberal/conservative divide. As a result of this concern, we proceeded in Chapter 6 to use an a priori measure of judicial attitudes to predict voting behaviour. Specifically, we adapted the successful approach of Segal and Cover (1989), subsequently developed by Ostberg and Wetstein (1999; 2007a) for Canada, that measures the attitudes of justices from an assessment of newspaper editorials at the time of appointment. Using measures of judicial attitudes derived from the *Globe and Mail*, the *Ottawa Citizen*, and seven regional newspapers, we uncovered evidence that their liberal/conservative attitudes have strong predictive power for voting in economic cases, criminal cases, and civil rights. These results reinforced the factor analysis in chapter 5, suggesting that the patterns of votes discovered there were not the result of circularity.

In the present chapter we adopt an alternative a priori approach to the measurement of judicial attitudes to provide an additional independent assessment of the influence of judicial attitudes on votes. Here, the focus is on the social backgrounds of the justices – such factors as religion, gender, and region. The analysis of the relationship between these attributes and behaviour on the court also sheds light on the possible political and social nature of the cleavages that arise in judicial policy making.

JUSTICES' BACKGROUNDS AND THE BASES OF DIVISIONS

Having examined individual differences among the justices and the relationship between a priori measures of judicial ideology derived from newspaper stories and their votes, we now look for any consistent commonalities in the backgrounds of the justices that are associated with the differences in the patterns of votes that emerged in the last chapter. Tate and Sittiwong (1989), in an analysis of voting patterns on the Supreme Court of Canada in the 1950s, 1960s, and 1970s, suggest that votes related strongly to three characteristics: the political party of the appointing prime minister, the justice's region, and the justice's religion.[1]

Finding measures of judicial attitudes that are both valid and reliable is a problem that has long plagued students of the courts. Most of the time, it is impossible to measure judges' attitudes directly. For example, most scholars assume that judges will be unwilling to discuss, openly and honestly, their private political views in an interview. However, as we noted in chapter 3, the justices did openly suggest that political views did, from time to time, influence their decision making. In addition, while a number of them have written on legal interpretation in law reviews and other contexts, few have published articles that advocate overtly political points of views. So their writings fail to provide good measures of their political attitudes.

One attempt to avoid this problem has been the development of personal attribute models. The model uses the judge's social background as a rough measure of ideology on particular issues (Schmidhauser 1961; Ulmer 1973; Tate 1981; Tate and Handberg 1991). In this vision of judicial behaviour, the judge brings an ideology or a set of political preferences to the bench that is the result of "birth, upbringing, socialization, career, and partisan affiliation" (Tate and Handberg 1991, 461). As Justice (then Judge) Rosalie Abella noted, every judge "who walks into a courtroom to hear a case is armed not only with the relevant legal texts but with a set of values, experiences and assumptions that are thoroughly embedded" (Hausegger et al. 2009, 130). This ideology is often representative of widespread cleavages that exist in a particular society. In turn, ideology may determine how the judge votes in the case (Schubert 1965; Peck 1969; Segal and Spaeth 1993; Robertson 1998), subject to judicial restraints that may exist. The central insight here is that "precourt life experiences play a prominent role in shaping the personal values and policy preferences of judges, and that such biographical factors can be useful in predicting judicial decisions" (Brudney et al. 1999, 1682).

Use of judicial attributes as measures of, or surrogates for, judicial attitudes has the advantage that the attributes exist independent of judicial votes and thus avoid the problems of circularity. Background attributes also come into being before judicial votes. This time sequence increases the reasonableness of inferring that if attitudes (as measured by attributes) correlate with votes, they may be inferred to have a causal effect on the votes. Finally, judicial attributes frequently are readily available and can be observed and recorded inexpensively and measured reliably. The roughness of the measurement, however, presents problems. It may introduce substantial amounts of random error into the subsequent analyses. Such random error makes it difficult to achieve standard levels of statistical significance even when a relationship may in fact exist among the variables in the model.

However, if one is able to discover statistically significant relationships among variables despite substantial amounts of random error, one may have more confidence that there is actually a relationship among key concepts (i.e., using variables with substantial random error "stacks the deck" against confirming the theoretically derived hypotheses). Thus positive relationships should reflect a "real" relationship between attitude and behaviour. Following the theory and practice of previous scholars, we developed several attribute models of voting in the Charter period from multiple indicators of political philosophy drawn from insights about the cleavages in Canadian politics and the differences in the types of socialization that are common in the legal community.

Party of Prime Minister

As we noted above, earlier studies (e.g., Tate and Sittiwong 1989) suggest that votes of the justices are strongly related to three characteristics of their background: political party of the appointing prime minister, region, and religion. Thus our model includes measures of the religion of the justice and the political party of the appointing prime minister. In order to gain a fuller understanding of regional cleavages on the Supreme Court, we categorize judicial origins into four regions: Quebec, Ontario (since by law and practice each of these provinces has three justices on the court), the "east," or Atlantic provinces, and the "west," or all provinces west of Ontario. We begin by examining the individual direct effects of each of these background characteristics on judicial voting and then proceed to determine whether those effects remain constant in multivariate analyses once we add control variables for case characteristics and additional judicial attributes.

Before analysing the relationship between background characteristics and voting tendencies, we note that the justices on the Charter-era court have come from a diverse array of social backgrounds, resulting in robust degrees of variation on our independent variables. Throughout the past twenty years the court has been bipartisan, has represented all the regions of Canada, has been nearly equally divided between Catholics and non-Catholics, and, compared to many other common law countries (e.g., Australia, England, and the United States), has had substantial gender diversity.[2] The distributions of each characteristic are presented in Table 10.

One of the most obvious a priori measures used in political science is the party affiliation of the appointing official (for US examples, see Tate and Handberg 1991; Wasby 1993; in Canada, see Tate and Sittiwong 1989; Ostberg and Wetstein 1998; 2007a; Wetstein and Ostberg 1999; Songer and Johnson 2007). The presumption here is that political conflict in other arenas is often structured along party lines, and so policy-oriented presidents or prime ministers probably choose justices who mirror their own political preferences and ideological beliefs. In line with past research in this area, we included in the analysis a measure of party of prime minister, which we coded as a dichotomous variable (1 = Conservative appointee, 2 = Liberal appointee). Our use of the measure here essentially replicates our use of it in chapter 6. The expectation of an attitudinal interpretation of

Table 10
Backgrounds of justices serving 1984–2003

Variable	*Number*	*Percentage*
Party		
Conservative	11	45.8
Liberal	13	54.2
Region		
West	6	25.0
East	3	12.5
Ontario	5	20.8
Quebec	10	41.7
Religion		
Catholic	12	52.1
Other	11	47.8
Gender		
Male	19	79.2
Female	5	20.8
Law professor?		
Yes	12	50.0
No	12	50.0

Table 11
Differences in policy positions of justices appointed by Liberal versus Conservative prime ministers in non-unanimous votes in three policy areas, 1984–2003

Party of prime minister	*For defendant (N)*	*Civil liberties liberal (N)*	*For economic underdog (N)*
Conservative	48.0%	43.4%	54.0%
	(1067)	(263)	(176)
Liberal	53.7	45.4	46.0
	(503)	(108)	(64)
Chi square	4.43*	0.13	0.95

* p < .05.

differences on the court is that appointment by a Liberal prime minister should be associated with more "liberal" policy choices by the justices, including support for economic underdogs, criminal defendants, and rights claimants.

The relationship between judicial votes and the political party of the appointing prime minister is presented in Table 11. The results suggest that over the 20 years that we studied there was a moderately strong relationship between party and the policy positions supported by the justices in divided decisions in only one of the three policy areas – criminal cases – that we examined. They were significantly more likely to support criminal defendants, yet the party difference is modest – a 6 percentage-point differential in the tendency to support the petitions of criminal defendants. Differences in civil liberties cases are in the predicted direction (i.e., Liberals supporting rights claimants more frequently) but are not statistically significant. For economic cases, there was no evidence that Liberal justices were more likely to support economic underdogs.

The results for criminal cases suggest different patterns of attitudinal voting by the justices from different party backgrounds, but the absence of a partisan relationship in economic cases suggests a reduced significance for partisan appointment over time. Thus disclaimers by government officials that there are no partisan-based ideological criteria for the selection of justices receives partial support in the economic realm in recent years. Also paralleling the earlier findings of Tate and Sittiwong (1989), the differences between parties in criminal cases, while too large to have occurred by chance, are relatively modest. That is, there are definite party-based differences, but party cohorts on the court are far from monolithic, the average members of each party tend to be different, but there is considerable variation within each party as well.

Region

The logic behind using political party to assess differences that might be related to policy preferences is then extended to include other judicial attributes. Since regional conflict has permeated much of Canadian politics, it is natural to ask if regionally based differences in political perspective extend to policy-relevant behaviour on the Supreme Court.

An examination of regional origins of the justices reveals statistically significant differences in two of the three policy areas we examined – criminal cases and civil liberties. In criminal cases, justices from Ontario stand out as substantially different from the others. In fact, Ontario justices were one-and-a-half times as likely as eastern justices to support criminal defendants, and the propensities of justices from Quebec were only marginally different from eastern

Table 12
Differences in policy positions of justices from different regions in non-unanimous votes in three policy areas, 1984–2003

Region	*For defendant (N)*	*Civil liberties liberal (N)*	*For economic underdog (N)*
West	54.2%	47.8%	45.4%
	(494)	(115)	(77)
East	42.9	34.1	50.0
	(168)	(44)	(26)
Ontario	67.3	53.3	59.2
	(336)	(75)	(49)
Quebec	37.8	38.7	54.6
	(572)	(137)	(88)
Chi square	81.29***	6.60#	2.60

*** $p < .001$.
# $.05 < p < .10$.

justices. Justices from the western provinces have a record that is intermediate compared to the other provinces. In other words, western justices could be found in the middle of their more liberal Ontario counterparts and their more conservative colleagues from Quebec and the east. The magnitude of these regional differences is substantial – roughly three times that of the differences related to party.

In civil liberties cases, the differences are also substantial, though not as great as for criminal appeals. Once again, justices from Ontario were the most liberal, with justices from both Quebec and the eastern provinces supporting rights claims only 60 per cent as often. The western provinces were again intermediate. For private economic cases, the pattern is somewhat similar, although the magnitude of regional differences is smaller than in the other two areas and fails to reach statistical significance.

Scholars and journalistic accounts have largely assumed that the regional effect that mattered most was between Quebec and "English" Canada. But the data in Table 12 suggest that, in terms of actual differences in judicial behaviour on the Supreme Court, it is Ontario justices who stand apart. In three important areas of judicial policy making, they were on average substantially more likely to support liberal outcomes than the justices from any other provinces.

Table 13
Differences in policy positions of Catholic and non-Catholic justices in non-unanimous votes in three policy areas, 1984–2003

Religion	*For defendant (N)*	*Civil liberties liberal (N)*	*For economic underdog (N)*
Non-Catholic	50.6%	52.7%	51.1%
	(633)	(150)	(92)
Catholic	45.8	37.2	54.5
	(820)	(196)	(132)
Chi square	3.16#	8.20**	0.26

** $p < .01$.
# $.05 < p < .10$.

In contrast, the voting behaviour of justices from Quebec was largely indistinguishable from the voting of justices from at least one of the other two regions in each of the three policy areas examined.

Religion

When asked, particularly in reference to the earlier findings of judicial attribute models (Tate and Sittiwong 1989), the justices whom we interviewed for this project were unanimous in their conclusion that while religious differences may have helped to shape differences in judicial philosophy in the past, religion no longer mattered. The data in Table 13 suggest that the justices were wrong and underestimated religion's impact. In both criminal appeals and in civil liberties cases, the differences between the voting records of Catholics and non-Catholics were at or near statistical significance. Non-Catholics were moderately more likely than Catholics to support criminal defendants and substantially more likely to support rights claimants in civil liberties cases. While the magnitude of the differences is not as great as those associated with regional origins, the relationship of religion to judicial voting appears to be about as strong as the relationship of political party to voting.

In summary, when the justices cannot agree on a unanimous approach to resolve the case before them, the differences among them that emerge appear to be related to partisan, regional, and religious variation. While there are some differences, as we noted above, these results suggest that the cleavages on the court in the Charter era resemble those in earlier years (Tate and Sittiwong 1989). Of these bases of the divisions on the Charter-era court, region appears to have the greatest effect.

Gender: A New Basis for Division

A major change in the Supreme Court's composition occurred shortly before the Charter came into effect and the first Charter litigation reached the court. Prime Minister Pierre Trudeau in March 1982 appointed Bertha Wilson, the first woman to serve on the court. Gender diversification has continued, with seven women appointed by 2010. At the time we wrote this book, the Supreme Court consisted of five men and four women.

Will women justices decide cases differently from their brethren? According to Bertha Wilson, there is "overwhelming evidence that gender-based myths, biases, and stereotypes are deeply embedded in the attitudes of many male judges" and that "gender difference has been a significant factor in judicial decision-making, particularly in the areas of tort law, criminal law, and family law" (Wilson 1990, 512). She argues that women view the world differently from men and that female judges often bring this alternative perspective to bear on the cases they decide (Wilson 1990). She maintains that the addition of more women to the bench could make a difference in the law, if "women judges, through their differing perspectives on life, can bring new humanity to bear on the decision-making process" (Wilson 1990, 522). Supreme Court Justice Claire L'Heureux-Dubé points to her own opinions as evidence. In *R v. Seaboyer* she argued in dissent that the "rape-shield" law under consideration was the product of decades of myths and stereotypical thinking about sexual assault. Similarly, in *Symes v. Canada*, she disagreed with her male colleagues about whether provisions in income tax law about business expenses were based on the experiences of only businessmen (L'Heureux-Dubé 1997).

But not everyone agrees that women will produce different decisions. For instance, Sandra Day O'Connor, the first woman on the US Supreme Court, argues that gender makes no difference in judging (Sandra Day O'Connor 2003, 190–3; Woodruff 2003). Indeed, several analyses of her voting tend to support that view in her instance (Karen O'Connor and Segal 1990; Davis 1993). However, Davis (1993) finds her more supportive of claims involving equality than of claims brought against criminal defendants.

Unfortunately, larger-scale studies of gender disparities in other appellate courts have been limited primarily to US judges. This research has generally produced mixed results. Some scholars find evidence that the effects of gender vary across issues, and specifically that female judges are more likely to support women's rights claimants (Cook 1981; Allen and Wall 1987; Martin 1993; Songer et al. 1994; Palmer 2002). In addition, an analysis of female decision making on US district courts finds them more supportive of personal liberties and minority groups (Johnson et al. 2008). An earlier study, however, shows them more sympathetic only to economic regulation, not to civil liberties claims and criminal and women's rights cases (Walker and Barrow 1985). Another study of US courts of appeals uncovers significant differences vis-à-vis employment discrimination but not obscenity and search and seizure (Songer et al. 1994).

Two studies of gender in Canadian courts have also come to different conclusions. Candace C. White (2002) examines the Charter opinions of women on the Supreme Court between 1993 and 1996. Based on this limited sample, she concludes that no gender difference existed in Charter cases dealing with legal rights but that the female justices were more supportive than their male colleagues of rights claimants in cases involving fundamental freedoms and equality rights. Ostberg and Wetstein (2007a; 2007b) uncover significant gender differences in several issue areas, including equality and labour relations. In contrast, McCormick and Job (1993), in their analysis of criminal cases in Alberta, discover little gender difference even in issues such as sexual assault, and women slightly more conservative in criminal cases than their male colleagues.

To explore the impact, if any, of gender diversification on the division of the Supreme Court of Canada, we first look at the simple differences in the overall voting patterns of male and female justices in our three policy areas of interest. The results are in Table 14.

An examination of these first-order differences suggests that gender may be the most significant cleavage on the court. However, gender differences do not fall neatly into the sort of liberal/conservative split found in the United States. The largest gender differences occur in criminal cases. In contrast to expectations derived

Table 14
Differences in policy positions of male and female justices in non-unanimous votes in three policy areas, 1984–2003

Gender	*For defendant* (N)	*Civil liberties liberal* (N)	*For economic underdog* (N)
Male	54.1%	40.8%	47.4%
	(1195)	(277)	(173)
Female	36.0	53.2	64.2
	(375)	(94)	(67)
Chi square	37.58***	4.38*	5.45*

* p < .05.
*** p <.001.

from gender difference in the United States, Canadian male justices are substantially more likely than their female colleagues to support criminal defendants. The "gender gap" there is 18 percentage points, and the difference is significant at the 99.9-per-cent confidence level.

A nearly identical margin separates the genders in private economic cases, but with women more "liberal." Women's support for economic underdogs is 17 percentage points higher than men's, and the difference is statistically significant. This overall pattern of gender differences mirrors earlier work by Ostberg and Wetstein (2007b) on specific labour disputes.

Studies of the effects of gender in US courts generally detect the greatest differences in civil liberties cases, with women more likely to support an expansion of civil liberties. The data in Table 14 show that Canadian female justices, like their US counterparts, more frequently support liberal positions. By US standards, the differences are substantial and statistically significant. But the 12-percentage-point gap between the votes of male and female justices is actually the smallest gender difference on the Supreme Court of Canada for any issue examined.

MULTIVARIATE MODELS OF JUDICIAL BEHAVIOUR

Having established that the patterns of division on the Supreme Court of Canada relate to partisan selection, region, religion, and gender, we now construct multivariate models of judicial behaviour in each of our three policy areas. In each area, we examine the effect of each of these four sources of cleavage in a multivariate model that allows us to explore the impact of each variable while controlling simultaneously for the effects of all the others in addition to several control variables. Since the dependent variable is dichotomous and ordinary-least-squares models are inappropriate, we use logistic regression to model the likelihood of a "liberal" vote in each policy area (Aldrich and Nelson 1984). We create four dichotomous variables to permit assessment of regional effects. The variable "east" is the excluded category in each table, so that the coefficients for "Quebec," "Ontario," and "west" indicate the effect of being from that region compared to being from the eastern, or Atlantic provinces.

For readers unfamiliar with logistic regression, we offer an introductory primer (see Aldrich and Nelson 1984). The technique presumes mathematically predictable relationships between a set of indicators – in this case pertaining to the background characteristics of justices of the Supreme Court of Canada and their individual votes in particular cases. We score votes as zero or one depending on ideological direction (1 = liberal). We can likewise score justices' background characteristics as zero or one, depending on whether or not they possess that attribute. Logistic regression relies on a model of hypothesized effects on votes, with indicators tending to predict either greater or lesser probabilities of a liberal vote, based on the relationships found across all the justices simultaneously. Moreover, the model presumes that one can control for each indicator while looking at the effect of the others. In effect, if we can hold constant the religion, gender, and region of each justice – meaning that all the justices are the same on these three variables – we can assess the odds of a liberal vote among Liberal appointees. If we assume that all justices are from the same region, religion, and party, what are the odds of Conservatives voting liberally (i.e., while we hold all other factors constant)? That ability to control for the effects of rival variables, while simultaneously estimating the impacts of each, is what makes multivariate logistic regression so useful to quantitative researchers.

Criminal Cases

We begin our analysis with an examination of the model of decisions in criminal cases (Table 15). The findings suggest that the effects

Table 15
Logistic-regression model of the likelihood of a pro-defendant vote by justices, 1984–2003

Variable	*Maximum likelihood estimate*	*Standard error*	*Odds ratio*
Party of PM	0.393**	0.126	1.482
Quebec	0.487*	0.206	1.627
Ontario	2.731***	0.316	15.353
West	1.847***	0.243	6.341
Catholic	1.069***	0.176	2.913
Female	–0.840***	0.139	0.431
Law professor	0.790***	0.135	2.203
Federal govt	–0.437*	0.187	0.645
Lower court	–0.122	0.127	0.884
Intercept	–7.846	1.087	

N = 1,399.
-2Log L = 1764.92.
Chi square = 143.30.***
* p < .05.
** p <.01.
*** p < .001.

of political party, region, religion, and gender that we noted in the analyses above are all independent of each other and operate jointly. In addition to the variables for party, region, religion, and gender, we add controls to reflect whether each justice had been a law professor, the lower court's decision, and whether the federal or the provincial government had prosecuted the crime. Vis-à-vis these control variables, former law professors were more likely to support criminal defendants, and the federal government won more criminal appeals than provincial governments. However, the direction of the lower court's decision was unrelated to the justices' decisions.

When these basic variables are controlled, each indicator of judicial attitudes has the expected relationship to votes. First, even after we control for region and religion, Liberal appointees were more likely to support criminal defendants. While the magnitude of partisan effects is moderate, it is significant at the 99-per-cent confidence level. The odds ratios in Table 15 report the change in the probability of a liberal vote associated with a one-unit change in the dependent variable. Thus the odds ratio of 1.48 for "political party" indicates that the odds of a liberal vote increase by 48 per cent if the justice is a Liberal rather than a Conservative. Thus party differences are greater than chance would suggest, and the differences are relatively large.

Regional effects also remain robust even after addition of all the controls. Justices from Ontario were significantly more likely than those from both the Atlantic provinces and Quebec to support criminal defendants. Western justices were also substantially more likely than Atlantic colleagues to support criminal defendants. While justices from Quebec tended to be more moderate than their colleagues from Ontario and the west, even they were more pro-defendant to a statistically significant degree than Atlantic justices. In fact, the odds ratio suggests that the odds of a pro-defendant vote by a Quebec justice are more than 60 per cent greater than the odds of such a vote from an Atlantic colleague (even after we control for party, gender, and so on). This intermediate position on criminal appeals reinforces the findings above that suggest that, in contrast to findings about earlier periods (Tate and Sittiwong 1989), Quebec justices no longer manifest a distinctive pattern of judicial behavior.

When we add controls for other relevant influences, Catholic justices were *more likely* than non-Catholics to support criminal defendants. This finding is directly opposite to the apparent relationship between religion and voting in criminal cases in Table 13, where we examine the relationship between religion and voting in isolation from other influences. That is to say, when one compares (as in Table 13) all Catholic justices to all non-Catholic justices without regard to region, gender, or party, the non-Catholics are more likely to support criminal defendants. But Table 15 suggests that this apparent difference is the result not primarily of religion but of the fact that non-Catholics have other characteristics that lead them to support criminal defendants. Therefore Catholic justices are more likely to support criminal defendants than are their non-Catholic colleagues who share the same other characteristics with them (e.g., both are males from Quebec). This finding demonstrates the importance of looking at the impact of variables simultaneously.

As we noted above, gender diversification of the Supreme Court began approximately when the first Charter cases reached the court. The analysis in Table 15 indicates that in criminal cases there are sharp differences in the voting patterns of male versus female justices. Gender differences are statistically significant at the 99.9-per-cent confidence level, with a female justice being less than half as likely as a male to support a criminal defendant once we control for party, region, and religion.

Civil Rights and Liberties Cases

In contrast to the findings for criminal cases, it appears that partisan selection does not have a substantial effect on judicial votes in civil rights and liberties cases. Liberal appointees were no more likely than their Conservative colleagues to support a rights claim. Similarly, Catholics did not support rights claims more than Protestants. While there is some indication that regional cleavages matter, the effect of region is much lower in civil liberties cases than in criminal cases. However, as in the model for criminal appeals, justices from Ontario were substantially more liberal than their colleagues from elsewhere.

In contrast to those studies examining pre-Charter periods, the Charter-era divisions on the court now appear to centre around a new regional split, with Ontario rather than Quebec as the most distinctive region, along with the emergence of gender as a basis of cleavage. The data in Table 16 show that the votes of male and female justices differed significantly, with women more willing to support rights claimants in non-criminal cases. Specifically, a female justice was 61 per cent more likely to support a rights claimant than was a male justice of the same party, region, and religion.

Each of the control variables in the model has the predicted results. Consistent with past studies of party-capability theory in Canada as well as in the United States and the United Kingdom, litigants with greater resources were more likely to win civil liberties cases than litigants with fewer resources (e.g., see Atkins 1991; Songer and Sheehan 1992; McCormick 1993). And, as in the model of criminal appeals that we discussed above, former law professors were more likely than other litigants to support liberal outcomes.

Economic Cases

As for economic cases, Table 17 also indicates a substantial change over time in the bases of cleavages in the divided private economic cases. This result is somewhat surprising, since the issues in these cases should not have been affected very much by the Charter. In

Table 16
Logistic-regression model of the likelihood of a pro-rights claimant vote by justices in civil rights and liberties cases, 1984–2003

Variable	*Maximum likelihood estimate*	*Standard error*	*Odds ratio*
Party of PM	0.143	0.252	1.153
Quebec	0.330	0.424	1.391
Ontario	1.035*	0.590	2.814
West	0.422	0.488	1.525
Catholic	–0.352	0.332	0.703
Female	0.479*	0.255	1.614
Law professor	0.312	0.265	1.365
Litigant difference	0.284***	0.073	1.328
Intercept	–3.083	2.090	

N = 372.
-2Log L = 475.66.
Chi square = 30.96.***

* p < .05.
*** p < .001.

Table 17
Logistic-regression model of the likelihood of a pro-underdog vote by justices in private economic cases, 1984–2003

Variable	*Maximum likelihood estimate*	*Standard error*	*Odds ratio*
Party of PM	–0.633	0.361	0.530
Quebec	–0.015	0.563	0.984
Ontario	0.510	0.737	1.665
West	–0.801	0.577	0.448
Catholic	0.211	0.384	1.235
Female	0.627**	0.316	1.872
Private practice	–2.011*	1.017	0.133
Law professor	–1.966*	0.940	0.139
Litigant difference	0.229*	0.107	1.257
Lower court	0.044	0.285	1.045
Intercept	2.124	2.584	

N = 234.
–2Log L = 299.90.
Chi square = 21.38.**

* p < .05.
** p <.01.

sharp contrast to studies from the pre-Charter period, none of the hypothesized relationships remains the same. Party, region, and religion appear not to affect the pattern of voting to any substantial degree. In each of these cases, the effect of the judicial characteristic on voting fails to reach standard levels of statistical significance.

The characteristic that does stand out in this area of law is gender. Even when we add all the controls, female justices were substantially more (87 per cent more) likely than men to support economic underdogs. In addition, justices from private practice with corporate law firms were also substantially less likely to support economic underdogs than were colleagues without such a background.

CONCLUSION

Taken together, earlier studies demonstrate that in the pre-Charter era divisions on the court related to party, region, and religion. However, the only ones that carried on after 1982 were in criminal law. But even in criminal appeals, there is evidence that it is the distinctiveness of Ontario origins rather than Quebec origins that is driving the significance of region for the structuring of disagreement. There is also some evidence of this Ontario distinctiveness in civil liberties cases and perhaps a slight hint of it in private economic conflicts. We think that this Ontario distinction is worthy of further study, and we speculate that its roots may lie in the greater exposure that justices there might have received to an urban-metropolitan culture that sets them apart from justices that hail from less populated provinces and from the distinctive culture of Quebec. Perhaps more important, the bases of cleavages of the Charter period are definitely not similar across the three issue areas, as party, region, and religion appear to have lost their ability to structure division in either civil liberties or private economic conflicts. And perhaps most important, with the gender diversification of the court, gender has emerged as a primary distinction in all three areas. However, the addition of female justices has not moved the court in a consistent "liberal" direction. Instead, while female justices provided more support for rights claimants and economic underdogs, they were substantially less supportive of criminal defendants.

In summary, a justice's gender has emerged as a significant new basis for differences on the Supreme Court of Canada in the Charter period. Before 1982, conflict was structured by party, region, and religion. But in the Charter era, divisions are more frequently structured along gender lines, and the effect of gender remains strong even after one controls for all the traditional bases of disagreement that dominated earlier courts. The results appear to confirm, at least in the Canadian context, the early prediction of Justice Bertha Wilson that the addition of women to the courts would indeed make a difference.

The evidence of this chapter reinforces the findings of the previous two chapters to provide strong evidence that the attitudes and policy preferences of the justices have a substantial relationship to their decisions. Despite denials that judicial ideology is not actively considered in their selection, the evidence is clear that their actual voting relates to the party of the appointing prime minister, at least in the important area of criminal appeals. And as the relevance of religion appears to have waned, gender has now emerged as a substantial basis of judicial decision making.

However, despite the strong evidence of attitudinal impact on decision making in this chapter, one very strong caveat is in order. All the analyses above were based only on cases in which the Supreme Court divided. Since most of its cases result in unanimous decisions, one should not jump to conclude that our attempts to explain divided decisions necessarily illuminate decision making in all cases. Instead, what can be said is that when the court splits, the division appears to reflect attitudinal or ideological divisions among the justices. To conclude our analysis of the attitudinal model as an explanation of judicial behaviour on the Supreme Court of Canada, we take a look at unanimous decisions in chapter 8.

8 The Attitudinal Model and the Puzzle of Unanimity

In sum, the analyses of the past three chapters provide strong evidence that the political attitudes of the justices have a substantial effect on their decisions across many of the politically salient issues addressed by the Supreme Court of Canada under the Charter. When the court divides, the votes of the justices frequently fall into consistent patterns that reflect the ideological and partisan divisions of the court. But when these findings are combined with the well-known phenomenon that in a large majority of cases the court is unanimous, a puzzle emerges. If it is attitudinal differences among the justices that drive the outcomes, why is the court so frequently unanimous?

The high rate of unanimity has been a consistent characteristic of the court's decision making for many years, under many chief justices. The annual rate of unanimity from 1970 through 2004 is plotted in Figure 4. It has fallen below 60 per cent only once and in many years exceeded 70 per cent. For the Charter period as a whole, 76 per cent of the court's decisions have been unanimous.

To explore this puzzle of unanimity on a court that reflects attitudinal decision making, we first examine the perspectives of the justices themselves on the subject. Next, we examine their actual behaviour to see if the data are consistent with their perceptions. Thus we turn to our interviews for clues about factors that might produce unanimity and find two consistent themes. First, the justices believed that unanimity was the end result of serious discussion and debate about the meaning of law and precedent for a particular decision. Second, most of the justices suggested that informal norms of collegiality and respect for the opinions of colleagues often resulted in deliberate efforts to find acceptable compromise. No justice reported that

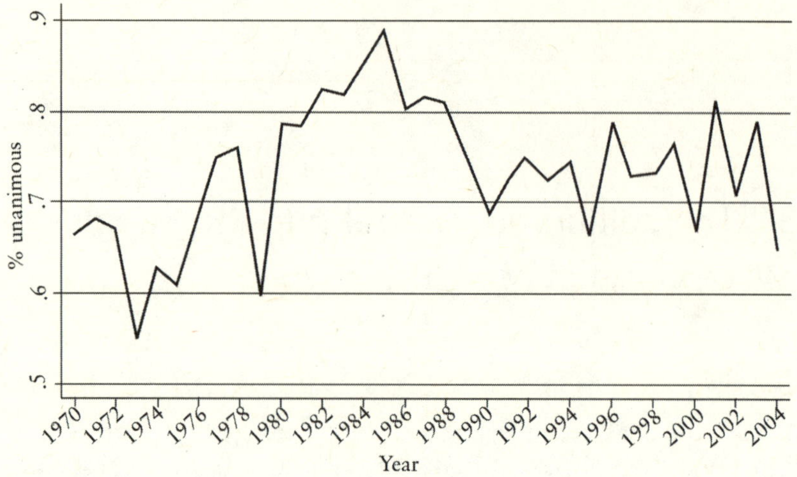

Figure 4
Unanimous decisions, change over time, 1970–2004

strategic reactions to external actors had a substantial effect on the rate of unanimity. We now analyse the justices' observations about unanimity and test some of their beliefs.

EXPLAINING UNANIMITY: JUSTICES' PERCEPTIONS

Several justices reported informal pressure to work out differences among court members. Justice F recalled that in conference the person designated to write the majority opinion would frequently say something such as, "If I write the opinion in thus and such a way, would that satisfy the concerns that have been expressed?" Similarly, Justice B indicated that he thought that most of his colleagues shared his belief that it was important to "get a blend of individuality and collegiality." He constantly reminds himself that "we are not just soloists" but a choir. Consequently, while he feels free to dissent when his differences on principle are "major," he "looks first to try to get consensus." Justice G agreed: "Justices have a commitment whenever principle doesn't require them to divide to give a little and take a little to try to reach agreement." Justice F, when asked to describe the typical process in opinion writing, said that there is frequently a deliberate attempt to increase consensus and that the person originally selected to write the opinion of the court frequently moderates his original draft in order to obtain unanimous support. When asked directly about Justice F's statement, Justice A agreed and added that the chief justice made it clear that she favoured consensus when it was possible. Both justices E and H reported informal pressure to work out differences, although Justice E characterized it as "gentle" pressure.

The comments thus suggest that informal norms of collegiality play a large role in unanimity. When asked directly about the cause of unanimity, Justice I responded that in general "the unanimity that emerges at the *end* of the process is probably equal parts deference to and accommodation of the views of your colleagues and persuasion about what the proper resolution of the issues is."

Similarly, Justice H suggested that "everyone understands that there are differences in approaches to the law – differences in jurisprudence, if you will – and these often colour how we each interpret the legal questions." But he added that there is also a substantial collegiality that generally leads to attempts at finding a statement that everyone can live with. "I suppose you would call that compromise, but it is at least in part a recognition that each of your colleagues has preferences and points of view that are as legitimate as your own – so in part it is less deliberate compromise in a political sense as it is respect for the values and points of view of your colleagues."

Justice D picked up on this general point and suggested that he thought that the justices generally agreed that one should try to reach consensus when there were not major differences on principle and thus were most likely to be unanimous on questions that did not raise major policy issues or extensive controversy in the "political sphere." Justice F concurred, noting that Charter issues were the types of matters on which members were most likely to have firm, "principled" positions that were most difficult to compromise. When this comment was relayed to Justice H, he agreed in general but noted that sometimes questions of statutory interpretation were as controversial and principled as Charter questions. Significantly, no justice indicated that he ever sought to create only a minimum winning coalition, which would be the rational approach of justices if they were motivated solely by policy preferences.

When asked more generally about how they approached their decision-writing chores, both Justices C and D indicated that there was often fairly direct bargaining among the justices (see chapter 3 above). Justice C said that although the justices generally approach each other tactfully, one frequently receives a memo after the initial draft of the opinion has circulated that says something along these lines: "I think that the analysis in section 3 could be strengthened if you approached it in the following way." And everyone understands that such a memo indicates the possibility of an implicit bargain, whereby the responding justice would drop initial opposition in return for the indicated change. Moreover, he commented, most of the time such implicit bargains are accepted, unless the opinion writer has very strong feelings about the original position. Justice D agreed that such implicit bargaining went on but added that sometimes it was explicit; that is, a justice's memo stated that unless such and such a change was made he would have to write separately. Such bargaining, according to several justices, often narrowed the scope of the original opinion in order to gain unanimous support.[1] Several other justices agreed that one form of "compromise" was simply to leave out resolution of the specific point that was most contentious if the case could be resolved without it. Thus consensus was sometimes reached via a narrower opinion than the writer initially preferred.

Related to the acceptance of such bargaining, several justices indicated that, especially on complex cases, the give and take in conference and in opinion writing often led justices to change their personal positions. That is, discussion of the legal issues often resulted in sincere agreement about the proper outcome despite initial disagreement in conference. Justice D reported that he was convinced to change his mind on the meaning of precedent more often by discussion with his colleagues than from listening to the arguments of counsel. Justice A indicated that, even on hard cases, justices often eventually came to a consensus that the lower court should be reversed after they had carefully worked through all the legal issues. And at least two of the justices commented that sometimes one realizes that an initial dissenting position "just won't write" and thus accepts the legal reasoning of the majority.

Finally, several justices (J, K, and C) suggested that it was sometimes easier to reach consensus when the court wanted to affirm the decision below than when a majority wanted to reverse it. Justice K suggested that this was in part due to the reluctance of anyone to stand out completely alone. For instance, if seven or eight colleagues favoured a position that was in concert with one or more three-judge panels on the courts of appeal and they also had affirmed the trial judge, simple modesty might lead a justice to question whether he was sure that he was right to disagree. Alternatively, even if he were confident of his own position, it would feel lonely to cast a dissent in such a case. Justice C agreed with Justice K's analysis but added that at least on occasion the court would hear a case in which there was little question about the accuracy of the legal analysis in the court below, but the justices simply felt that the principle announced below was important enough that it should be given the "seal of approval" of the Supreme Court. In such cases, the chief would usually try to seat the full nine members to hear the case, and such decisions were usually unanimous.

But even though the justices agreed that unanimous decisions were most likely in cases in which the legal issues were straightforward and/or there was agreement on which precedents should control the outcome, unanimity was also reached in some of the hard cases. Justice F observed that even unanimous reversals sometimes occurred in hard cases where consensus was eventually reached through the *process* of the court. He noted that this "often reflects a good bit of give and take. We all recognize that we all come to the court with different points of view – different approaches to the law – and these always will affect our judgment of how a case should be decided when the legal issues are complex or murky." Nevertheless, "we respect these different approaches and see if we can work out an opinion that everyone can live with – you have to have some degree of humility and accept that the approaches of the others are as legitimate as your own."

TESTING JUSTICES' PERCEPTIONS OF UNANIMITY

Simple Empirical Testing

We next attempt to test empirically these predictions about unanimity derived from the perspectives of the justices. Unfortunately, some of the suggestions offered in the interviews cannot be easily tested with empirical data derived from case outcomes. Some concepts suggested by the justices, such as collegiality, are difficult to measure; others, such as perception of the degree of constraint imposed by precedent in a given case or willingness to accept specific compromises offered by other justices to a first-draft opinion, are simply not available from the final opinions. However, a few implications of the perspective offered by the justices can be tested.

The idea that some opinions become unanimous once the justices have thoroughly talked through the legal issues involved is difficult to test directly. While conceptually it makes sense that cases in which the legal issues are relatively clear and straightforward will be among the ones in which consensus is easiest to obtain, there is no completely satisfactory, objective indicator of which cases have such issues. However, one objective characteristic of opinions in which the legal issues may reasonably be thought to be less complex relates to the length of the opinion. Short opinions are likely to reflect the view that the legal issues are not difficult. Moreover, the justices noted that in order to reach consensus they frequently simplified the opinions, dropping collateral issues on which the justices disagreed but that were not essential to resolution of the basic dispute between the litigants. Thus one would expect, based on the views expressed by the justices, that unanimity would be more frequent in shorter opinions, either because the issues were inherently less complex or because bargaining produced consensus by reducing the initial complexity of the issues.

We test this implication of the interviews first by simply computing the average length of opinions in unanimous versus divided decisions. This simple comparison provides strong support for the justices' perspective. The mean (i.e., average) length of divided decisions is 52.6 pages, and of unanimous decisions, 19.6 pages.

To further explore this idea, we examine the distribution of very short opinions, which we define as two pages or less. These are the opinions that most likely resolve those cases in which the law is so straightforward that little explanation is needed. We compare the prevalence of such short opinions versus all other opinions in unanimous and divided decisions in Figure 5. Once again, the empirical results strongly support the perspectives of the justices. Specifically, 92 per cent of these short opinions came in unanimous decisions, while the distribution of cases with opinions longer than two pages was similar to that of all decisions. Thus the data do provide some confirmation of the justices' assertion that some cases present issues in which the law is rather straightforward and that the justices frequently can all agree that there is clearly one legally correct outcome.

Another expectation of the justices' perception that there are some cases in which the law is relatively straightforward and in those cases there is likely to be a unanimous decision relates to panel size. Particularly, we saw in chapter 3 that the chief justice will often seat

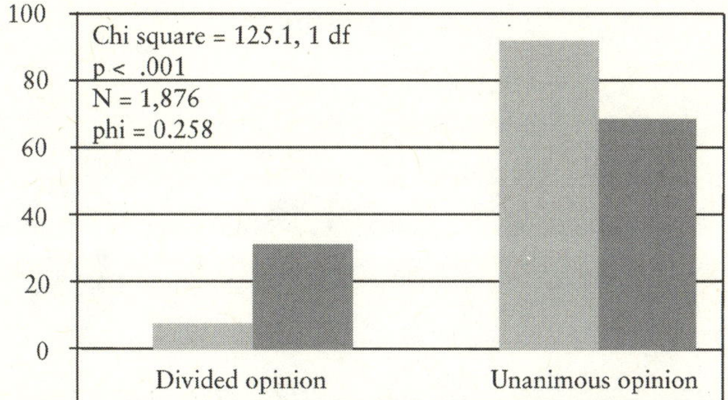

	Divided opinion	Unanimous opinion
Up to two pages	8.2	91.8
More than two pages	31.5	68.5

Figure 5
The relationship between opinion length and unanimous outcomes (% divided or unanimous)

a five-judge panel in cases reaching the court as of right when the chief justice perceives the issues raised by the appellant to be not of great consequence. Given this correlate of panel selection, one would expect that five-judge panels would be particularly likely to render unanimous decisions.[2]

The data in Figure 6 provide strong confirmation of these expectations. The relationship between panel size and unanimity is significant at the 99.9-per-cent-confidence level. Five-judge panels produce unanimous decisions in almost 88 per cent of cases, compared to 66 per cent when the whole court sits.

Multivariate Analysis

Following these preliminary examinations of the data, we seek to test more systematically some of the implications of the justices' perspective with a multivariate analysis. Since the dependent variable (unanimous versus divided decision) is dichotomous, we create a logistic-regression model in which the independent variables consist of those factors that the justices said should make unanimity more likely and others that they thought would make it less likely. The model thus represents an attempt to test partially their perspective on unanimity. In line with our discussion of logistic regression in chapter 7, we seek here to predict whether a case is unanimous,

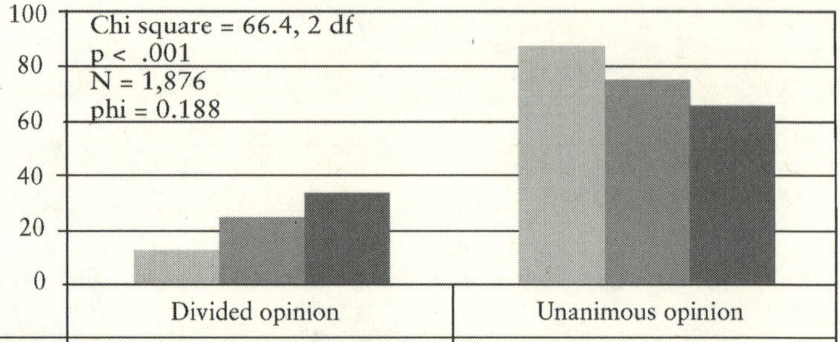

	Divided opinion	Unanimous opinion
Five	12.1	87.9
Seven	24.4	75.6
Nine	33.7	66.3

Figure 6
The relationship between panel size and unanimous outcomes (% divided or unanimous)

using seven traits about it to guide that predictive model (they all appear below in Table 18).

First, a consistent theme in the interviews was that collegiality and mutual respect encouraged justices to work towards compromise, but not without limits. Justices all indicated that they would work towards mutual accommodation "when they could" or when such a compromise "did not go against strongly held principles." This suggests that unanimous decisions were most likely when the perceived stakes were not as high. Several justices suggested that accommodation would be easier when the cases did not involve a Charter issue. Thus the first independent variable in the model was simply whether or not a constitutional issue arose in the opinion. We expected the presence of constitutional issues to decrease the likelihood of a unanimous ruling.

Second, at least one justice suggested that cases involving construction of a federal statute might also appear to have high stakes. To test this possibility, we add to the model a dichotomous variable noting the presence or absence of an issue of statutory construction. We expect the complexity of such cases to lessen the chances of unanimity.

Third, an alternative way of assessing the political stakes in a case is to see whether or not non-parties (e.g., interest groups or other governments) appear as interveners. The model includes simply the number of interveners listed as appearing before the court. We anticipate that interveners reduce the odds of a unanimous decision.

Fourth, justices also indicated that they sometimes strove to achieve unanimity by narrowing the scope of the opinion. They might delete issues that some justices wanted to address but which justices decided, after some give and take, were not essential for resolution of the appeal. To assess this possibility, we use the tag lines of the opinion to identify the number of paragraphs raising separate legal issues.[3] Narrow opinions would tend to have fewer paragraphs indicating separate issues, and thus we expect a positive coefficient for these types of cases.

Fifth, as we noted above, the difficulty of finding reliable empirical indicators of the influence of precedent and other legal factors has long inhibited analysis of judicial voting. While no completely satisfactory indicator is available, one partial indicator may be agreement between different levels of courts.[4] The fact that two sets of judges ultimately reach the same conclusion may thus be at least a rough indicator that law or precedent constrained the justices. This may be more likely in a court that controls its own docket, since a court may grant leave to appeal partly because it appears as if the case was decided wrongly below. When that initial presumption is overcome after further consideration and deliberation on the case, it may indicate that justices concluded that the law constrained their ability to overturn the decision. Thus the model includes a dichotomous variable indicating whether or not the Supreme Court affirmed the lower court's decision.

Sixth, alternatively, our interviews indicated that panel size may also be an indicator of both the legal complexity and the political salience of a case. The justices agreed that five-judge panels were usually set to hear a case when the justices initially thought the case relatively straightforward legally. Yet the chief justice was expected to have the whole court sit for a particularly important or controversial issue. Moreover, even with random behaviour, agreement should be more frequent in smaller panels. To test these observations, we also include panel size as a variable in the model.

Seventh and finally, while the justices downplayed the role of political preferences in unanimous decisions, a proponent of the attitudinal model would expect more unanimous decisions as ideological agreement among justices increased. To test this idea, we include a measure of the ideological diversity of the members of the panel that decided each case.[5] If the implications of the attitudinal model are correct, then increasing ideological diversity should reduce the proportion of unanimous decisions.

To measure ideological range, we use the measure of Supreme Court ideology devised by Ostberg and Wetstein (1998; 2007a) and discussed above in chapter 6. Ostberg and Wetstein adapt the measure developed by Segal and Cover (1989), which has become the most widely used measure of US Supreme Court ideology. Our content analysis of editorials and articles at the time of appointment for each justice in the nine leading national and regional newspapers of Canada produced a cumulative measure of the frequency with which new justices were referred to as "liberal" or "conservative," resulting in a scale running from most liberal (+2) to most conservative (-[minus]2). To construct our measure of the ideological range on the panel deciding each case we simply subtract the value of the most conservative member from the value for the most liberal.

A MODEL OF UNANIMITY

As we explained above, we create a logistic-regression model to test justices' perspectives on the conditions that they thought made unanimous decisions more or less likely. We run our model using all published decisions of the Supreme Court from 1984 through 2005.The dependent variable is dichotomous – whether the decision was unanimous or divided (1 for unanimous and 0 for divided). The independent variables include four factors that the justices predicted would have a negative relationship with unanimity (i.e., make it less likely): the presence of a constitutional issue, of a statutory construction issue, or of interveners, and a large panel. Two factors are predicted to make unanimous decisions more likely: the decision to affirm the decision below and the writing of a narrow opinion. The justices predicted that the panel's ideological diversity would not affect the likelihood of a unanimous decision, although the attitudinal perspective would have it do so (in other words, greater ideological range would decrease the odds of unanimity). The results of this analysis appear in Table 18.

The results provide strong support for the justices' perspectives. Two of the three indicators of the salience of the issue make a unanimous decision much less probable. The coefficients for constitutional issue and statutory interpretation are both statistically

Table 18
Logistic-regression models of the likelihood of a unanimous decision under the Charter, 1982–2004

Variable	*Maximum likelihood estimate*	*Standard error*	*Odds ratio*
Constitutional issue	–0.469***	0.119	0.625
Statute interpretation	–0.316**	0.121	0.729
No. of interveners	–0.011#	0.008	0.989
Narrow opinion	0.306**	0.114	1.358
Affirm	0.202*	0.109	1.224
Panel size	–0.239***	0.043	0.787
Ideological range	0.105	0.106	1.111
Intercept	2.561	0.289	

N = 1,950.
–2Log L = 2,065.47.
Chi square = 104.74.***

* p < .05.
** p <.01.
*** p < .001.
# .05 < p < .10.

significant and in the direction predicted by the justices. Unanimous decisions are substantially less likely if either a constitutional issue or a statutory interpretation is involved. Moreover, the more attention the case attracts from interest groups and other interveners, the slightly less likely the justices are to resolve the dispute unanimously.

In addition, both of the factors predicted to make unanimous decisions more likely also are consistent with the justices' predictions. The positive and statistically significant coefficient for a narrow opinion supports their suggestion that initial conflicts are sometimes resolved by a narrower resolution that everyone can accept. Similarly, the positive and statistically significant coefficient for decisions that affirm the ruling of a lower court supports their predictions.

The coefficient for panel size indicates that, as the size of the panel increases from five to nine justices, the likelihood of a unanimous decision declines. As we commented above, this effect may reflect the chief justice's tendency to name five members when she perceives a high degree of legal constraint (e.g., clear precedent controls the outcome), or it may simply reflect the mathematically easier task of getting five people to agree than nine.

In addition to providing support for the justices' perspective on factors that make unanimous decisions more likely, the statistically non-significant coefficient for ideological range supports their assertions that perceived differences in ideological preferences have little to do with whether or not a decision is unanimous.

Our interviews with the justices suggest that some unanimous decisions are the result of their perception of legal constraints that lead them all to support the same outcome regardless of their political preferences. Other justices indicate that unanimity may have to do with informal norms relating to collegiality. They note "gentle pressure" sometimes for them to try to work out differences if they can do so without sacrificing strong principles.

These notions of collegiality and perceptions of legal constraint are very difficult to test with quantitative methods. Nevertheless, a substantial part of what the justices suggested was tested, and those tests were consistent with the justices' perspectives. The results implied that unanimity is more difficult to reach on crucial political issues (especially interpretations of the Charter) and on issues that attract the widest interest from the broader political community (as when the presence of interveners reduces the likelihood of unanimity). The finding that narrow opinions are more likely to be unanimous is consistent with the justices' contention that they sometimes compromise and accept an opinion narrower than they would ideally prefer in order to achieve unanimity. And finally, while the finding that five-judge panels are the most likely to be unanimous does not provide direct evidence that legal constraint influences unanimity, it does provide indirect evidence, since justices generally believe that, when legal constraints appear especially clear and unambiguous at the time they grant leave, the chief justice is most likely to appoint a five-justice panel to hear the case.

Nevertheless, our finding – that each of the justices' perspectives that we could test empirically received empirical support – provides some added measure of confidence in the accuracy of the justices' perspectives that we could not directly test. Thus, in the absence of any empirical evidence to the contrary, it is reasonable to give substantial credence to their untested conclusions that collegiality and gentle pressure to compromise when possible, along with the notion that reasonable people who respect their colleagues can often reach agreement about the meaning of law and precedent, all play a part in the high level of unanimity on the Supreme Court of Canada.

9 Conclusions: Attitudinal Decision Making and the Supreme Court

We began this study by noting that a July 2005 article in the *Globe and Mail* cautions readers that the prime minister's selection of justices to serve on the Supreme Court of Canada is of profound importance because "the court's rulings have far-reaching effects, particularly in the age of the Charter of Rights and Freedoms." But at the court's inception in 1875, no newspaper would have made such a claim. In fact, it is doubtful that many would have made such a claim as late as the mid-1970s. However, since adoption of the Charter in 1982, it is not uncommon to note the significance of the Supreme Court for the resolution of politically important issues. Since then, the court has played an integral role in the resolution of some of the most divisive issues in Canadian politics, including Quebec's potential secession, abortion, child pornography, gay rights, and the role of women. Many of its decisions have provoked both passionate support and intense disagreement; however, there is no debate about the court's pivotal role in the wake of the Charter's adoption.

The increased political role of the Supreme Court and the growing activism of its justices appear to be part of a worldwide phenomenon in which courts have become increasingly active in the politics of both well-established and emerging democracies around the globe. As we noted above, scholars in many countries have recently been studying the "judicialization of politics," or the "rights revolution" (Tate and Vallinder 1995; Epp 1998; Hirschl 2004; 2010). In Canada, the increased attention to the court has resulted in a spate of studies analysing its doctrinal development and providing normative commentary on the appropriate exercise of power by the court. Specifically, scholars have debated whether the court has superseded legislatures in making policy or whether it is merely engaging in a running dialogue with Parliament and the prime minister and cabinet (see Manfredi 1993; 2001; Hogg and Bushell 1997; Manfredi and Kelly 1999; Morton and Knopff 2000; Roach 2001; Kelly 2005).

In this debate, Morton and Knopff (2000, 149) argue that the Charter-era court has too frequently endorsed the arguments of "court party" advocates and usurped the majoritarian preferences of elected legislators in a representative democracy. Other commentators have been more supportive of the court's increasing role in protecting rights and liberties in the Charter, applauding its independence and courage for supporting rights claims that are unpopular or advanced by disadvantaged groups (see Roach 2001, ix). Moreover, some scholars have contended that in this dialogue legislatures have the power to respond to the court's policy announcements with new legislation to reframe the discussion about Charter principles. As such, the policy-making process becomes a dialogue that goes back and forth between and within political institutions (see Kelly 2005). Indeed, Kelly (2005, 256) suggests that the dialogue over the Charter originates within the cabinet and the federal Department of Justice, which try to craft legislation that squares with Charter values. Regardless of where the dialogue originates, it is clear that Charter vetting is the result of institutions interacting with each other and responding to a rights culture that has emerged in Canadian society.

Underlying this discussion is the question of whether the court's new mandate to protect Charter rights and freedoms has triggered greater attitudinal disagreement among its justices. Given the transformation in the court's role, it is not surprising that justices frequently disagree over the proper resolution of significant disputes. Even the justices themselves have taken notice of the degree of conflict within their own court, with one suggesting that academics need to devote more energy to understanding the nature of conflict that has emerged on the court since the Charter's adoption (Iacobucci 2002; see Ostberg and Wetstein 2007a).

This book sought to take up this charge by exploring the relevance of the attitudinal model of judicial decision making in the Supreme Court of Canada and by examining what the justices themselves have to say about their work and the patterns of conflict and consensus that emerge in their rulings. Specifically, we employed three distinctive quantitative research strategies to investigate the extent to which ideology influences judicial decision making in non-unanimous cases and explored the differences that divide the justices. We applied factor analysis, bivariate correlation analysis, and logistic regression to explore the effects of ideology on judicial voting in the Charter era. Moreover, we added qualitative research that relies on extensive interviews with the justices to provide behind-the-scenes insight into their own thinking about the decisions they hand down.

The blending of these four methods provided a comprehensive assessment of the impact of attitudinal behaviour, and the data and interviews helped to answer the central questions of the book: what is the nature and extent of attitudinal decision making in the Supreme Court, and what evidence can be marshalled to suggest that the justices decide cases along ideological lines? Although the impact of ideology played out differently in each of the substantive chapters, and there are important nuances throughout, the overarching conclusion boils down to the following claim: the personal political preferences and ideologies of Canadian justices do influence how they approach different policy issues and why they resolve cases in a divided manner. Thus attitudinal decision making does seem to be alive and well on a prominent high court outside the United States.

ATTITUDINAL EXPLANATIONS OF JUDICIAL VOTES

Despite disclaimers that in Canada justices' ideology is not actively considered in their selection, the evidence from other countries sharing Canada's common law heritage is clear: the actual behaviour of the justices is related to their political attitudes. There seems to be little doubt that in both the United States and Australia, the political preferences of the justices strongly affect their judicial behaviour (e.g., see Galligan 1987; Segal and Spaeth 2002), and there is even accumulating evidence that the behaviour of the Law Lords in England is influenced at least in part by their political ideology (Robertson 1998).

This evidence from the common law world has begun to challenge traditional understandings of judicial decision making – most notably, the legal model of judicial behaviour, which we discussed in chapter 3. While that approach is satisfying for some legal scholars, social scientists have increasingly turned to more political explanations of judicial behaviour that incorporate factors such as social background, attitudes, and small-group dynamics (see Schubert

1965; Rohde and Spaeth 1976; Robertson 1982; 1998; Tate and Handberg 1991; Segal and Spaeth 1993; 2002; Epstein and Knight 1998; Maltzman et al. 2000; Ostberg and Wetstein 2007a). According to one recent analysis of these factors' effect on decision making in Canadian courts, "law and judicial process are indeed political" (Hausegger et al. 2009, 25). Even though each factor influences judicial decision making, we sought to focus on the degree to which attitudes account for judicial conflict.

The review of recent scholarship that we presented in chapter 3 indicated that in the past half-century a competing attitudinal model has emerged, especially for students of the US Supreme Court, and that model has become the dominant theory guiding research on US courts. After tracing the development of this model and evidence from US and British studies of its utility, we asked whether such an attitudinal model might explain the votes of the justices on the Supreme Court of Canada. In other words, do the justices' own political preferences drive the bulk of disagreement on the Charter-era court, or do other factors play a stronger role in shaping such patterns of disagreement? The empirical analysis of chapters 5–7 attempted to answer this question.

Given controversy in previous studies over the best way to assess whether the political attitudes of judges affect their decision making, we investigated the question of ideological influence from a multifaceted perspective. First, we interviewed the justices themselves to obtain their perceptions about attitudinal differences among them. We supplemented these observations with empirical analyses of the actual decisions of the justices, using three different approaches to assess attitudinal influence. The application of three methods, which each independently demonstrated a connection between judicial attitudes and votes on case outcomes, produced strong evidence that attitudinal decision making does indeed play an important role in the Canadian context.

Before analysing the justices' voting patterns, we noted that scholars who have examined attitudinal voting elsewhere argue that such voting is possible only when a court possesses a series of institutional features that give justices the freedom and incentive to make decisions consistent with their private preferences. Specifically, Segal and Spaeth propose that members of the US Supreme Court are free to vote their policy preferences without constraint from precedent because "they lack electoral or political accountability, ambition for higher office, and comprise a court of last resort that controls its own jurisdiction" (1993, 69). Furthermore, the absence of these factors hinders attitudinal voting by judges. The implication of this view is that if other courts possessed these institutional features, judges would be more likely to make their decisions based on their attitudes.

By 1983, the Supreme Court of Canada possessed all the institutional features critical to the existence of attitudinal voting. Most important, its level of judicial independence appears to be comparable to that enjoyed by the US Supreme Court. Both countries boast a strong tradition of judicial independence (Manfredi 1993), and all the justices we interviewed stoutly maintained that independence remains strong today. In order for attitudinal voting to occur, judicial independence must reflect practical political realities as well as formal institutional structures. Accounts from many other judicial systems drive home the point that one cannot simply assume judicial independence from formal constitutional "guarantees." For instance, constitutional guarantees of life tenure for Supreme Court justices did not prevent new regimes in a number of countries, including Argentina and Venezuela, from replacing the entire Supreme Court as soon as they took power (Helmke 2005). And in some regimes (e.g., Uganda in the 1970s) justices who opposed the government even risked being shot, despite firm constitutional guarantees of independence (Widner 2001). But in Canada, the justices unanimously expressed the view that the culture supporting the rule of law was so strong that the justices possessed substantial independence in fact as well as in law. Thus, given the similarities in institutional structures in the United States and Canada, one can expect that Canadian justices are as free as their counterparts to the south to vote their attitudinal preferences.

In the light of these arguments, this study set out to examine two questions – namely, 1) does the Supreme Court of Canada exhibit patterns of attitudinal decision making, and 2) if so, are the nature of those attitudinal cleavages similar to or different from those exhibited by US Supreme Court justices? To achieve this goal, we employed three different strategies to measure attitudinal disagreement. The first part of the analysis (in chapter 5) employed factor-analytic techniques to examine the attitudinal conflicts that divided members of the Lamer court between 1992 and 1997 in three important areas of law (economic policy, criminal, and civil rights and liberties). We chose this time frame because it displayed the most stable membership of the Charter era. In chapter 6, we applied the techniques developed by Segal and Cover (1989), using independent assessments of judicial ideology by newspaper writers and editors at the time of the appointment of new justices to assess the relationship between justices' attitudes and votes. Finally, in chapter 7, we used a judicial-attributes model to examine career liberalism patterns of 22 justices serving in the Charter period across these three issue areas, while controlling for various background characteristics of the justices. The three methods, working together, provided a powerful strategy for assessing the degree of attitudinal conflict on the Charter-era court, because it allowed for triangulation of the results. The findings reveal that ideological disagreement emerges as a prominent feature regardless of the method that we used for assessing attitudinal conflict.

In the factor-analysis section (chapter 5), the results show that an ideological divide helps account for differences that emerge between members of the Lamer court in all three issue areas of the study. Indeed, the most prominent factor in each of the issue areas is dominated by ideological conflict. Put simply, disagreement among the justices in the economic, criminal, and civil rights and liberties cases was structured primarily along ideological lines. While the first factor in the economic area pertains to liberalism in private law disputes, in the criminal cases it deals with a liberal/conservative struggle over the treatment of the accused, and in the civil liberties area, a similar divide dominates the first factor over discrimination and liberty claims. These findings suggest that when attitudinal conflicts emerged in the Lamer natural court they were driven principally by ideological discord. Although one must acknowledge that publicly expressed disagreement occurs less often on the highly collegial Charter-era court, it seems that the Lamer court justices, when they did disagree, were influenced by their own political preferences in a manner somewhat similar to their American counterparts.

While the results from the factor analyses in chapter 5 are potentially subject to questions about circular logic – namely, that judicial ideology derived from case outcomes is related to judicial decisions in those same cases – the second and third phases of our analysis largely put such concerns to rest. Both the newspaper measures of judicial ideology (see chapter 6) and justices' attributes (see chapter 7), while admittedly providing only rough approximations of the "real" attitudes of the justices, have the advantages of being independent of and prior in time to the votes of the justices on the Supreme Court. The importance of the newspaper measures cannot be overlooked, because they provide a rigorous assessment of ideology at the time of the justices' appointment that future scholars can use in research both within Canada and in comparative studies of judicial behaviour. Moreover, the findings from the chapter analysing judicial attributes are significant, because they provide new and compelling evidence that attributes can serve as useful predictors of judicial ideology in the Canadian context. Thus the findings enhance prior work by Tate and Sittiwong (1989) that has been widely cited by scholars interested in comparative research on the US and Canadian Supreme Courts. The results on newspaper ideology and judicial attributes in chapters 6 and 7 demonstrated statistically significant relationships between political preferences and judicial voting patterns, and our use of multiple measures reinforces the conclusions that emerged from the scaling and factor analysis of judicial decisions in chapter 5. The overall conclusion from our multi-faceted analysis is that the attitudinal model provides a robust explanation of voting behaviour in the Supreme Court of Canada.

Even though both US and Canadian high courts exhibit ideological discord in the three areas analysed, they do not march to the same ideological drumbeat. Indeed, there is an underlying complexity to the way that Canadian justices approach cases in these three disparate areas of law that provides a valuable theoretical contribution to the attitudinal model and provides insight for further research in comparative law. Scholars of public opinion argue that elites in democratic societies will be consistent in their ideological beliefs across different issue areas (see Campbell et al. 1960; Sniderman et al. 1996). What is striking about several of the justices on the Lamer natural court is the lack of ideological consistency apparent in their decisions across contested economic, criminal, and civil rights and liberties cases. In fact, their voting patterns in such cases reflect a greater amount of ideological complexity than is found in the US Supreme Court. This complexity is grounded in the fact that more than half of the justices scoring most extremely on the factors in chapter 5 take far more nuanced ideological positions than their US counterparts. For example, Justices Gonthier, LaForest, and L'Heureux-Dubé, who were found at the most liberal extreme of the economic ideological dimension, turned out to be the least liberal justices on the criminal factor. In contrast, Justices Major and Sopinka, who occupied the most conservative position on economic cases, turned out to be the most liberal justices on criminal decisions that scored strongly on the ideological factor. These findings indicate that, unlike most members of the US Supreme Court today, justices of the Lamer natural court did not simply adhere to rote liberal or conservative stances across multiple issue dimensions. Rather, their voting behaviour reflected a more nuanced, multi-dimensional ideological approach to the contested cases in these three distinct legal areas. These findings are critical for comparative scholars studying high courts around the world, because they suggest that a more sophisticated analysis of attitudinal decision making is warranted to assess whether other common law high courts follow the rote ideological patterns of the US Supreme Court or reflect a more nuanced style of decision making like that of the Supreme Court of Canada.

The Canadian voting patterns were also different from the patterns discovered in the United States in two additional, important ways. In the United States, the nature of disagreement in appellate courts is highly structured by the party of the appointing president and has only very tenuous relationships, if any, to a judge's gender. In Canada, the opposite appears to be true. The differences between the judicial cohorts appointed by Conservative and Liberal prime ministers were more modest than those dividing Republican and Democratic appointees in the US context. In contrast, gender differences among the justices on the Supreme Court of Canada were evident in all three issue areas. In both countries there is some evidence of greater support for equality and civil liberties among female justices, although the relationship is stronger in Canada. However, in stark contrast to US patterns, Canadian female justices were much more likely than their male colleagues to support the prosecution in criminal appeals. Collectively, these two caveats highlight important differences in attitudinal voting in these two high courts.

From a broader perspective, the use of three distinct research strategies has allowed us to demonstrate that the Supreme Court of Canada does exhibit patterns of attitudinal decision making but that the cleavages that divide Charter-era justices are more nuanced than those found on the US Supreme Court. It is particularly compelling that our multi-faceted research methods independently highlight political preferences or ideology as a prominent source of conflict on the Canadian court. When the statistical models derived from each of these three approaches independently point to a significant role for judicial attitudes, the conclusions on the role of attitudes in judicial decision making rest on much firmer grounds than in previous studies.

The impact of ideology is reinforced to some degree by our interviews with the justices themselves. Our research is the first to combine insights gained from in-depth interviews with a series of quantitative analyses of judicial decisions. Those interviews (in chapter 3) provided partial, though somewhat ambiguous support for the empirical analyses of the justices' actual voting presented in the subsequent chapters (5 through 7). All the justices admitted to understanding that there were differences in "judicial philosophy" and/or "ideas about justice" among them, and all appeared to understand that such differences were the basis for the splits on the court on at least some issues. The justices freely admitted that their political attitudes do have some impact on their decision making, but there is consensus among them that they do not try to shape the court's output to support their private political preferences. In both direct and indirect ways they indicated that law and precedent also matter and that unanimity is sometimes the result of agreement on what the law should mean. In addition, the justices are often willing to compromise their differences, not just to produce a "minimum winning coalition," but more frequently to achieve unanimity. One theme that was consistent in their comments was a belief that the attitudinal differences among them were more complex and multifaceted than would be suggested by a simple liberal/conservative ideological divide.

However, despite the strong evidence of attitudinal impact on decision making presented in chapters 5–7, one very strong caveat is in order. Most of the analyses were based primarily on those cases in which the justices disagreed with each other. Yet three-fourths of all the cases decided by the court in the Charter period have been unanimous decisions. Since a substantial majority of all cases do not generate dissent, one should not jump to the conclusion that what has been found to explain the divided decisions necessarily serves as an explanation of decision making in all cases. It seems clear, however, that when there is division on the court it appears to reflect attitudinal or ideological discord.

Even though a large majority of the decisions are unanimous, the influence of judicial attitudes found in divided cases is not incompatible with the notion that other factors, such as building consensus and writing good law, are prominent in the Canadian context. This notion aligns well with the statements of the justices, who recognize that attitudinal differences emerge from time to time but do not overwhelmingly drive decision making on the court. This interpretation is also consistent with the fact that the regression coefficients in our analyses are much smaller than those found in attitudinal studies of the US Supreme Court. Thus both the evidence from the judicial interviews and the empirical analyses of votes indicate that, while ideological factors are important, their effects are far more muted in the Canadian high court than in its US counterpart.

IMPLICATIONS FOR THE FUTURE: WHY ATTITUDINAL DECISION MAKING MATTERS

Our findings on judicial decision making have the most obvious relevance for current debates about potential changes in the judicial selection process in Canada. Despite the oft-repeated disclaimer that judicial ideology is not actively considered in judicial selection, the evidence throughout this book makes it clear that the actual voting behaviour of the justices is related to the political attitudes they bring to the court. When attitudinal influences are understood in combination with the now well-established premise that in the Charter period justices have become major policy makers, the implication is that the policy views of prospective justices may be worth examining. The link is straightforward. The policy preferences of justices affect their decisions, which in turn shape public policy in ways that have far-reaching consequences for society at large. Since justices on the Canadian court may serve until the age of 75, the choices that prime ministers make in the selection process are likely to influence public policy long after they have left office. Because of this lasting policy impact, some reformers believe that the current selection process is flawed and requires more transparent discussion about prospective nominees. Although the existence of attitudinal decision making guarantees that the selection of a justice is a political decision, the question remains whether the discussion of a nominee's values is open, deliberate, and democratically accountable, or whether it will take place behind the closed doors of elite decision makers within the Prime Minister's Office, the cabinet, and the Department of Justice.

As a way of reflecting on the significance of our attitudinal findings for the appointment process of high court justices, consider two likely scenarios – cursory participation of Parliament in the questioning of nominees, or a lengthy set of televised hearings that allow for public inquiry into the attitudes and values of a potential justice. The latter approach may be more transparent and democratic but may also devolve into an American style free-for-all among different ideological camps in the House of Commons. The former approach may be quieter and less messy politically but deprives elected officials of an active voice in the process and deprives the public of the opportunity to learn more about the future direction the law may take.

The relevance of political attitudes for the appointment process does not necessarily negate the significance of other important considerations that prime ministers must keep in mind when making appointments to the Supreme Court. It is clear that prime ministers pay attention to a host of judicial attributes that are not considered by US presidents. For example, it is difficult to conceive of a US president considering bilingual (English–French) capabilities for a Supreme Court appointment, while this is a crucial consideration in Canada. Similarly, legal mandate and political considerations keep prime ministers mindful of maintaining regional representation on the court. Other important factors in the Canadian appointment process include gender, legal specialization, and the past custom of ensuring that at least one justice comes directly from private law practice. Taken together, these factors demonstrate that the Canadian appointment process, unlike the US approach, is far more complex than simply looking at the ideological proclivities of a potential justice. Yet our findings demonstrate that ideology plays a significant role in structuring court rulings and merits greater attention in the scholarly literature and assessment of the appointment process.

From a broader theoretical perspective, our book does not contend that judicial attitudes and values are the only factors that influence decision making on high courts. We acknowledge, and the interviews with the justices themselves confirm, that other factors also play an important role in the voting behaviour of justices once they are elevated to the high court. Prior scholarship has shown that appellate justices are influenced by their colleagues on the bench (Murphy 1964; Epstein and Knight 1998; Ostberg et al. 2004; Songer 2008). Indeed, the norm of consensus and collegiality prevails much more frequently in Canada than in the United States, which is illustrated by the high rates of unanimity on the Canadian high court. This finding, along with the fact that particular justices in Canada have made strategic alterations in their voting and writing behaviour while on the high court (Wetstein and Ostberg 2005), indicates that small-group interaction plays a more dominant role in the Canadian setting than in the US Supreme Court. Thus we believe that while attitudes and values have a prominent impact on judicial behaviour in Canada, we acknowledge that other considerations play a major role as well.

In the end, our results suggest that Canadian scholars should pay attention to the patterns of attitudinal decision making that appear in the Canadian court in order to gain a better understanding of the ideological divisions that animate conflict within that body. Since the evidence from our book demonstrates that judicial disagreements are often sparked by complex ideological differences, it makes sense to assess such differences in an effort to obtain a richer and more holistic understanding of the development of law and politics in the Charter era. Our findings also imply that scholars studying other high courts should devote greater attention to the patterns of ideological conflict that are evident in those settings to assess whether the attitudinal model could be useful in understanding judicial decision making of other common law high courts.

APPENDIX A

Interviews with Justices by Donald R. Songer: Letter, Names and Dates, Protocol

Interviews with the justices of the Supreme Court of Canada were solicited by Donald Songer as part of a larger study of judicial decision making on the top courts of common law countries funded by a 2001 grant from the US National Science Foundation.[1] Interviews were first solicited with a letter that promised that no comments would be attributed to a specific justice, a procedure suggested by the chief executive legal officer of the court, who was consulted in advance of our first contact with the justices. There follow here pertinent parts of the letter, a list of the justices who accepted the invitation (with the dates of the interview), and the protocol, which focused on the process of decision making.

LETTER

Dear Justice ____

My name is Donald Songer. I am a Professor of Political Science at the University of South Carolina in the United States. I am conducting not-for-profit academic research sponsored by a grant from the United States National Science Foundation. This project is a collaborative effort with professors at Michigan State University, Louisiana State University, and the University of North Texas to study the highest appellate courts in ten nations. My primary responsibilities relate to the appellate courts in Canada, England, and the United States. Part of this research is to conduct interviews with judges on those Top Courts and with other elites involved in the selection of the justices and the disposition of cases in those courts. From these interviews, I hope to gain a better understanding of the process of decision making in the formally decided cases, the factors that influence the decisions of the judges, and the strategies used by judges on the Top Courts to maintain coherence within their judicial hierarchy.

I need only 45 minutes of your time and I guarantee complete confidentiality for your comments. I am interested in discovering general patterns of approaches to judging on courts in different countries, rather than the opinions of particular judges. Combined with statistical analyses of the data from the cases we are coding, these interviews will form the basis of an academic book that compares the roles of judges on the top courts in the judicial systems of the ten nations we are studying. No judge will be identified by name or by any characteristics (e.g., gender, home province) that will make it possible for readers to identify a particular judge. Moreover, no judge will be asked to reveal any information about any specific case on the docket or any previously decided case. Quotations will be attributed to a named judge only if that judge gives written permission to be quoted.

NAMES AND DATES

Ten of the justices serving on the court between 2002 and 2007 consented to interviews:

Michel Bastarache (interview 2 July 2002)
William Binnie (4 July 2002)
Louise Charron (14 May 2007)
Marie DesChamps (20 July 2004)
Morris Fish (19 July 2004)
Frank Iacobucci (2 July 2002)
Louis LeBel (3 July 2002)
John Major (2 July 2002)
Chief Justice Beverly McLachlin (2 July 2002)
Marshall Rothstein (7 May 2007)

All the interviews took place at the justices' offices in the Supreme Court building on Wellington Street in Ottawa, just west of the Parliament Building. Almost all the justices, once they started talking, were willing to go beyond the 45 minutes originally suggested for the interview, and the interviews in practice averaged about 75–80 minutes.

INTERVIEW PROTOCOL: DECISION MAKING

The interview protocol that served as the basis for the interviews is printed below. However, while the protocol formed a basic outline for the interview, I tried to keep the interview as informal and conversational as possible. Consequently, I frequently asked follow-up questions to gain clarification of initial comments and would skip some questions if the justice had already answered the question in effect in an earlier comment.

1 *I'm going to ask you to think about how you decided three cases.*
a) Criminal case; b) Charter of Rights case; c) Complex private litigant case. Each time, I'm going to describe a type of case that you see on the Supreme Court and I would like you to think about a particular case you remember that you've decided in the past year or so. I don't want you to tell me any specific details that would identify the case or the litigants; instead I'm going to ask you some general questions about how you go about deciding cases, but as you answer these general questions I want you to be thinking in your own mind about how you approached that particular case. OK?

1-1 *Now first, I'd like you to think about a* ***routine criminal case.*** Could you begin by telling me in your own words how you approached that case and how you made up your mind? What were the important influences on your decision? What was the process like? How many judges heard the case, how did the Court reach its decision and decide who would write the opinion?

1-2 *Next, I'd like you to think about an important* ***Charter of Rights case.***
Once again, could you begin by telling me in your own words how you approached that case and how you made up your mind? What were the important influences on your decision? What was the process like? How many judges heard the case, how did the Court reach its decision and decide who would write the opinion?

1-3 *For the third case, I'd like you to think about a complex piece of* ***civil litigation involving private litigants*** *(for example a contract dispute or a tort).*

Once again, could you begin by telling me in your own words how you approached that case and how you made up your mind? What were the important influences on your decision? What was the process like? How many judges heard the case, how did the Court reach its decision and decide who would write the opinion?

Now, if you can recall those same three cases, I'd like to ask you some specific questions about the way you and your panel reached its decision. The way I'd like to proceed is to ask about the specific factor, and then have you tell me separately how you would answer for each of the three cases, so if there were differences in the three cases, you can point that out.

2 First, **how soon** in the process were you pretty sure how you were going to decide? a) Criminal case; b) Charter of Rights case; c) Complex private litigant case
3 How would you characterize the **degree of discretion** you had in this case versus the extent to which you felt you were constrained to decide the case a specific way? Were you constrained just to decide the case in favor of one side with some freedom to decide how broad or narrow the ruling would be or the particular basis of the opinion, or did you feel that the basic thrust of the opinion was also constrained? (follow up – so would you say there was/was not a clear "right answer"?) a) Criminal case; b) Charter of Rights case; c) Complex private litigant case
4 How important were the ***legal arguments*** and discussion of precedent in the briefs? Did you go with the side that had the stronger brief? a) Criminal case; b) Charter of Rights case; c) Complex private litigant case
5 *What about* ***oral argument****? How much did it influence the way you decided?* a) Criminal case; b) Charter of Rights case; c) Complex private litigant case
6 *How much of an influence were the* ***views of your colleagues*** *on the Court? Did you discuss the case before oral arguments? What type of communication was there after conference? Did the views of colleagues not hearing the argument affect your thinking?* a) Criminal case; b) Charter of Rights case; c) Complex private litigant case

7 *Was there much* ***bargaining*** *over the opinion?* a) Criminal case; b) Charter of Rights case; c) Complex private litigant case

8 How constraining was existing precedent for the decision you reached in this case? Would the outcome have been different if a different size panel of court had heard the case? a) Criminal case; b) Charter of Rights case; c) Complex private litigant case

Now let me shift the focus and ask you some more general questions not tied to the three specific cases we've been discussing.

9 First, I'd like to ask you about the way the court sets its agenda, that is, the way it decides petitions for leave to appeal.
   - a) *Are there any important informal practices that modify in practice the formal rules?*
   - b) *What are the most important criteria for granting leave petitions? What are you looking for?*
   - c) *How much interaction is there between the 3 judge panels and the rest of the court? How autonomous are those panels?*
   - d) *What about the identity/reputations of either the attorneys seeking or opposing leave to appeal or the reputation of the judge below? (do you have a feel for the jurisprudence/leanings of most appeals court judges?)*

10 *What is the nature of the influence of interveners – especially those from interest groups?*

11 The final topic I'd like to explore is the problem of maintaining coherence in the Judicial Hierarchy.
   - a) *How effectively do you think the Supreme Court is in monitoring the courts below?*
   - b) *Are there particular courts (e.g., the court of appeals of a particular province) or particular judges below viewed as needing close scrutiny?(possibly mention 9th circuit in US)*
   - c) *Is there a problem with information asymmetry?*
   - d) *Do possible reactions from other political actors merit attention (e.g., the possibility of the use of the Notwithstanding Clause or legislative override of statutory interpretation or non-enforcement by the government)?*

e) Is there much communication, especially informal communication, among judges on different levels or between judges and the government?

f) Are the policy preferences of judges or courts below known? If so, is there a tendency to "give the benefit of the doubt" when a judge below makes a decision contrary to their normal political or jurisprudential leanings? (e.g., a staunch Charter supporter rules against the charter claimant in a case)

APPENDIX B

Factor Analysis of Cases

This table lists the cases – economic, criminal, and civil rights and liberties – that scored most positively and negatively in the factor analysis.

Case rank	Factor score	Name and citation
Economic cases		
Factor 1+		
1-1	+ 1.74	*R. v. Hydro-Québec*, [1997] 3 SCR 213 (environmental regulation, federalism)
1-2	+ 1.70	*Galaske v. O'Donnell*, [1994] 1 SCR 670 (tort, motor vehicle accident)
1-3	+ 1.67	*Winnipeg Child and Family Services (Northwest Area) v. G. (D.F.)*, [1997] 3 SCR 925 (tort, *parens patriae* doctrine)
1-4	+ 1.46	*Hodgkinson v. Simms*, [1994] 3 SCR 377 (tort, contracts)
1-5	+ 1.43	*Royal Oak Mines Inc. v. Canada (Labour Relations Board)*, [1996] 1 SCR 369 (labour dispute, jurisdiction)
Factor 1–		
1-42	– 2.06	*RJR-MacDonald Inc. v. Canada (Attorney General)*, [1995] 3 SCR 199 (regulation of commercial advertising)
1-41	– 1.81	*Royal Bank of Canada v. Sparrow Electric Corp.*, [1997] 1 SCR 411 (bankruptcy, federal priority)
1-40	– 1.32	*Finlay v. Canada (Minister of Finance)*, [1993] 1 SCR 1080 (disability benefits)
1-39	– 1.31	*Cunningham v. Wheeler*, [1994] 1 SCR 359 (tort, damages)
1-38	– 1.15	*Béliveau St-Jacques v. FEESP*, [1996] 2 SCR 345 (workers compensation, damages, sexual harassment)
Factor 2+		
2-1	+ 1.60	*Hy & Zel's Inc. v. Ontario (Attorney General)*, [1993] 3 SCR 675 (business regulation, Sunday closing laws, standing)

Case rank	Factor score	Name and citation
2-2	+ 1.60	*Symes v. Canada*, [1993] 4 SCR 695 (tax deductions, child care expenses)
2-3	+ 1.48	*Slattery (Trustee of) v. Slattery*, [1993] 3 SCR 430 (bankruptcy, tax)
2-4	+ 1.44	*Wallace v. United Grain Growers Ltd.*, [1997] 3 SCR 701 (tort, wrongful dismissal, bankruptcy)
2-5	+ 1.28	*Canadian Broadcasting Corp. v. Canada (Labour Relations Board)*, [1995] 1 SCR 157 (labour, scope of labour board's jurisdiction)
Factor 2–		
2-42	– 1.83	*Hickman Motors Ltd. v. Canada*, [1997] 2 SCR 336 (tax deduction)
2-41	– 1.48	*Zeitel v. Ellscheid*, [1994] 2 SCR 142 (tax assessment, property dispute)
2-40	– 1.43	*Friesen v. Canada*, [1995] 3 SCR 103 (tax deduction)
2-39	– 1.36	same as 1-41
2-38	– 1.34	*Gold v. Rosenberg*, [1997] 3 SCR 767 (tort, breach of trust, estates)
Criminal cases		
Factor 1+		
1-1	+ 1.32	*R. v. R. (D.)*, [1996] 2 SCR 291 (hearsay evidence, sexual assault)
1-2	+ 1.32	*Dagenais v. Canadian Broadcasting Corp.*, [1994] 3 SCR 835 (publication ban in criminal trial, jurisdiction)
1-3	+ 1.30	*R v. Osolin*, [1993] 4 SCR 595 (presumption of innocence)
1-4	+ 1.30	*R. v. P. (M.B.)*, [1994] 1 SCR 555 (trial procedure, sexual assault)
1-5	+ 1.30	*R. v. Heywood*, [1994] 3 SCR 761 (sexual offender, loitering, Charter section 7)
1-6	+ 1.30	*R. v. McIntosh*, [1995] 1 SCR 686 (self defence, jury instructions, murder)
1-7	+ 1.30	*R. v. St. Pierre*, [1995] 1 SCR 791 (blood alcohol, statutory interpretation)
1-8	+ 1.30	*R. v. Pontes*, [1995] 3 SCR 44 (strict liability offence, motor vehicle act, Charter section 7)
1-9	+1.30	*R. v. Carosella*, [1997] 1 SCR 80 (right to full defence, gross indecency, Charter section 7)
1-10	+ 1.30	*R. v. McDonnell*, [1997] 1 SCR 948 (sentencing, sexual assault)
Factor 1–		
1-75	– 1.95	*R. v. MacGillivray*, [1995] 1 SCR 890 (dangerous operation of vessel)
1-74	– 1.93	*R. v. S. (R.D.)*, [1997] 3 SCR 484 (judicial apprehension of bias)

Case rank	Factor score	Name and citation
1-73	– 1.93	*R. v. O'Connor*, [1995] 4 SCR 411 (discovery of evidence, sexual assault)
1-72	– 1.86	*R. v. Jones*, [1994] 2 SCR 229 (dangerous sex offender proceedings, Charter sections 7, 10b)
1-71	– 1.72	*R. v. E. (A.W.)*, [1993] 3 SCR 155 (sexual offence, jury instructions)
Factor 2+		
2-1	+ 1.41	*R. v. Feeney*, [1997] 2 SCR 13 (unlawful search and seizure, right to counsel, exclusion of evidence)
2-2	+ 1.40	*R. v. Felawka*, [1993] 4 SCR 199 (concealed weapon, statutory interpretation)
2-3	+ 1.37	*R. v. Noble*, [1997] 1 SCR 874 (evidence, Charter sections 7, 11)
2-4	+ 1.20	same as 1-75
2-5	+ 1.16	*R. v. Dawson*, [1996] 3 SCR 783 (child abduction, statutory interpretation)
Factor 2–		
2-75	– 3.18	same as 1-1
2-74	– 2.95	*R. v. Collins*, [1995] 2 SCR 1104 (speedy trial, Charter section 11b)
2-73	– 2.19	*R. v. Swietlinski*, [1994] 3 SCR 481 (parole eligibility, evidence, victim impact statements)
2-72	– 2.15	*R. v. Power*, [1994] 1 SCR 601 (exclusion of evidence, appellate review)
2-71	– 1.91	*R. v. Belnavis*, [1997] 3 SCR 341 (search and seizure, exclusion of evidence)
Civil rights and liberties cases		
Factor 1+		
1-1	+ 1.45	*Egan v. Canada*, [1995] 2 SCR 513 (gay discrimination, old age benefits)
1-2	+.977	*Opetchesaht Indian Band v. Canada*, [1997] 2 SCR 119 (aboriginal land use)
1-3	+.962	*Rodriguez v. British Columbia (Attorney General)*, [1993] 3 SCR 519 (assisted suicide for terminally ill, equality)
1-4	+.759	*Hy and Zel's Inc. v. Ontario (Attorney General)*, [1993] 3 SCR 675 (Sunday closing laws, religion)
1-5	+ .759	*Symes v. Canada*, [1993] 4 SCR 695 (sex discrimination, childcare tax deductions)
1-6	+ .759	*Gould v. Yukon Order of Pioneers*, [1996] 1 SCR 571 (sex discrimination, private fraternal club)
1-7	+ .759	*R. v. Nikal*, [1996] 1 SCR 1013 (aboriginal fishing rights, licensing)
1-8	+ .759	*R. v. Van der Peet*, [1996] 2 SCR 507 (aboriginal fishing rights, licensing)
1-9	+ .759	*R. v. N.T.C. Smokehouse Ltd.*, [1996] 2 SCR 672 (aboriginal fishing rights, licensing)

Case rank	*Factor score*	*Name and citation*
1-10	+ .759	*Adler v. Ontario*, [1996] 3 SCR 609 (funding for religious schools)
Factor 1–		
1-26	– 2.48	*Miron v. Trudel*, [1995] 2 SCR 418 (common law spouses, insurance benefits)
1-25	– 2.25	*Dagg v. Canada (Minister of Finance)*, [1997] 2 SCR 403 (access to information)
1-24	– 1.48	*Dagenais v. Canadian Broadcasting Corp.*, [1994] 3 SCR 835 (free press, media ban)
1-23	– 1.15	*RJR-MacDonald Inc. v. Canada (Attorney General)*, [1995] 3 SCR 199 (free expression, commercial advertising)
1-22	– .763	*University of British Columbia v. Berg*, [1993] 2 SCR 353 (discrimination in public facilities)
Factor 2+		
2-1	+.911	same as 1-25
2-2	+.761	same as 1-4
2-3	+.761	same as 1-5
2-4	+.761	same as 1-6
2-5	+.761	same as 1-7
2-6	+.761	same as 1-8
2-7	+.761	same as 1-9
2-8	+.761	same as 1-10
Factor 2–		
2-26	–.3.02	*Weber v. Ontario Hydro*, [1995] 2 SCR 929 (Supreme Court's jurisdiction, labour law)
2-25	-1.94	*Haig v. Canada*, [1993] 2 SCR 995 (powers of chief electoral officer, election law)
2-24	-1.66	*Canadian Pacific Ltd. v. Matsqui Indian Band*, [1995] 1 SCR 3 (tribunal jurisdiction, administrative law)
2-23	-1.28	*P. (D.) v. S. (C.)*, [1993] 4 SCR 141 (trial judge's divorce decree, family law)
2-22	–.780	same as 1-1

Notes

CHAPTER ONE

1 One scholar makes a similar argument for the influence of judges' political preferences in the top court (Law Lords) in Britain (Robertson 1998).

CHAPTER THREE

1 See also Maltzman and Wahlbeck 1996a; 1996b; Wahlbeck et al. 1998; Spriggs et al. 1999.
2 In the Supreme Courts in both the United States and Canada, justices now have close to complete discretion as to which cases to hear. In the US court, all nine justices vote on each petition, and four votes guarantees a hearing (i.e., the "petition for certiorari" – cert for short – will be granted). In Canada, petitions for "leave to appeal" determine acceptance of a case for the court's docket. While all judges may informally influence the decision, a three-justice panel makes the decision (see chapter 4).
3 While a strategic understanding of judicial behaviour might suggest that external political forces might also constrain judges from following precedent or other legally relevant considerations, virtually all studies of US courts study constraint simply on judges' expression of their political preferences.
4 In one instance that Widner reports, the government of Uganda executed the chief justice of the supreme court for the court's failure to follow its orders.
5 In both the United States and Canada, subsequent legislation can overturn decisions based on statutory construction, but such overrides are uncommon.
6 *United States v. Butler*, 297 US 1 (1936), at 62.

CHAPTER FOUR

1 Details of the interviews appear below in Appendix A. Since the justices were promised anonymity as a condition of the interviews, two conventions are adopted in reporting the results: justices are referred to as simply "Justice A," "Justice B," and so on, and the masculine pronoun is used for all justices (even though both male and female justices were interviewed) to prevent their identification.

2 Interviews with Donald Songer in Vancouver, 14–17 June 2005. Interviews were conducted with the understanding that comments would not be attributed to specific justices by name.

3 A new section 691(2) of the *Criminal Code* now requires a dissent on a question of law in the Court of Appeal for an automatic right of appeal to the Supreme Court, even when the Court of Appeal has reversed an acquittal at trial.

4 Similarly, the chances that the US Supreme Court will hear a request for review are substantially increased if the circuits split in their interpretation of some aspect of law.

5 Three other justices also spontaneously used the phrase "fact driven" when describing the types of cases the court was not interested in taking. Such cases by their nature tend to be of significance only for the litigants, because whichever way the court would decide such a case, the law would remain the same for future litigants.

6 Before 1999, they were sent to the Registrar's Legal Service.

7 Leave applications contain records from the courts below, citations and/or copies of relevant precedent and other authorities, and a factum (similar to an appellate brief in the United States) that provides a written argument by counsel. Factums are limited to twenty pages, but the whole package supporting the petition is usually much larger (see Greene et al. 1998).

8 In the United States, all justices formally vote on all cert petitions brought to conference, and the decision rule is that cert will be granted, placing the case on the court's docket, if at least four of the nine justices vote to hear the case.

9 On rare occasions, a decision will be made by a panel of six or eight justices, but typically only when one judge assigned to hear a case becomes unavailable through illness or death. If a panel with an even number of justices is evenly split, the appeal fails and the decision of the lower court stands.

10 Conversely, at least in the Lamer court, if a case involved solely an interpretation of common law and was to be decided by less than the whole

court, the chief justice would typically leave two of the Quebec justices off the panel (Greene et al. 1998, 116).

11 The percentage of cases with dissent but a margin of victory greater than one is not presented in the table but can easily be computed by subtracting the sum of the two listed votes (i.e., unanimous and minimum winning) from 100 per cent.

12 Interveners play a role that is essentially the same as that of *amici curiae* in the United States. Interveners are groups, government officials, or individuals who are not formally litigants in the case but have a concern about the resolution of the case and/or the legal rule that may emerge from the court's decision. In Canada, interveners may participate by submitting a factum for the court's consideration and/or by participating in oral argument with the approval of the court.

13 And the authors' observations of a dozen or so hearings confirm that when the justices speak during oral argument they usually ask a question.

14 There were interveners in only 49 per cent of the Charter cases in 1996.

15 What is more frequently referred to as the "opinion of the court" in the United States.

16 But even Justice E characterized the chief justice's expressions as "gentle" pressure.

17 Example provided by Justice G.

CHAPTER FIVE

1 Throughout this chapter, we identify this period as the "Lamer natural court," which began with the arrival of Justice Major in November 1992 and closed with the retirement of Justice LaForest in September 1997, a period in which there were no changes in the membership.

2 Since we focused on cases that had written reasons for judgment, we reduced the N in the criminal area from 92 to 75 because 17 involved oral judgments. We did not reduce the N vis-à-vis economic and civil rights and liberties cases, because they did not have any non-unanimous oral judgments during the period studied.

3 The inclusion of the zero score for non-participation is an intuitively conservative solution to the confounding problem of missing data. Other options were available, such as inserting a mean "liberalism" score for a particular justice or a score of a neighbouring justice in an ideological space (see McIver 1976), but we rejected these ideas because they superimpose a liberal–conservative dimension on the data. Our application of the factor-analytic approach departs somewhat from prior studies that

used this technique because of data constraints imposed by two sources: 1) the non-participation of judges in cases and 2) the low number of cases (N) in the three areas of law studied. Therefore we limited our analysis to the top two factors in each area of law for consistency purposes and because we wanted to identify the two most salient dimensions that divided the justices in these legal fields. For each area of law, the two principal factors accounted for roughly 50 per cent of the voting variance in the court (46, 50, and 47 per cent in economic, criminal, and civil rights cases, respectively). Moreover, we limited our discussion to analysing the five most positively and negatively scoring cases on each of the factors because we wanted to focus our reading on the subset of decisions that loaded most prominently on each dimension. Since there were only 26 non-unanimous cases in civil liberties, for purposes of consistency we limited our analysis to the five cases that featured the largest positive and negative scores on the factors across all three areas of law. When we examined the cases scoring below the "top five" in the criminal and economic areas, which featured larger Ns, the underlying dimension of conflict that was identified remained the same. This decision to focus in on the top five or ten scoring cases departs from prior studies that typically examined cases with factor scores above +1 and below –1. While the factor scores for four of the six factors met this traditional rule of thumb, the two factors in civil rights and liberties did not, because of the particularly few cases in this area. None the less the top-scoring cases in civil rights and liberties highlighted obvious patterns of disagreement that we felt comfortable identifying.

4 Since we are not using this technique for the statistical analysis of interval-level data, the traditional rules of thumb used to select factors (Eigen values above 1.0) are not technically relevant (see Kim and Mueller 1978a; 1978b).

5 Only ten of the cases in our data set fell into two different legal areas, with all ten featuring civil rights and liberties. Eight of these cases also addressed economic issues, while two featured criminal concerns. None of the cases spanned all three areas of law.

6 The varimax rotation produced three factors with Eigen values above 1.0, but we forced a two-factor solution because of the low N and our desire to highlight the two principal dimensions of conflict in each area of law. The third factor would have added only about 14 per cent more explained variance and would have made detection of the factors much more difficult, given the small number of cases. The votes included in our analysis are derived from Chief Justice Lamer and Justices LaForest, L'Heureux-

Dubé, Sopinka, Gonthier, Cory, McLachlin, Iacobucci, and Major. While the first factor accounted for just over half of the explained variance (55 per cent, Eigen value = 2.28), the second accounted for the balance (Eigen value = 1.87).

7 Many readers might perceive the court's ruling as one that advances a woman's reproductive rights over the state interests in protecting the fetus. However, the court classified this as a tort law case because it involved an analysis of the scope of the duty-of-care doctrine as it applied to an unborn child.

8 The factor analysis produced three factors with Eigen values in excess of one, but we chose to identify a two-factor solution because the third factor's Eigen value barely exceeded 1.0 and explained only 11 per cent more of the variance. Additionally, analysis of the scree plot of Eigen values suggested that a two-factor solution was more appropriate, because the slope of the plot diminished considerably after the second factor's Eigen value. The first factor accounted for 66 per cent of the explained variance (Eigen value = 3.01), while the second explained the remaining variance (Eigen value = 1.53).

9 Although we chose to review the five cases scoring most positively and negatively on a given factor, on the first criminal factor there were eight cases that tied for third in the ranking (+1.30), and thus we analysed a total of 10 cases on the positive side of this factor. The eight cases featuring "tied scores" essentially featured the same voting blocs opposed to each other.

10 A total of 10 cases was discussed on the positive side of factor 1 because of tie scores on the third through tenth most extremely scoring disputes.

11 We are analysing a justice's liberalism score in only non-unanimous cases or in cases that have triggered attitudinal conflict on the court in each of the three areas of law. An analysis of the larger set of unanimous and non-unanimous cases would generate different loadings and results.

CHAPTER SIX

1 The description of this measure and the scoring of the justices are drawn largely from research by Ostberg and Wetstein (2007a, chap. 3) and were first presented in Ostberg et al. 2004. Data collection for the newspaper ideology measures was supported by the Canadian Embassy Faculty Research Award Program in 2004, Media Analysis of Supreme Court Nominations, C.L. Ostberg, principal investigator. We are grateful for permission to revise and reprint material from our earlier work; see C.L.

Ostberg and Matthew E. Wetstein, *Attitudinal Decision Making in the Supreme Court of Canada* (Vancouver: University of British Columbia Press, 2007). Scores were not presented for the *National Post*, because although it has provided extensive coverage of the Supreme Court and its justices in recent years, it was not published at the time of the appointment of many of the justices included in our analyses.

2 The number of justices analysed for each correlation entry varies, depending on the number of justices with full information across the two measures being correlated. For example, since 22 have scores on both the *Globe and Mail* and the *Ottawa Citizen* measures, the N for that correlation is 22 (see Table 8).

3 Weighting the ideology data makes sense, because Canadian justices often sit in panels of fewer than nine justices and because mandatory retirement at age 75 or early retirement can create large disparities in the number of cases that a particular justice participates in while sitting on the court. An example of the importance of this weighting scheme: Justice Stevenson served just two years, and Justice L'Heureux-Dubé, 15. Obviously, her career record of voting should carry more weight in the data analysis.

4 By referring to statistical significance, we mean that the relationship is so strong that it almost certainly did not occur by chance.

5 The chance that this conclusion is wrong for the *Ottawa Citizen*'s measure is less than one out of 100; we are 99 per cent sure the results are not due to some random occurrence.

CHAPTER SEVEN

1 Tate and Sittiwong also suggest that prior judicial experience and association with political groups is related to judicial voting. However, secondary analysis indicates too little variation in the measure of political associations to make it a useful explanatory factor, and preliminary analysis suggests that whatever power a measure of prior judicial experience had for the earlier period, it is no longer a significant predictor of voting behaviour. Consequently, these two variables are not included in the analyses reported in this chapter.

2 In the history of their courts, only one woman has served as a justice in the House of Lords in Britain. Four women have served on the High Court of Australia, but only one before 2005. Only four have served on the US Supreme Court, with two of those joining since 2009.

CHAPTER EIGHT

1 See the comments of Justice C in chapter 3 above about compromise leading to '*fudgier*' opinions.
2 In addition, of course, it is simply easier on average for five people to reach agreement than for nine people to all agree.
3 "Tag lines" – roughly analogous to West's categories of "topics" and "key numbers" at the top of decisions of US appellate courts – are produced by the professional staff of the Supreme Court of Canada to provide a brief overview of the primary legal issues addressed in each opinion.
4 Carl Baar (1999), though not directly testing reasons for unanimous decisions, does find congruence between trial and appellate courts in Canada, and he does so by examining both unanimous and divided decisions. He finds that in criminal cases, trial and appellate courts – including the Supreme Court of Canada – dispose of cases similarly, with a "drop-off" of cases at each court level resulting in a disproportionate number of cases decided in favour of the crown.
5 That is, we used the ideological range on the panel that made each decision. Therefore, for any given year or natural court, the ideological range would vary considerably, depending on the combination of justices in a case.

APPENDIX A

1 "Collaborative Research: Fitting More Pieces into the Puzzle of Judicial Behavior: A Multi-Country Database and Program of Research," SES-9975323.

Bibliography

Aldrich, John H., and Forrest D. Nelson. 1984. *Linear Probability, Logit, and Probit Models*. Beverly Hills, CA: Sage.

Allen, David W., and Diane E. Wall. 1987. "The Behavior of Women State Supreme Court Justices: Are They Tokens or Outsiders?" *Justice System Journal* 12 (2): 232–45.

Atkins, Burton M. 1991. "Party Capability Theory as an Explanation for Intervention Behavior in the English Court of Appeal." *American Journal of Political Science* 35 (Nov.): 881–903.

Baar, Carl. 1988. "The Courts in Canada." In Jerold L. Waltman and Kenneth M. Holland, eds., *The Political Role of Law Courts in Modern Democracies*. New York: St Martin's Press. 53–82.

– 1991. "Judicial Activism in Canada." In Kenneth M. Holland, ed., *Judicial Activism in Comparative Perspective*. New York: St Martin's Press. 53–69.

– 1999. "Courts as State Actors: Comparing Appeal and Trial Courts." In Joseph F. Fletcher, ed., *Ideas in Action: Essays on Politics and Law in Honour of Peter Russell*. Toronto: University of Toronto Press. 188–204.

Baum, Lawrence. 1980. "Response of Federal District Judges to Court of Appeals Policies: An Exploration." *Western Political Quarterly* 33 (June): 217–24.

– 1997. *The Puzzle of Judicial Behavior*. Ann Arbor: University of Michigan Press.

Becker, Theodore L. 1970. *Comparative Judicial Politics: The Political Functionings of Courts*. Chicago: Rand McNally & Co.

Brace, Paul, and Melinda Gann Hall. 1993. "Integrated Models of Judicial Dissent." *Journal of Politics* 55 (Nov.): 914–35.

– 1995. "Studying Courts Comparatively: The View from the American States." *Political Research Quarterly* 48 (March): 5–29.

– 1997. "The Interplay of Preferences, Case Facts, Context, and Rules in the Politics of Judicial Choice." *Journal of Politics* 59 (Nov.): 1206–31.

– Melinda Gann Hall and Laura Langer. 1998. "Formal Models of Judicial Decisionmaking in Comparative Perspective." Presented at the Annual Meeting of the American Political Science Association, Boston.

Brenner, Saul, and Marc Stier. 1996. "Retesting Segal and Spaeth's Stare Decisis Model." *American Journal of Political Science* 40 (Nov.): 1036–48.

Brodie, Ian. 2002. *Friends of the Court: The Privileging of Interest Group Litigants in Canada*. Albany: State University of New York Press.

Brudney, James J., Sara Schiavoni, and Deborah J. Merritt. 1999. "Judicial Hostility toward Labor Unions? Applying the Social Background Model to a Celebrated Concern." *Ohio State Law Journal* 60 (5): 1675–1771.

Bushnell, Ian. 1992. *The Captive Court: A Study of the Supreme Court of Canada*. Montreal and Kingston: McGill-Queen's University Press.

Bushnell, S.I. 1982. "Leave to Appeal Applications to the Supreme Court of Canada: A Matter of Public Importance." *Supreme Court Law Review* 3: 479–558.

Bzdera, Andre. 1993. "Comparative Analysis of Federal High Courts: A Political Theory of Judicial Review." *Canadian Journal of Political Science* 26 (March): 3–29.

Cairns, Alan C. 1998. *Constitution, Government and Society in Canada*. Toronto: McClelland & Stewart.

Campbell, Angus, Phillip E. Converse, Warren E. Miller, and Donald E. Stokes. 1960. *The American Voter*. Chicago: University of Chicago Press.

Canada Supreme Court Reports. Ottawa: Registrar of the Supreme Court of Canada.

Canadian Who's Who, The. Toronto: University of Toronto Press.

Carter, Lief H. 1998. *Reason in Law*. 5th ed. New York: Longman.

Coffin, Frank M. 1980. *The Ways of a Judge: Reflections from the Federal Appellate Bench*. Boston: Houghton Mifflin.

– 1994. *On Appeal: Courts, Lawyering, and Judging*. New York: W.W. Norton.

Cook, Beverly. 1981. "Will Women Judges Make a Difference in Women's Legal Rights? A Prediction from Attitudes and Simulated Behavior." In Margherita Rendel and Georgina Ashworth, eds., *Women, Power, and Political Systems*. New York: St Martin's Press. 216–39.

Danelski, David J. 1969. "The Supreme Court of Japan: An Exploratory Study." In Glendon Schubert and David J. Danelski, eds., *Comparative Judicial Behavior: Cross-cultural Studies of Political Decision-Making in the East and West*. New York: Oxford University Press. 121–56.

Davis, Sue. 1993. "The Voice of Sandra Day O'Connor." *Judicature* 77 (Nov.–Dec.): 134–9.

Dion, Stéphane. 1992. "Explaining Quebec Nationalism." In R. Kent Weaver, ed., *The Collapse of Canada?* Washington, DC: Brookings Institution Press. 13–23.

Dodek, Adam. 2001. Interview (former law clerk, Supreme Court of Canada). Toronto, July.

Ducat, Craig R., and Robert L. Dudley. 1987. "Dimensions Underlying Economic Policymaking in the Early and Later Burger Courts." *Journal of Politics* 49 (May): 521–39.

Dudley, Robert L., and Craig R. Ducat. 1986. "The Burger Court and Economic Liberalism." *Western Political Quarterly* 39 (June): 236–49.

Dworkin, Ronald. 1988. *Law's Empire*. Cambridge: Belknap Press.

Dyck, Perry Rand. 2000. *Canadian Politics: Critical Approaches*. Scarborough, ON: Nelson Thomson Learning.

Epp, Charles R. 1996. "Do Bills of Rights Matter? The Canadian Charter of Rights and Freedoms." *American Political Science Review* 90 (Dec.): 765–79.

– 1998. *The Rights Revolution: Lawyers, Activists, and Supreme Courts in Comparative Perspective*. Chicago: University of Chicago Press.

Epstein, Lee, and Jack Knight. 1998. *The Choices Justices Make*. Washington, DC: Congressional Quarterly Press.

– 2000. "Toward a Strategic Revolution in Judicial Politics: A Look Back, a Look Ahead." *Political Research Quarterly* 53 (Sept.): 625–61.

– and Carol Mershon. 1996. "Measuring Political Preferences." *American Journal of Political Science* 40 (Feb.): 261–94.

Ferejohn, John, and Charles Shipan. 1990. "Congressional Influence on Bureaucracy." *Journal of Law, Economics, and Organization* 6: 1–20.

Flango, Victor F., and Theodore L. Becker. 1967. "Judicial Decision-Making in the Philippines and in Hawaii." Unpublished paper, Department of Political Science, University of Hawaii. Reported in Theodore l. Becker, ed., *Comparative Judicial Politics: The Political Functioning of Courts*. Chicago: Rand McNally and Company, 1970.

Flango, Victor E., and Craig R. Ducat. 1977. "Toward an Integration of Public Law and Judicial Behavior." *Journal of Politics* 39 (Feb.): 41–72.

Flemming, Roy B. 2000. "Processing Appeals for Judicial Review: The Institutions of Agenda Setting in the Supreme Courts of Canada and the United States." In Martin Westmacott and Hugh Mellon, eds., *Political Dispute and Judicial Review: Assessing the Work of the Supreme Court of Canada*, ed. Scarborough, ON: Nelson-Thompson Learning.

– 2004. *Tournament of Appeals: Granting Judicial Review in Canada*. Vancouver: University of British Columbia Press.

– and Glen S. Krutz. 2002. "Repeat Litigators and Agenda Setting on the Supreme Court of Canada." *Canadian Journal of Political Science* 35 (4): 811–33.

Fletcher, Joseph F. 1999. *Ideas in Action: Essays on Politics and Law in Honour of Peter Russell*. Toronto: University of Toronto Press.

Foglesong, Todd. 2001. "The Dynamics of Judicial (In)dependence in Russia." In Peter Russell and David O'Brien, eds., *Judicial Independence in the Age of Democracy: Critical Perspectives from Around the World*. Charlottesville: University Press of Virginia. 62–88.

Forsyth, C.F. 1985. *In Danger for Their Talents: A Study of the Appellate Division of the Supreme Court of South Africa from 1950 to 1980*. Cape Town: Juta & Co., Ltd.

Fouts, Donald E. 1969. "Policy Making in the Supreme Court of Canada, 1950–1960." In Glendon Schubert and David J. Danelski, eds., *Comparative Judicial Behavior: Cross-cultural Studies of Political Decision-Making in the East and West*. New York: Oxford University Press. 257–92.

Gadbois, George H., Jr. 1969. "Selection, Background Characteristics, and Voting Behavior of Indian Supreme Court Judges." In Glendon Schubert and David J. Danelski, eds., *Comparative Judicial Behavior: Cross-cultural Studies of Political Decision-Making in the East and West*. New York: Oxford University Press.

Galligan, Brian. 1987. *Politics of the High Court*. St Lucia: University of Queensland Press.

George, Tracey E., and Lee Epstein. 1992. "On the Nature of Supreme Court Decision Making." *American Political Science Review* 86 (June): 323–37.

Globe and Mail. 2005. Toronto.

Goldman, Sheldon. 1966. "Voting Behavior on the United States Courts of Appeals, 1961–1964." *American Political Science Review* 60 (June): 374–83.

– 1975. "Voting Behavior on the United States Courts of Appeals Revisited." *American Political Science Review* 69 (June): 491–506.

Greene, Ian, Carl Baar, Peter McCormick, George Szablowski, and Martin Thomas. 1998. *Final Appeal: Decision-Making in Canadian Courts of Appeal*. Toronto: James Lorimer & Co., Ltd.

Gruhl, John. 1980. "The Supreme Court's Impact on the Law of Libel: Compliance by Lower Federal Courts." *Western Political Quarterly* 33 (Dec.): 502–19.

Guarnieri, Carlo. 2001. "Judicial Independence in Latin Countries of Western Europe." In Peter Russell and David O'Brien, eds., *Judicial Independence in the Age of Democracy: Critical Perspectives from Around the World*. Charlottesville: University Press of Virginia. 111–30.

Hagle, Timothy M., and Harold J. Spaeth. 1992. "The Emergence of a New Ideology: The Business Decisions of the Burger Court." *Journal of Politics* 54 (Feb.): 120–34.

– 1993. "Ideological Patterns in the Justices' Voting in the Burger Court's Business Cases." *Journal of Politics* 55 (May): 492–505.

Hall, Melinda Gann. 1987. "Constituent Influence in State Supreme Courts: Conceptual Notes and a Case Study." *Journal of Politics* 49 (Nov.): 1117–24.

– and Paul Brace. 1992. "Toward an Integrated Model of Judicial Voting Behavior." *American Politics Quarterly* 20 (April): 147–68.

– 1994. "The Vicissitudes of Death by Decree: Forces Influencing Capital Punishment Decisionmaking in State Supreme Courts." *Social Science Quarterly* 75 (March): 136–51.

Hart, H.L.A. 1961. *The Concept of Law*. Oxford: Clarendon Press.

Hausegger, Lori. 2000. "Panel Selection in the Canadian Supreme Court: Neutral Assignments or the Exercise of Power." Presented at the annual meeting of the Southern Political Science Association, Atlanta.

– and Stacia Haynie. 2003. "Panel Assignments in Appellate Courts: Influences on Judicial Decision Making in South Africa and Canada." *Law and Society Review* 37: 635–57.

– Matthew Hennigar, and Troy Riddell. 2009. *Canadian Courts: Law, Politics, and Process*. Don Mills, ON: Oxford University Press.

Haynie, Stacia L. 2003. *Judging in Black and White: Decision Making in the South African Appellate Division, 1950–1990*. New York: Peter Lang Publishing, Inc.

Heard, Andrew D. 1991. "The Charter in the Supreme Court of Canada: The Importance of Which Judges Hear an Appeal." *Canadian Journal of Political Science* 24 (June): 289–307.

Helmke, Gretchen. 2002. "The Logic of Strategic Defection: Court–Executive Relations in Argentina under Dictatorship and Democracy." *American Political Science Review* 96 (June): 291–303.

– 2005. *Courts under Constraints: Judges, Generals, and Presidents in Argentina*. Cambridge: Cambridge University Press.

Hennigar, Matthew. 2004. "The Canadian Government's Litigation Strategy in Sexual Orientation Cases." Presented at the annual meeting of the Canadian Political Science Association, Winnipeg, 4 June.

Hiebert, Janet L. 2001. "Wrestling with Rights: Judges, Parliament and the Making of Social Policy." In Paul Howe and Peter H. Russell, eds., *Judicial Power and Canadian Democracy*. Montreal and Kingston: McGill-Queen's University Press.

– 2002. *Charter Conflicts: What Is Parliament's Role?* Montreal and Kingston: McGill-Queen's University Press.

Hirschl, Ran. 2004. *Towards Juristocracy: The Origins and Consequences of the New Constitutionalism*. Cambridge, MA: Harvard University Press.

– 2010. *Constitutional Theocracy*. Cambridge, MA: Harvard University Press.

Hogg, Peter W., and Allison A. Bushell. 1997. "The Charter Dialogue between Courts and Legislatures." *Osgoode Hall Law Journal* 35: 75–124.

Horowitz, Donald L. 1977. *The Courts and Social Policy*. Washington, DC: Brookings Institution Press.

Howard, A.E. Dick. 2001. "Judicial Independence in Post-Communist Central and Eastern Europe." In Peter Russell and David O'Brien, eds., *Judicial Independence in the Age of Democracy: Critical Perspectives from Around the World*. Charlottesville: University Press of Virginia. 89–110.

Howard, J. Woodford, Jr. 1981. *Courts of Appeals in the Federal Judicial System*. Princeton, NJ: Princeton University Press.

Humphries, Martha Anne, and Donald R. Songer. 1999. "Law and Politics in Judicial Oversight of Federal Administrative Agencies." *Journal of Politics* 61 (Feb.): 207–20.

Iacobucci, Frank. 2002. Remarks delivered to a conference commemorating the 20th anniversary of the Charter of Rights and Freedoms, Association of Canadian Studies, Ottawa, March.

Jackson, Donald W., and C. Neal Tate. 1992. *Comparative Judicial Review and Public Policy*. Westport, CT: Greenwood Press.

Johansen, David, and Philip Rosen. 2008. "The Notwithstanding Clause of the Charter." Library of Parliament, Parliamentary Research Branch, Law and Government Division, Ottawa.

– 1997. "The Notwithstanding Clause of the Charter." Library of Parliament, Parliamentary Research Branch, Law and Government Division, Ottawa.

Johnson, Susan W., Ronald Stidham, Kenneth Manning, and Robert Carp. 2008. "The Gender Influence on U.S. District Court Decisions: Updating the Traditional Judge Attribute Model." *Journal of Women, Politics and Policy* 29: 497–526.

Kawashima, Takeyoshi. 1969. "Individualism in Decision-Making in the Supreme Court of Japan." In Glendon Schubert and David J. Danelski, eds., *Comparative Judicial Behavior: Cross-cultural Studies of Political Decision-Making in the East and West*. New York: Oxford University Press. 103–20.

Kelly, James. B. 2005. *Governing with the Charter: Legislative and Judicial Activism and Framers' Intent*. Vancouver: University of British Columbia Press.

Kim, Jae-On, and Charles W. Mueller. 1978a. *Factor Analysis: Statistical Methods and Practical Issues*. Sage University Paper Series on Quantitative Applications in the Social Sciences, 07-014. Beverly Hills, CA: Sage Publications.

– 1978b. *Introduction to Factor Analysis: What It Is and How to Do It*. Sage University Paper Series on Quantitative Applications in the Social Sciences, 07-013. Beverly Hills, CA: Sage Publications.

Klein, David, and Stefanie A. Lindquist. 2002. "The Influence of Jurisprudential Considerations on Supreme Court Decision Making: A Study of Conflict Cases." Presented at the Political Science Research Workshop, University of South Carolina, Columbia.

Klein, David E. 2002. *Making Law in the United States Courts of Appeals*. New York: Cambridge University Press.

Knopff, Rainer. 2001. "Courts Don't Make Good Compromises." In Paul Howe and Peter H. Russell, eds., *Judicial Power and Canadian Democracy*. Montreal and Kingston: McGill-Queen's University Press. 87–93.

Knopff, Rainer, and F.L. Morton. 1992. *Charter Politics*. Toronto: Nelson.

Kozinski, Alex. 1997. "What I Ate for Breakfast and Other Mysteries of Judicial Decision Making." In Lawrence 1994.

Langer, Laura. 2002. *Judicial Review in State Supreme Courts: A Comparative Study*. Albany: SUNY Press.

Lawrence, Susan E. 1994. "The Supreme Court and the Attitudinal Model: Introduction to the Symposium." *Law and Courts* 4: 3.

Lebel-Grenier, Sebastien. 2001. "The Charter and Legitimization of Judicial Activism." In Paul Howe and Peter H. Russell, eds., *Judicial Power and Canadian Democracy*. Montreal and Kingston: McGill-Queen's University Press. 94–8.

Leeson, Howard. 2001. "Section 33: The Notwithstanding Clause: A Paper Tiger?" In Paul Howe and Peter H. Russell, eds., *Judicial Power and Canadian Democracy*. Montreal and Kingston: McGill-Queen's University Press. 297–311.

L'Heureux-Dubé, Claire. 1997. "Making a Difference: The Pursuit of a Compassionate Justice." *University of British Columbia Law Review* 31 (1): 1–15.

Maltzman, Forrest, James F. Spriggs II, and Paul J. Wahlbeck. 2000. *Crafting Law on the Supreme Court: The Collegial Game*. New York: Cambridge University Press.

– and Paul J. Wahlbeck. 1996a. "May It Please the Chief? Opinion Assignments in the Rehnquist Court." *American Journal of Political Science* 40 (May): 421–43.

– 1996b "Strategic Policy Considerations and Voting Fluidity on the Burger Court." *American Political Science Review* 90 (Sept.): 581–92.

Mandel, Michael. 1989. *The Charter and the Legalization of Politics in Canada*. Toronto: Wall and Thompson.

– 1994. *The Charter of Rights and the Legalization of Politics in Canada*. Rev. ed. Toronto: Thompson Educational.

Manfredi, Christopher P. 1989. "Adjudication, Policy-Making and the Supreme Court of Canada: Lessons from the Experience of the United States." *Canadian Journal of Political Science* 22: 313–35.

– 1990. "The Use of United States Decisions by the Supreme Court of Canada under the Charter of Rights and Freedoms." *Canadian Journal of Political Science* 23 (Sept.): 499–518.

—.1993. *Judicial Power and the Charter: Canada and the Paradox of Liberal Constitutionalism*. New York: Oxford University Press.

– 2001. *Judicial Power and the Charter: Canada and the Paradox of Liberal Constitutionalism*. 2nd ed. New York: Oxford University Press.

– and James B. Kelly. 1999. "Six Degrees of Dialogue: A Response to Hogg and Bushnell." *Osgoode Hall Law Journal* 37: 513.

Martin, Elaine. 1993. "The Representative Role of Women Judges." *Judicature* 77 (Dec.–Jan.): 166–73.

McCormick, Peter. 1993. "Party Capability Theory and Appellate Success in the Supreme Court of Canada, 1949–1992." *Canadian Journal of Political Science* 26 (Sept.):523–40.

– 1994. *Canada's Courts*. Toronto: James Lorimer & Company.

– 1998. "Birds of a Feather: Alliances and Influences on the Lamer Court 1990–1997." *Osgoode Hall Law Journal* 36 (summer): 339–68.

– 2000. *Supreme at Last: The Evolution of the Supreme Court of Canada.* Toronto: James Lorimer & Company.

– and Ian Greene. 1990. *Judges and Judging: Inside the Canadian Judicial System.* Toronto: James Lorimer & Company.

– and Twyla Job. 1993. "Do Women Judges Make a Difference? An Analysis of Appeal Court Data." *Canadian Journal of Law and Society* 8 (spring): 135–48.

McIver, John P. 1976. "Scaling Judicial Decisions: The Panel Decision-making Process of the U.S. Courts of Appeals." *American Journal of Political Science* 20 (Nov.): 749–61.

McWhinney, Edward. 1987. "Judicial Review in a Federal and Plural Society: The Supreme Court of Canada." In John R. Schmidhauser, ed., *Comparative Judicial Systems: Challenging Frontiers in Conceptual and Empirical Analysis.* Boston: Butterworths. 1–4.

Monahan, Patrick J. 1999. "The Supreme Court of Canada's 1998 Constitutional Cases: The Debate over Judicial Activism Heats up." *Canada Watch* 7: 4–5.

– 2000. "The Supreme Court of Canada in the 21st Century." Prepared for the Supreme Court Centennial Symposium, Ottawa.

Morton, F.L., ed. 2002. *Law, Politics and the Judicial Process in Canada.* 3rd ed. Calgary: University of Calgary Press.

– and Rainer Knopff. 2000. *The Charter Revolution and the Court Party.* Peterborough, ON: Broadview Press.

– Peter H. Russell, and Troy Riddell. 1994. "The Canadian Charter of Rights and Freedoms: A Descriptive Analysis of the First Decade." *National Journal of Constitutional Law* 5: 1–58.

– Peter H. Russell, and Michael J. Withey. 1992. "The Supreme Court's First One Hundred Charter of Rights Decisions: A Statistical Analysis." *Osgoode Hall Law Journal* 30 (spring): 1–56.

Murphy, Walter F. 1964. *Elements of Judicial Strategy.* Chicago: University of Chicago Press.

O'Brien, David M. 1996. *Storm Center: The Supreme Court in American Politics.* 4th ed. New York: Norton.

– and Yasuo Ohkoshi. 2001. "Stifling Judicial Independence from Within: The Japanese Judiciary." In Peter Russell and David O'Brien, eds., *Judicial Independence in the Age of Democracy: Critical Perspectives from Around the World.* Charlottesville: University Press of Virginia. 37–61.

O'Connor, Karen, and Jeffrey A. Segal. 1990. "Justice Sandra Day O'Connor and the Supreme Court's Reaction to Its First Female Member." *Women and Politics* 10 (2): 95–104.

O'Connor, Sandra Day. 2003. *The Majesty of the Law*. New York: Random House.

Ostberg, C.L., Susan W. Johnson, Donald R. Songer, and Matthew E. Wetstein. 2004. "The Nature and Extent of Attitudinal Conflict in the Supreme Court of Canada." Presented at the annual meeting of the American Political Science Association, Chicago.

– and Matthew Wetstein. 1998. "Dimensions of Attitudes Underlying Search and Seizure Decisions of the Supreme Court of Canada." *Canadian Journal of Political Science* 31 (Dec.): 767–87.

– 2006. "Judicial Behavior on the Canadian Supreme Court: Attitudinal Conflict in Right to Counsel Cases, 1984–2002." *Political Science Quarterly* 121 (4): 677–97.

– 2007a. *Attitudinal Decision Making in the Supreme Court of Canada*. Vancouver: University of British Columbia Press.

– 2007b. "Examining Gender Differences in the Canadian and U.S. Supreme Courts in Economic Disputes." Prepared for presentation at the annual meeting of the Canadian Political Science Association, Saskatoon, 1 June.

Ostberg, C.L., Matthew E. Wetstein, and Craig R. Ducat. 2002. "Attitudinal Dimensions of Supreme Court Decision Making in Canada: The Lamer Court, 1991–1995." *Political Research Quarterly* 55 (March): 235–56.

– 2004. "Leaders, Followers, and Outsiders: Tasks of Social Leadership on the Canadian Supreme Court in the Early Nineties." *Polity* 36 (3): 505–28.

Packer, Herbert L. 1968. *The Limits of the Criminal Sanction*. Palo Alto, CA: Stanford University Press.

Palmer, Barbara. 2002."Justice Ruth Bader Ginsberg and the Supreme Court's Reaction to Its Second Female Member." *Women and Politics* 24 (1): 1–23.

Peck, Sidney. 1969. "A Scalogram Analysis of the Supreme Court of Canada, 1958–1967." In Glendon Schubert and David J. Danelski, eds., *Comparative Judicial Behavior: Cross-cultural Studies of Political Decision-Making in the East and West*. New York: Oxford University Press. 293–334.

Perry, H.W., Jr. 1991. *Deciding to Decide: Agenda Setting in the United States Supreme Court*. Cambridge, MA: Harvard University Press.

Posner, Richard A. 1990. *The Problems of Jurisprudence*. Cambridge, MA: Harvard University Press.

– 1997. "What Am I, a Potted Plant? The Case against Strict Construction." In David M. O'Brien, ed., *Judges on Judging: Views from the Bench*. Chatham, NJ: Chatham House. 165–70.

Pritchett, C. Herman. 1941. "Divisions of Opinion among Justices of the U.S. Supreme Court, 1939–1941." *American Political Science Review* 35 (Oct.): 890–8.

– 1948. *The Roosevelt Court: A Study in Judicial Politics and Values, 1937–1947*. New York: MacMillan Co.

Richards, Mark J., and Herbert M. Kritzer. 2002. "Jurisprudential Regimes in Supreme Court Decision Making." *American Political Science Review* 96 (June): 305–20.

Richardson, Richard J., and Kenneth N. Vines. 1970. *The Politics of Federal Courts: Lower Courts in the United States*. Boston: Little, Brown and Co.

Roach, Kent. 2001. *The Supreme Court on Trial: Judicial Activism or Democratic Dialogue*. Toronto: Irwin Law.

Robertson, David. 1982. "Judicial Ideology in the House of Lords: A Jurimetric Analysis." *British Journal of Political Science* 12 (Jan.): 1–25.

– 1998. *Judicial Discretion in the House of Lords*. New York: Oxford University Press.

Rohde, David W. 1972. "Policy Goals, Strategic Choice, and Majority Opinion Assignments in the U.S. Supreme Court." *Midwest Journal of Political Science* 16 (Nov.): 652–82.

Rohde, David W., and Harold J. Spaeth. 1976. *Supreme Court Decision Making*. San Francisco: W.H. Freeman and Co.

Russell, Peter H. 1969. *The Supreme Court of Canada as a Bilingual and Bicultural Institution*. Documents of the Royal Commission on Bilingualism and Biculturalism. Ottawa: Queen's Printer.

– 1983. "The Supreme Court Decision: Bold Statecraft Based on Questionable Jurisprudence." In Keith Banting and Richard Simeon, eds., *And No One Cheered: Federalism, Democracy, and the Constitution Act*. New York: Methuen. 217.

– 1993. *Constitutional Odyssey: Can Canadians Become a Sovereign People?* 2nd ed. Toronto: University of Toronto Press.

– 1995. "Canadian Constraints on Judicialization from Without." In C. Neal Tate and Torbjörn Vallinder, eds., *The Global Expansion of Judicial Power*. New York: New York University Press. 137–50.

Russell, Peter, and David M. O'Brien. 2001. *Judicial Independence in the Age of Democracy: Critical Perspectives from Around the World*. Charlottesville: University Press of Virginia.

Samonte, Abelardo G. 1969. "The Philippine Supreme Court: A Study of Judicial Background Characteristics, Attitudes, and Decision Making." In Glendon Schubert and David J. Danelski, eds., *Comparative Judicial Behavior: Cross-cultural Studies of Political Decision-Making in the East and West*. New York: Oxford University Press. 157–96.

Schmidhauser, John R. 1961. "Judicial Behavior and the Sectional Crisis of 1837–1860." *Journal of Politics* 23 (Nov.): 615–40.

Schubert, Glendon A. 1965. *The Judicial Mind: The Attitudes and Ideologies of Supreme Court Justices, 1946–1963*. Evanston, IL: Northwestern University Press.

– 1968. "Opinion Agreement among High Court Justices in Australia." *Australian and New Zealand Journal of Sociology* 4: 2–17.

– 1969a. "The Dimensions of Decisional Response: Opinion and Voting Behavior of the Australian High Court." In Joel B. Grossman and Joseph Tanenhaus, eds., *Frontiers of Judicial Research*. New York: John Wiley and Sons. 163–95.

– 1969b. "Two Causal Models of Decision-Making by the High Court of Australia." In Glendon Schubert and David J. Danelski, eds., *Comparative Judicial Behavior: Cross-cultural Studies of Political Decision-Making in the East and West*. New York: Oxford University Press. 335–66.

– 1974. *The Judicial Mind Revisited: Psychometric Analysis of Supreme Court Ideology*. New York: Oxford University Press.

– 1985a. *Political Culture and Judicial Elites: A Comparative Analysis*. Vol. 1 of *Political Culture and Judicial Behavior*. Lanham, MD: University Press of America.

– 1985b. *Subcultural Analysis of Judicial Behavior: A Direct Observational Study*. Vol. 2 of *Political Culture and Judicial Behavior*. Lanham, MD: University Press of America.

– 1987. "Subcultures and Judicial Background: A Cross-cultural Analysis." In John R. Schmidhauser, ed., *Comparative Judicial Systems: Challenging Frontiers in Conceptual and Empirical Analysis*. Boston: Butterworths. [pp?]

Segal, Jeffrey A. 1984. "Predicting Supreme Court Cases Probabilistically: The Search and Seizure Cases, 1962–1981." *American Political Science Review* 78 (Dec.): 891–900.

– 1997. "Separation-of-Powers Games in the Positive Theory of Congress and Courts." *American Political Science Review* 91 (March): 28–44.

– and Albert D. Cover. 1989. "Ideological Values and the Votes of U.S. Supreme Court Justices." *American Political Science Review* 83 (June): 557–65.

– and Harold J. Spaeth. 1993. *The Supreme Court and the Attitudinal Model*. New York: Cambridge University Press.

– 1994. "The Authors Respond." *Law and Courts* 4: 10–12.

– 1996. "The Influence of Stare Decisis on the Votes of United States Supreme Court Justices." *American Journal of Political Science* 40 (Nov.): 971–1003.

– 2002. *The Supreme Court and the Attitudinal Model Revisited*. New York: Cambridge University Press.

Snell, James G., and Frederick Vaughan. 1985. *The Supreme Court of Canada: History of the Institution*. Toronto: University of Toronto Press.

Sniderman, Paul M., Joseph F. Fletcher, Peter H. Russell, and Philip E. Tetlock. 1989. "Political Culture and the Problem of Double Standards: Mass and Elite Attitudes toward Language Rights in the Canadian Charter of Rights and Freedoms." *Canadian Journal of Political Science* 22 (June): 259–84.

– 1996. *The Clash of Rights: Liberty, Equality, and Legitimacy in Pluralist Democracy*. New Haven, CT: Yale University Press.

Songer, Donald R. 1987. "The Impact of the Supreme Court on Trends in Economic Policy Making in the United States Courts of Appeals." *Journal of Politics* 49 (Aug.): 830–41.

– 2008. *The Transformation of the Supreme Court of Canada: An Empirical Examination*. Toronto: University of Toronto Press.

– Sue Davis and Susan Haire. 1994. "A Reappraisal of Diversification in the Federal Courts: Gender Effects in the Courts of Appeals." *Journal of Politics* 56 (May): 425–39.

– and Susan Haire. 1992. "Integrating Alternative Approaches to the Study of Judicial Voting: Obscenity Cases in the U.S. Courts of Appeals." *American Journal of Political Science* 36 (Nov.): 963–82.

– and Susan W. Johnson. 2007. "Judicial Decision Making in the Supreme Court of Canada: Updating the Personal Attribute Model." *Canadian Journal of Political Science* 40: 911–34.

– and Stefanie A. Lindquist. 1996. "Not the Whole Story: The Impact of Justices' Values on Supreme Court Decision Making." *American Journal of Political Science* 40 (Nov.): 1049–63.

– Jeffrey A. Segal and Charles M. Cameron. 1994. “The Hierarchy of Justice: Testing a Principal-Agent Model of Supreme Court–Circuit Court Interactions.” *American Journal of Political Science* 38 (Aug.): 673–96.

– and Reginald S. Sheehan. 1992. “Who Wins on Appeal? Upperdogs and Underdogs in the United States Courts of Appeals.” *American Journal of Political Science* 36 (Feb.): 235–58.

– Reginald S. Sheehan and Susan B. Haire. 2000. *Continuity and Change on the United States Courts of Appeals.* Ann Arbor: University of Michigan Press.

Sossin, Lorne. 1996. “The Sounds of Silence: Law Clerks, Policy Making and the Supreme Court of Canada.” *University of British Columbia Law Review* 30 (2): 279–308.

Spaeth, Harold J., and Jeffrey A. Segal. 1999. *Majority Rule or Minority Will? Adherence to Precedence on the U.S. Supreme Court.* Cambridge: Cambridge University Press.

Spriggs, James F., II, Forrest Maltzman, and Paul J. Wahlbeck. 1999. “Bargaining on the U.S. Supreme Court: Justices’ Responses to Majority Opinion Drafts.” *Journal of Politics* 61 (May): 485–506.

Statutes of Canada, 1974–75–76.

Stevens, Robert. 2001. “Judicial Independence in England: A Loss of Innocence.” In Peter Russell and David O’Brien, eds., *Judicial Independence in the Age of Democracy: Critical Perspectives from Around the World.* Charlottesville: University Press of Virginia. 155–72.

Stidham, Ronald, and Robert A. Carp. 1982. “Trial Court Responses to Supreme Court Policy Changes: Three Case Studies.” *Law and Policy Quarterly* 4 (April): 215–34.

Supreme Court of Canada. 2000. *The Supreme Court of Canada and Its Justices, 1875–2000.* Toronto: Dundurn Press.

Swinfen, David B. 1987. *Imperial Appeal: The Debate on the Appeal to the Privy Council, 1833–1986.* Manchester: Manchester University Press.

Tate, C. Neal. 1972. “Social Background and Voting Behavior in the Philippine Supreme Court.” *Lawasia* 3 (Aug.–Dec.): 317–38.

– 1981. “Personal Attribute Models of the Voting Behavior of U.S. Supreme Court Justices: Liberalism in Civil Liberties and Economic Decisions, 1946–1978.” *American Political Science Review* 75 (June): 355–67.

– 1993. “Courts and Crisis Regimes: A Theory Sketch with Asian Case Studies.” *Political Research Quarterly* 46 (June): 311–38.

– and Roger Handberg. 1991. "Time Binding and Theory Building in Personal Attribute Models of Supreme Court Voting Behavior, 1916–88." *American Journal of Political Science* 35 (May): 460–80.

– and Stacia L. Haynie. 1994. "The Philippine Supreme Court under Authoritarian and Democratic Rule: The Perceptions of the Justices." *Asian Profile* 22 (3): 209–26.

– and Panu Sittiwong. 1989. "Decision Making in the Canadian Supreme Court: Extending the Personal Attributes Model across Nations." *Journal of Politics* 51 (Nov.): 900–16.

– and Torbjörn Vallinder, ed. 1995. *The Global Expansion of Judicial Power*. New York: New York University Press.

Toharia, Jose J. 1975. "Judicial Independence in an Authoritarian Regime: The Case of Contemporary Spain." *Law and Society Review* 9 (spring): 475–96.

Ulmer, S. Sidney. 1973. "Social Background as an Indicator to the Votes of Supreme Court Justices in Criminal Cases: 1947–1956 Terms." *American Journal of Political Science* 17 (Aug.): 622–30.

– 1986. "Are Social Background Models Time-Bound?" *American Political Science Review* 80 (Sept.): 957–68.

Vaughan, Frederick. 2001. "Judicial Politics in Canada: Patterns and Trends." In Paul Howe and Peter H. Russell, eds., *Judicial Power and Canadian Democracy*. Montreal and Kingston: McGill-Queen's University Press. 3–26.

Volcansek, Mary L. 1991. "Judicial Activism in Italy." In Kenneth M. Holland, ed., *Judicial Activism in Comparative Perspective*. New York: St Martin's Press.

Wahlbeck, Paul J., James F. Spriggs, and Forrest Maltzman. 1998. "Marshalling the Court: Bargaining and Accommodation on the United States Supreme Court." *American Journal of Political Science* 42 (Jan.): 294–315.

Walker, Thomas G., and Deborah J. Barrow. 1985. "The Diversification of the Federal Bench: Policy and Process Ramifications." *Journal of Politics* 47 (June): 596–617.

Wallach, H.G. Peter. 1995. "Reunification and Prospects for Judicialization in Germany." In C. Neal Tate and Torbjörn Vallinder, eds., *The Global Expansion of Judicial Power*. New York: New York University Press. 325–42.

Waltman, Jerold L. 1991. "Judicial Activism in England." In Kenneth M. Holland, ed., *Judicial Activism in Comparative Perspective*. New York: St Martin's Press.

Wasby, Stephen L. 1993. *The Supreme Court in the Federal Judicial System*. 4th ed. Chicago: Nelson-Hall.

Weiler, Paul. 1974. *In the Last Resort: A Critical Study of the Supreme Court of Canada*. Toronto: Carswell/Methuen.

Weinrib, Lorraine Eisenstat. 2001. "The Activist Constitution." In Paul Howe and Peter H. Russell, eds., *Judicial Power and Canadian Democracy*. Montreal and Kingston: McGill-Queen's University Press. 80–6.

Wetstein, Matthew E., and C.L. Ostberg. 1999. "Search and Seizure Cases in the Supreme Court of Canada: Extending an American Model of Judicial Decision Making across Countries." *Social Science Quarterly* 80 (Dec.): 757–74.

– 2005. "Strategic Leadership and Political Change on the Canadian Supreme Court: Analyzing the Transition to Chief Justice." *Canadian Journal of Political Science* 38 (3): 653–73.

– C.L. Ostberg, and Craig R. Ducat. 1999. "The Bases of Conflict Underlying the Decision of Charter Cases in the Early and Late Dickson Courts." Paper presented at the annual meeting of the American Political Science Association, Atlanta.

Wheeler, Stanton, Bliss Cartwright, Robert A. Kagan, and Lawrence M. Friedman. 1987. "Do the 'Haves' Come Out Ahead? Winning and Losing in State Supreme Courts, 1870–1970." *Law and Society Review* 21 (3): 403–46.

White, Candace C. 2002. "Gender Differences on the Supreme Court." In F.L. Morton, ed., *Law, Politics and the Judicial Process in Canada*. 3rd ed. Calgary: University of Calgary Press. 85–90.

White, G. Edward. 1994. *Intervention and Detachment: Essays in Legal History and Jurisprudence*. New York: Oxford University Press.

Widner, Jennifer A. 2001. *Building the Rule of Law: Francis Nyalali and the Road to Judicial Independence in Africa*. New York: W.W. Norton & Co.

Williams, John M. 2001. "Judicial Independence in Australia." In Peter Russell and David O'Brien, eds., *Judicial Independence in the Age of Democracy: Critical Perspectives from Around the World*. Charlottesville: University Press of Virginia. 173–93.

Wilson, Bertha. 1990. "Will Women Judges Really Make a Difference?" *Osgoode Hall Law Journal* 28 (fall): 507–22.

Woodruff, Judy. 2003. "Sandra Day O'Connor: The Majesty of the Law." In CNN *Exclusive Interview*. 20 May. http://articles.cnn.com/2003-05-20/politics/judy.page.oconnor_1_individual-rights-supreme-court-justice-sandra-day-o-connor?_s=PM:ALLPOLITICS

Ziegel, Jacob S. 2001. "Merit Selection and Democratization of Appointments to the Supreme Court of Canada." In Paul Howe and Peter H. Russell, eds., *Judicial Power and Canadian Democracy*. Montreal and Kingston: McGill-Queen's University Press. 131–64.

Index